FAMILY
TREASON

FAMILY TREASON

THE WALKER
SPY CASE

Jack Kneece

STEIN AND DAY/*Publishers*

First published in 1986
Copyright © 1986 by Jack M. Kneece
All rights reserved, Stein and Day, Incorporated
Designed by Louis A. Ditizio
Printed in the United States of America

STEIN AND DAY/*Publishers*
Scarborough House
Briarcliff Manor, N.Y. 10510

Library of Congress Cataloging-in-Publication Data

Kneece, Jack.
  Family treason.

  Bibliography: p.
  Includes index.
  1. Walker, John Anthony, 1937-   . 2. Walker
family. 3. Whitworth, Jerry. 4. Espionage—Soviet
Union—History—20th century. 5. Espionage—United
States—History—20th century. 6. Anti-submarine
warfare. I. Title.
UB271.R92W344 1986   327.1'2'0924   85-40960
ISBN 0-8128-3095-4

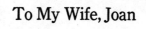
To My Wife, Joan

CONTENTS

ILLUSTRATIONS

ACKNOWLEDGMENTS

I am indebted to Jay Tolson, the literary editor of the *Wilson Quarterly,* for his initial support and enthusiasm for this book idea. Cara Saylor Polk and Joe Goulden, Washington authors of several good books of their own, helped me find an agent and publisher. My wife, Joan Mower, a journalist with the Associated Press in Washington, provided moral and financial support throughout this project.

I am deeply indebted to the Federal Bureau of Investigation and the Naval Investigative Service for their cooperation and assistance in my research. Particular thanks must be extended to Phil Parker, deputy director of the FBI, and to Lanny McCullah, assistant director of the Naval Investigative Service. The book would not have been possible without the cooperation of FBI agents Robert Hunter, Jack Wagner, Joe Wolfinger, and the Norfolk, Virginia, FBI office. I also appreciate the assistance of officials of the U.S. District Court in Baltimore and Norfolk, Assistant U.S. Attorney Michael Schatzow of Baltimore, and a number of newsmen and former newsmen in Norfolk, especially AP staffer Jean McNair and former *Norfolk Ledger-Star* reporter Fred Talbot. Laura Walker Snyder talked to me by telephone on key points.

Others who provided a substantial amount of assistance include former CIA official and author Robert Crowley, who helped me interpret much of what I had learned; Billy Wilkinson of Denham Springs, Louisiana, and Donald Clevenger of Odessa, Texas, the two men who served longest and closest with John Walker; Joseph Russinello of the U.S. District Court in San Francisco for invaluable help on the Whitworth case; Jody Olt, a reporter with the *Odessa American,* in Odessa, Texas, who helped me locate Clevenger; the U.S. Navy; Hugh Connor of Scranton, Pennsylvania; Rick Mates of Radio Station WEJL in Scranton; Vincent Tiberi of Scranton; Phil Prince of Bethesda; Anne Crowley Nelson, sister of Barbara Walker; Tom Stewart of the U.S. Justice Department; Don Morton of Muldrow, Oklahoma; Mr. and Mrs. Art Mower of Sacramento, California, and Tom Coakley, a staff writer with the *Sacramento Bee.*

Also, my thanks go to Attorney Louis Hiken of Davis, neighbors of Jerry Whitworth in the Rancho Yolo Mobile Home Park, Kathy Mayo, Mike Bell, Ted Uhlrich, several former CIA staffers, the CIA public information office, and Pamela K. Carroll.

Particular thanks also must go to Warren Hoffecker, who put me in touch with the right submarine authorities, and to a number of present and former Naval officers who asked not to be identified in the acknowledgments but who helped me understand the undersea world of John Walker. Nora Moody of St. Stephens, South Carolina, and Curly Houck of Ladson, South Carolina, also provided invaluable assistance about the South Carolina years of the Walker brothers.

I also am indebted to the photo staff of the Washington bureau of the Associated Press for helping me find photographs of the Walkers.

Thanks also to a number of people in Scranton, Pennsylvania, and Davis, California, who helped anonymously by providing information.

THE CHRONOLOGY

July 28, 1937— Birth of John Anthony Walker, Jr.

October 25, 1955—John Walker joins the Navy.

June 4, 1957—Marriage of John and Barbara Walker.

1968—John Walker and his brother, Arthur, overlap duty assignments in Charleston, South Carolina.

1968—Barbara Walker discovers John Walker is a Soviet spy.

1970—John Walker meets Jerry A. Whitworth in San Diego.

July, 1973—Arthur Walker retires from the Navy.

June 22, 1976—John Walker and Barbara are divorced after a year's separation.

August 1, 1976—John Walker retires from the Navy.

1978—John Walker attempts to recruit Laura Walker as a spy.

1980—Arthur goes to work for VSE, a defense contractor.

December 13, 1982—Michael Walker joins the Navy.

1983—Jerry A. Whitworth retires from the Navy.

November 23, 1984—Barbara Walker makes her first call to the FBI.

May 20, 1985—John Walker arrested.

May 22, 1985—Michael Walker arrested.

May 23, 1985—Soviet KGB agent Aleksey Tkachenko and his family flee Washington.

May 29, 1985—Arthur Walker arrested.

June 3, 1986—Jerry A. Whitworth arrested.

August 9, 1985—Arthur Walker convicted of seven counts of espionage.

Oct. 28, 1985—John and Michael Walker plead guilty.

March 10, 1986—Jerry A. Whitworth goes on trial in U.S. District Court in San Francisco.

July 24, 1986—Jerry A. Whitworth convicted on seven counts of espionage and five counts of tax fraud.

1

Walker Surfaces

He was a man who may have cost thousands of American lives in Vietnam, who had handed the Soviets years of submarine, missile, and communications technology, secret U.S. war contingency plans, and allowed the Soviets to decipher U.S. codes and duplicate U.S. cryptographic equipment.

Bruce Brahe and Douglas Stauffer flattened themselves in the underbrush when they heard the sound of the truck engine. They wore camouflage clothing and had camouflage makeup daubed on their faces and looked more like turkey hunters than FBI agents. They were grateful that there was no moon on this May 19, 1985. They checked almost involuntarily for the reassuring walnut grips of their revolvers.

They were waiting for a Soviet agent to pick up a packet of top-secret information, part of a "dead drop" that they had found only minutes before. It was an electric moment, a chance to arrest a KGB agent less than twenty-five miles from the White House.

This was the culmination of Operation Windflyer. It would result in the arrest of John Walker, a former Navy warrant officer; his son, Michael, a sailor aboard the aircraft carrier *Nimitz*; his brother, Arthur, a former submarine officer and authority on antisubmarine warfare; and a close friend of John Walker's, Jerry A. Whitworth, a retired navy communications specialist living in Davis, California. All would be charged with passing secret information to the Soviet Union.

The driver of the blue and white Chevrolet van parked the vehicle some distance away and began walking toward the hidden agents. He had a flashlight, and a .38 Smith & Wesson snubnosed pistol rested on his hip under his black windbreaker. He stopped at the base of a utility pole and played the light in small arcs at the base of the pole. He was just ten feet away. Stauffer and Brahe tried to slow their breathing. Their hearts beat almost audibly.

But rather than the KGB agent they expected, they were surprised to see John Walker, the retired Navy warrant officer who had dropped the package of classified information earlier in the night. Why did he return? Was he checking to see if the Soviets had picked up his package? Did something go wrong? Was he trying to retrieve the package the FBI had just picked up?

Brahe and Stauffer did not want to frighten away the suspect and ruin a chance for arrests in what the FBI would call the biggest espionage case in the history of the United States. They were hoping the man with the flashlight would meet with his Soviet contact.

The small, bearded man moved with birdlike motions. His black windbreaker and black running shoes looked more like the costume of a burglar than a spy. He seemed nervous as he probed the underbrush, searching with the flashlight. The agents hoped that he would not raise the yellow beam toward their hiding place in the sparse undergrowth. The sound of his walking in the brush was loud and surreal in the quiet night. There was no other traffic on the rural road.

Brahe and Stauffer knew a lot about John Walker—enough to recoil, not from fear, but from the dead soul that lived behind the happy-go-lucky public persona he had so carefully crafted.

He was a traitor to his country, a furtive coyote of a man whose ideology was money, whose religion was nihilism, and whose loyalties were none. He was a man who may have cost thousands of American lives in Vietnam, who had handed the Soviets years of submarine, missile, and communications technology, secret U.S. war contingency plans, and allowed the Soviets to decipher U.S.

codes and duplicate U.S. cryptographic equipment. And here he was almost within arm's reach. But they had to let him continue his puzzled search and watch silently as he walked back to his van and sped off again. The next six hours would probably make up the strangest night of their lives, a night that had its beginning in a small Hyannis, Massachusetts, apartment six months earlier.

2

The FBI Is Tipped

I wanted to give John a chance to run. That bond goes a lot deeper than you think. —Barbara Walker, June 1985

Barbara Walker was depressed. She was turning forty-seven, and her family was scattered, bitter, and unhappy. Her marriage had been over for a decade. Her job at a gift shop provided scarcely enough to pay her share of the groceries and rent for the apartment she shared with the one daughter, Cynthia, that she seemed to have left in her corner. She had begun to drink more heavily than usual. It was galling to think that the nice home she once had in Norfolk, Virginia, was now occupied by her former husband and a pretty twenty-four-year-old blonde who was young enough to be his daughter. Her bitterness had been building like a sealed volcano and was fed by the knowledge that her husband had been a Soviet spy for almost twenty years.

She was no longer sure whether she drank because of the rancorous rift in the family or whether she drank to forget that she had been married to a strange man who had betrayed his country, despised his three daughters, and only grudgingly tolerated his son. It was so different from the days when the family was

17

together—a Navy family who, for a time at least, did things together, who had lived and played in many Navy ports. She tried to convince herself that they had actually been happy for a few brief years.

On this evening, the telephone rang as Barbara Walker was well into one of several vodkas.

"Mother, it's Laura. I just wanted to wish you a happy birthday."

It was the first time Barbara had heard from her daughter in two years. The two women became emotional as Laura poured out her feelings. Laura missed her son, Christopher, who was living with her ex-husband, Mark Snyder, in a Maryland suburb of Washington, D.C. She felt like a part of her had been torn away. She tried to express to her mother what it was like, how much she missed the boy, how hard it had been to be separated from him and the rest of the family. It had been a severe test of her born-again Christian faith.

"Mother, you've got to turn him in to the FBI. You've got to for my sake and for Christopher's sake."

"Will you support me if I do?" Barbara Walker asked.

Laura assured her mother that she would. But she wondered later if her mother would keep her side of the bargain, whether it was the vodka that had given her the courage to agree or whether it was the resolve born of hearing her daughter's voice again. She knew that her mother had toyed with the idea before but had always backed out. She would not have been surprised had she done so once more. But she was glad she had called. It was worth it to hear the genuine affection in her mother's voice. It had been a long time.

The faded red and gold of New England's fall leaves blanketed the ground in Hyannis in November of 1984. A few burnt-sienna leaves clung tenaciously to the trees: a frail barrier to the beginning of the New England winter. Ronald Reagan had just been elected to a second term. The frenetic news coverage of the campaign was over, slipping into oblivion just as the fall leaves had slipped away. Chill winds swept down from Canada, and people on Cape Cod braced for a cold winter. It was that kind of day when Barbara Walker walked the few blocks home from her job in a gift shop, poured her first vodka, and readied herself for a telephone call to the FBI in Boston.

When she called, she spoke with a young clerk who referred her to the agent in charge of the Hyannis office, Walter Price. When she reached Price, he seemed skeptical, perhaps in part because she slurred her words as she said, "My former husband, John Walker, is a Russian spy." She told Laura later that Price did not take her seriously. Incredibly, it would be months before the agency placed any credence in her story. CIA officials would grumble privately that while the KGB checked out every casual call thoroughly, Barbara Walker had to hit the FBI on the head with a two-by-four several times to get their attention.

When she realized that Price didn't believe her, a feeling of helplessness swept over her. She had imagined that soon after she made the call, her small apartment would be swarming with FBI agents and that agents in Norfolk, Virginia, would immediately be dispatched to arrest her husband. But here was this faceless voice, a nice Southern baritone, talking to her as if she should go and sleep it off.

She talked to him by telephone several times after that, repeatedly telling him that her husband was, in fact, a Soviet spy, trying to add details each time that might convince him. It was frustrating, almost Kafkaesque. He still sounded skeptical, particularly after she admitted that she and John Walker had not lived together as husband and wife in ten years, and that, yes, she felt a great deal of anger toward him.

"Is there anyone else in your family who could verify this?" he had asked her after the first call. She had been irritated by the question, the tacit presumption that she was a middle-aged drunk who was trying to get even with her husband for some imagined wrong. "Yes, my daughter Laura," she said. She gave him Laura's number in Buffalo, New York.

"But they never called," Laura said later. "I had to take the initiative."

In January, twenty-five-year-old Laura Walker Snyder called her mother again and asked what had happened with the FBI. Barbara said she had talked to the FBI several times and nothing had happened. "Why don't you call them, Laura? Maybe they'll believe you." Laura agreed and called the next day, January 17, 1985. She was more convincing, and as a result Walter Price was soon on his way to see Barbara Walker.

Laura was initially ambivalent about her role with the FBI. "I had to think about it. I decided to pick up the phone one night. She [Mother] called in first, one night after drinking a little more than she should have. They didn't believe her. They didn't even act on it. No one called me. November went by. December, January. I asked my mother, 'When are they going to call?'"

FBI offices and newspapers both get "nut calls" on a routine basis, often several in any given week. But a good news-paperman—and a good FBI agent—learns how to spot the genuine, even though it is not always easy. Sometimes the caller sounds rational but turns out to be strange on closer examination. And somtimes a caller—or visitor—who sounds strange turns out to be the genuine article.

Price was known among his colleagues as a perceptive man. During his sixteen-year FBI career, he had been involved in virtu-ally every kind of case, and he had learned to be particularly wary of domestic cases. His initial assessment of Barbara Walker remained laced with doubt for some time after her first contact: "I thought she might be adding two and two and getting eight."

Price admitted that he originally considered the complaint with more than a jaundiced eye, his lack of belief increased because he had been by to see Barbara Walker several times and she was never there. Price was on the point of chalking the whole thing off as a kooky domestic case when he decided to try one more time. Barbara Walker promised that this time she would be at home.

She had a drink in her hand when she answered the door of the small apartment above a religious bookstore. Her hair had the slightly unkempt look of a woman who had just awakened after a brief nap. There was a vodka bottle and mixers on the Formica-topped kitchen table. She offered Price a drink and a seat. And she reiterated her claim that John Anthony Walker, Jr., had been a Soviet spy for most of his Navy career. The disclosure was the first loose thread in the unraveling of the most spectacular spy drama since the arrest of Julius and Ethel Rosenberg in 1950 on treason charges.

BARBARA WALKER HAD not slept well the night before she was to meet Price face to face to tell him the details of her former husband's activities. After all, many view treason as the worst crime of all, the betrayal of one's country.

She thought back over the years to 1956 when she was eighteen, a welder's daughter, and worked as a bank messenger in Boston. She was introduced to the earnest young sailor at a skating rink.

Though he was actually little more than a boy when he swept her off her feet, he was nonetheless a cocksure but charming young man, who swaggered as he told her how he planned to put in a few years in the Navy to learn communications and then make some real money. He still was not shaving every day, this young seaman, a nineteen-year-old radioman stationed aboard the USS *Johnnie Hutchins,* a destroyer escort. But he was more sensitive than the other young men she had met, and he seemed to be intelligent.

So she fell in love with a sailor, as young girls have been doing ever since young men have gone to sea. It all happened so fast that they didn't inform either family of the hasty wedding ceremony while he was on leave a few months later on June 4, 1957, in Durham, North Carolina. She had not yet met any of his family. Soon she would be following him to Navy bases and Navy towns on both coasts—Vallejo, Union City, and San Diego in California, Charleston, South Carolina, and Norfolk, Virginia. He would have nineteen duty assignments before he retired.

He had to borrow 100 dollars from his brother to pay the rent on their first apartment. Arthur Walker remembered that when John called to borrow the money he only incidentally informed him of the marriage to Barbara: "I was only getting about 150 dollars a month back then, and we decided to ask him if he was in trouble, and my wife, Rita, kept saying, 'If he got a girl pregnant, he doesn't have to marry her.' And he hesitated a bit, and then he said that he needed the money because he had quietly gotten married to Barbara and he needed the money for rent, so I wired it to him."

They would have three girls and a boy—Margaret, Laura, Cynthia, and Michael—and live in house trailers, quonset huts, Navy housing, and ramshackle old houses. The children attended a succession of schools near Navy bases on both coasts. They were living in a quonset hut when Michael, the youngest, was born in 1963.

It had been a tough life in many respects, but it had been a good life until 1967, when John became bitter and openly began seeing a succession of younger women. Their estrangement became deeper after Barbara began seeing his brother, Arthur, half out of retribution and half out of longing for male attention.

SHE WAS NERVOUS when she let Price into the small apartment, nervous despite the vodka, overcome with the enormity of what she was doing. There was also a nagging fear that she herself might be charged as an accessory for not having turned Walker in when she first found out about the espionage. Informing the FBI, she told Price, was not an easy thing to do, despite the animosity, the hurt, and the separation.

There were other reasons, family reasons, that precipitated her decision to inform on Walker. Barbara told Price about Laura's former husband, who had taken Laura's young son, Christopher, and threatened to tell the authorities about John Walker's spying if Laura tried to take the boy back. Now Laura could regain custody of her son without fear.

But would Price believe her?

LAURA WALKER SNYDER joined the Christian 700 Club after she and Mark Snyder were divorcd. She told the Christian organization that her husband was "blackmailing" her with her father's espionage. But the organization, ignorant of the gravity of the allegations against John Walker, simply urged her to reconcile with her mother and the rest of the family, to forget old wounds. More than two years before she persuaded her mother to call the FBI, a bitter time had begun for Laura Walker Snyder. She said her family at first "turned against me . . . My entire family thought that I should sit back and say nothing, to protect my father." The family rift occurred when she wanted to get her son back even though it meant that her father's espionage might be exposed. Her sisters and her mother urged her to try to live with the situation. Her mother was worried about the possibility of being charged as an accessory herself if Walker was turned in. "She said, 'You know, if you do this, you're going to destroy the family. I could go to jail, and who knows what else could happen . . .'"

Throughout this time the Walker family seemed more preoccupied with their differences and feuding than with anything else. Somehow, the fact that John Walker was a Soviet spy faded into the background. It was something they had learned to live with, a kind of familial affliction that was not as important in their lives as the more mundane hassles and worries of day-to-day living.

Laura did not believe she would have been able to turn John Walker in if her son had not been involved. "He was taken by his father when he was two. By this time he was five. I had to weigh ... make the decision whether my son was more important to me—and his love—than my father, who never really showed me much love anyway."

The family split up into feuding camps. John Walker, his son, Michael, Michael's wife, Rachel, and John's daughter Margaret became one faction. Laura was estranged from them all, and Barbara Walker and her daughter Cynthia made another faction. There was little communication between the sides. Laura made the Christian organization her surrogate family. A Christian Broadcast Network counselor urged her, eighteen months after the family estrangement, to reconcile with her family even if it meant that she had to take the first steps. But she couldn't bring herself to call her mother for another year because the hurt was so deep.

In one discussion with her father about the situation with her son and husband, he had told her to forget about getting her son back and accused her of giving her former husband "a hammer" that he could use on her and the family at any time. He also hinted at this time that he might kill Laura's husband.

When she did finally call on her mother's birthday in November 1984, "I think something within me wanted to say, 'Mother, you don't understand the pain I'm going through. You have never lost a child ...' " By not calling for two years, she had tried to show her mother how terrible losing her child was to her.

BARBARA WALKER HAD no suspicion that, in agreeing to tell the FBI all of the things she had been concealing about her former husband since 1968, she would lose her son, Michael, to a jail term and he would become estranged from her, nor did she dream she would step stage center into an international espionage drama.

She told Price that she had told each of the children when they were teenagers that John Walker was a Soviet spy. Michael, at seventeen, seemed particularly devastated by the knowledge, she recalled. She tried to describe what it was like, telling the children about their father. (Michael testified that he was thirteen when his mother told him, but he didn't believe her until a few years later.)

"All I tried to do was tell them their father was not a good person but he was still their father." It was a terrible and strange burden for the children to bear. John Walker always told his family that they must be close knit, closemouthed. Whatever they knew must remain within the family, just as within the Mafia.

He said that selling information was a common practice in the Navy. "Selling the yellow," he called it, referring to the color coding of classified documents. He told his children that the family needed the extra money, and he said the information he provided was really not all that valuable. He tried to make it seem as if it was not that big a deal, that the information was soon out of date anyway. But he warned that they must never breathe a word about it to anyone. On occasion he hinted broadly that he was actually a double agent. Many times, he would leave the family for several days, explaining that he was departing "on a secret mission for the Navy."

Barbara Walker told Price that she had once seen her husband pick up 35,000 dollars from a drop site after leaving information for the Soviets at another drop site. Once when Walker was transferred from the West Coast to Norfolk, Virginia, the family checked into a Washington, D.C., motel, and he made a drop and picked up a large sum of money. On another occasion, they picked up so much money that they were worried that someone might spot it when they flew back to California.

She went with him on dead-drop exchanges in 1969 and 1971 in the Washington, D.C., area. Each time, he filled a paper bag with trash and hid the classified information somewhere in the bag of trash. They would rent a car and a motel room, drive to a nearby rural area where they would look for a signal, then return to the motel. Later they would drive back in the dark and leave the paper bag. Still later, they would return to another site and pick up a bag full of money. Another time, when the couple flew back to Union City, California, where they were then living, they hid the money by taping some of it to their bodies and sewing the rest into the lining of a coat.

The FBI learned that the usual amount of payment was 50,000 dollars.

As she spoke, slurring her words a bit more with each drink, she stared off into the past with watery eyes, trying to recall bits and pieces of information that would have the ring of authenticity for Price.

Price saw that her brown eyes were glazed from the vodka. They were the eyes of a wounded doe. Her short, dark hair showed signs of gray. She chain-smoked as she talked.

He still doesn't believe me, she thought. She had to laugh to herself: all these years she had feared the FBI's knock on the door, and now she was struggling to convince them.

Barbara was right. Price remained dubious. A cursory check showed that John Walker had a flawless military career, retiring as a chief warrant officer after twenty years of service. He had indeed been a radioman, starting out with service on an old post-World War II diesel submarine and moving up to nuclear-powered submarines and then shore duty where he had access to the most sensitive of secrets in the Atlantic and Pacific fleets. Price knew that in order to serve in a sensitive communications post in any of the armed services, particularly where there was access to top-secret material, the Navy conducted a thorough background check. The Navy was very careful about the kind of person who was allowed to handle sensitive information. He also knew that the Navy conducted psychological testing of candidates to serve on board submarines.

Barbara was vague about the kind of information allegedly passed along and about other things, too, including exactly how and precisely when her husband began spying. And when she said that her husband was constantly bragging about his espionage activities and trying to make them seem glamorous, that didn't ring true to Price either. It didn't sound like a man who had been a successful spy for almost twenty years. Successful espionage agents kept their mouths shut tight. Bragging ones wound up dead or jailed.

Price was also puzzled about the fact that the Walkers had joined the John Birch Society with some Navy friends in 1965. That didn't seem to jibe with espionage either.

So Price continued to wonder whether Barbara Walker was not just another disgruntled, angry ex-spouse trying to get her husband in trouble. He could not help but consider how it would look to his superiors if he took the whole thing seriously and it turned out that she was simply another nut case? Wouldn't the boys in Washington get a big chuckle out of that? Yet, there was something sincere about her.

She claimed to have first found out about the espionage when the family moved into a luxurious high-rise apartment building in Norfolk, the Algonquin House, far more expensive than they normally could afford. It was then, in April of 1968, that Walker also bought two sailboats, all new furniture, and some unimproved real estate and generally began spending far in excess of their income, especially on his girlfriends.

Wondering where all the money was coming from to pay for this, Barbara, one day when her husband was away, broke into a locked desk drawer and began a search. She found a tin box shoved far back in the drawer, hidden under some papers. In it were about 2,000 dollars in cash and a large manila envelope. Inside the envelope she found photographs of wooded areas with instructions written on the pictures and more detailed instructions on the backs of the pictures. One of the things in the envelope was a map with the words *PLEASE DESTROY* printed at the top. A circuitous route was marked on the map.

There was also a note that someone had written to him saying they were dissatisfied with the previously furnished material and asking for specific information "on rotor." She wondered what the rotor was and thought it might perhaps be part of a submarine. She would not find out until years later that it was the key part of a highly secret method of sending and receiving encrypted messages that uses the mathematical laws of probability to make it virtually impossible for any one to break U.S. radio codes—without espionage.

It was the kind of experience designed to give anyone goose bumps. For a split second she was afraid Walker would come home suddenly and find out that she knew he was a Soviet spy. But a few weeks later, when she and John got in an argument, she blurted out, "You're a spy! You're nothing but a traitor to your country. I found the stuff in your desk—the money, the pictures, the instructions."

He became furious, angrier than she had ever seen him, scowling darkly. He began hitting her in the face with his fists until she thought she would pass out, blackening both of her eyes. He warned her that someone might have overheard her accusation. He said he could go to jail for the rest of his life, leaving her to take care of the children. Although he was furious that she had found him out, he braggingly told her that he had begun his espionage activity while based in Charleston. He later explained the operation to her and made her accompany him on some of his drops.

"I walked around with these two big shiners for days," she remembered. "If he was such a great spy, how did I find out? He wasn't too damn bright. He used to tell me one of my problems is that I was too smart. I just figured he was too dumb." The way she described her confrontation with her husband convinced Price.

She had been torn between love of family and love of country while agonizing over the years about what she should do. And she had also worried about being charged as an accessory not only because she had not turned him in when she first found out but because he had entrapped her into being a participant. She loved her country and considered herself a patriot, and had felt especially guilty when she visited other nations in the company of other Navy wives. "I've seen how other people have to live, Mr. Price, and I can't imagine not being grateful to be an American."

She believed that her brother-in-law, Art, was probably helping her ex-husband pass information to the Soviets. Art had retired from the Navy after twenty-one years, his last grade having been lieutenant commander, and he now worked for a defense contractor in Norfolk, the VSE Corporation, and still had access to classified information. (She neglected to mention, at that point, that she had once had an affair with Art and felt bitter toward him even though she described him as "a real sweet guy.")

In 1966, to make extra money, Barbara told Price that she and her husband had started the Bamboo Snack Bar in Ladson, South Carolina—a Charleston suburb. Originally, it had catered to teenagers, but later when they got a beer and wine license the clientele changed to servicemen and local blue-collar workers.

John started passing secrets to the Soviets before they left Charleston when the snack bar began to fail. But she was not positive that he had not been spying even earlier. Money was his motive, but according to Barbara they really had not suffered too much financially. "There was never a reason for John to do what he did. If the business failed, it was no big deal. We were thirty years old. We could start again."

Barbara had spent a lot of time thinking back on those days. They had hired a cook, Nora Moody, to help make pizzas and hamburgers. "Aunt Nora" lived next door to their bar. They paid her three dollars an hour, a salary that was then higher than minimum wage and generous by local standards. Nora became one of the family, and her small sons, Randy and Richard, played with the Walker children. The Walkers lived in a house trailer behind the bar.

That's when the first signs of a sea change in John's life became apparent: he became different, cruel and unfaithful; sarcasm turned to heated criticism. He told Barbara she could sleep with bar customers to raise extra money if she wanted to. The remark was designed to hurt.

Barbara had tried on several occasions in Norfolk, California, and in Maine to turn in her former husband, but she could never muster enough resolve to go through with it. Once, she started to tell a good family friend, Don Clevenger, but decided not to at the last moment. "Cleve" Clevenger was a radioman who had served with Walker on two submarines, the *Razorback* and the *Andrew Jackson*. Barbara was a good friend of Cleve's wife, Kathy.

Barbara explained that her husband was not an ideologue, but a very greedy person, while she cared nothing for the luxuries that Walker coveted. She valued friends and family above all. "John is a very materialistic man," she said. "He could never understand why I couldn't care about the money, that money didn't have any meaning. I practically threw it away."

Despite her growing dislike of her husband, "We talked about this frequently. Why did we talk about it? It was a way of life. Adaptability, or you go stark raving mad."

At times she tried to believe that perhaps he was a double agent. "I tried to convince myself that was what he was doing—that he was being very patriotic."

On two occasions she thought that Walker had been caught or was about to be arrested. "Once, a man came to the door in Union City in 1973 and warned John to stop having an affair with his wife." Because the man looked official, dressed in a suit, she feared he might be an FBI agent. Later, in Norfolk, she thought that her husband's executive officer had realized that John was spying but "was not smart enough" to piece it together.

She began to drink more after she found out about Walker's espionage. "Liquor was the only way I could get to sleep." After the divorce she had moved to Skowhegan to be near her brothers, a sister, and other relatives, and because "it was as far away from John as I could get." By the time she and Walker were divorced on June 22, 1976, her drinking had become severe and his affairs with other women had become more brazen and more frequent. They lived apart for some time prior to the divorce, but he would sometimes visit her and the four children. She knew then where he kept the secret documents in the house—even after they separated—for eventual sale to the Russians.

When she moved to Maine, she told Walker she was leaving on a Friday but had the moving truck come on the preceding Wednesday so that she could leave without harassment. She took Michael and the girls to Skowhegan, where she hoped to get some support from her family. Soon Cynthia left the household to work, and Laura joined the Army. Margaret went back to Norfolk and stayed for a time with her father while she looked for work. Walker would call from time to time to inquire about the children. She finally agreed to let Michael, who adored his father and disliked the New England winters, join Walker in Norfolk and go to school there. Walker pestered all the children to go into either the military or a police force. He wanted his son to enter the SEALS, the elite Navy frogman unit, but he did not have the qualifications.

She was particularly worried about how an investigation of John Walker would affect her twenty-two-year-old son, who was now serving aboard the aircraft carrier *Nimitz*. She told Price that Michael was a wholesome, decent youth. John Walker's arrest would be a blow to him, but it was something he would have to learn to live with, even though it might adversely affect his Navy career. But Barbara thought that he didn't really like the Navy anyway, that he wanted to go home to his young wife, Rachel, and move to California where he could surf. He had loved California when the family lived in San Diego in the early 1970s.

WHEN BARBARA WALKER first arrived in Maine, she moved in with her sister and brother-in-law. Anne Crowley Nelson and her hus-

band, Robert, lived about thirty miles from Skowhegan, in a rural area near Anson and Waterville.

"They all moved in here," said Robert Nelson, who works at a paper mill. "All of them—Barbara, her son, and all three daughters. They were city kids, and they had never lived in the country before. I can tell you it was hard getting along with them for a while. I couldn't get used to them. They stayed with us for six months. Then they moved to Skowhegan where Barbara got a job."

After the move to Skowhegan, a mill town of 7,500 along the Kennebec River, Barbara got a job as a "gluer" with the Dexter Shoe Company. It was hard work, the hardest work of her life. In some ways, she felt that her life was behind her, but she would at least make a good home for her children. A neighbor once asked her to go to communion, and Barbara replied, "There's a reason why I can't, for my own conscience." It seemed a puzzling statement at the time.

Relatives and friends agree that Barbara worked hard, coming home each night to her 35-dollar-a-week apartment with glue smeared on her clothing. According to one neighbor, "She worked faster than two men. She brought home 250 to 300 dollars a week, but she really worked for it. She was so exhausted that all she could do was lie on the couch and sleep until it was time to go to work the next day."

"My sister worked very hard to support her family and maintain a nice clean home," concurs Anne Nelson. "She had a family to raise and had put that top priority. My sister was like the rest of us. We keep a lot of things inside. We keep our troubles inside ourselves unless we need each other. She put up with a lot from that man over the years."

According to Royce Knowles, principal of Skowhegan Area Junior High School, Michael had behavioral problems as an eighth grader, which didn't make Barbara's home life very pleasant. After a hard day at work she would return to a sullen, griping son who whined about missing Norfolk, his dad, and the ocean. But despite his whining, he was a loving youth who did much of the housework for his mother and even some of the cooking. She clung to him and tried to talk him out of returning to Norfolk to be with his father. But there was something in her air of desperation that made Michael want to escape all the more. "He was different," Knowles said. "He was probably more street wise. He didn't dress or behave as our kids did."

"He was real bitter about being up here," said Paul Vestal, a former youth services worker. "He wanted to stay in Virginia with his father."

Michael was suspended from junior high school for a brief time because of behavioral problems and was placed in an alternative tutorial program for adults seeking general equivalency diplomas. "What he found in social life elsewhere doesn't fit into Skowhegan," Marti Stevens, who ran the program, reported. "He was much more sophisticated and mature than his cohorts. He was here with his mom without friends. He was very impressed with his dad. He knew that he was heading in a direction that would mean trouble. He was bright, quick, and helpful, and nonjudgmental with the adults, very agreeable, very personable. The adults liked him."

Barbara Walker couldn't pay for Michael's tutoring, so a barter arrangement was made and Michael fed Marti Stevens's thirty cows and cleaned out her barn, matching each hour she tutored him. Despite his unhappiness, Michael was a good student who tried hard in her class.

"He stopped me on the street a year later. His hair had been cut. He looked different. He put his hand out and said, 'Marti, you don't recognize me, but I want to thank you. I think I learned something. Now my dad is bringing me back to Virginia and has arranged to pay for me for a military academy.'"

NOW PRICE DECIDED to question Laura, too. "I can tell you, he really drilled me over and over. His questions were very thorough."

Laura told the FBI that when she was an Army communications specialist at Fort Polk, Louisiana, in 1978 and 1979, she was approached by her father, who had flown his airplane to Baton Rouge. He tried to recruit her as a Soviet spy, and she had refused, although not immediately. Walker wanted her to think it over. It was then that she told her husband about her father.

Barbara Walker had called Walker and told him that his efforts to recruit Laura were a "cheap shot." He had just giggled in that strange way of his.

Price now informed his superiors in Washington, who suggested that before they made a major move Barbara Walker and her daughter should be given lie-detector tests. Barbara and Laura agreed without hesitation.

BARBARA WALKER AND Laura Walker Synder passed the polygraph. Barbara's answers indicated no deception, and the agent giving the test even paid her an offhand compliment: "You have difficulty dealing with lies don't you?"

"Windflyer," the FBI's code name for the investigation, was to be a four-month surveillance of the man who masterminded what FBI Deputy Director Philip Parker would term the most damaging, biggest, and longest-lasting spy network in this century. Before it was over, more than one-hundred agents would participate in the operation, coordinating with the CIA and Navy intelligence. FBI Director William Webster and Parker both instructed the Norfolk FBI office, counterintelligence agents, and the Washington field office to make Windflyer their number one priority. "Whatever you want, you'll get it."

"We knew this was big—very big—from the beginning," said Parker, who played a key role in coordinating the Washington and Norfolk offices. The day-to-day operation was led by Jack Wagner, who was in charge of the Norfolk office, Joseph Wolfinger, supervisor, and Robert W. Hunter, an agent who worked the case almost eighteen hours a day. There were dozens of others, including FBI counterintelligence specialists, lab technicians, and cryptographers borrowed from Naval intelligence.

Wagner, Wolfinger, and Hunter were painfully aware that they had nothing on Walker but the recollections of his former wife, admittedly a disgruntled and angry woman, and his estranged daughter. Even an inept defense lawyer could beat this kind of evidence. Initially, there was also a lingering doubt, based on the possibility that Barbara Walker and her daughter, although they passed the polygraph, might have been deceived by a prank pulled by John Walker, a man, the FBI soon learned, who enjoyed cruel practical jokes.

The FBI sought permission, for national security reasons, for a covert wiretap of John Walker's office and home telephones, and the tap was approved after a brief secret session with a federal judge specializing in foreign surveillance. The FBI's electronics experts were unhappy to learn that Walker was the co-owner, with Laurie Robinson, of one detective agency, Confidential Reports, and owned another that specialized in debugging and sweeps to check for tapped telephones and other kinds of electronic surveillance. This firm, Electronic Counterspy, was known to be effective. One of its biggest clients was the Portsmouth Naval Shipyard, a facility teeming with classified projects and data, a gold mine for espionage. It was a place to which Walker's contract gave him unhampered access without suspicion.

Because of Walker's expertise at detecting telephone taps, the FBI sought the cooperation of the telephone company in putting a tap on his home and office telephones that could not be detected. Use of any of the telephones automatically activated a tape, and agents could also monitor it live. It was tedious work, and they knew that Walker was probably too smart to say anything incriminating on the telephone, but in the end it did pay off.

The FBI also rented an office downstairs in the same two-story brick office building on Parliament Drive in Virginia Beach where Walker had his detective agency. They rented it under the name of a Norfolk construction company.

In addition, the FBI staked out Walker's two-story brick and frame Old Ocean View Avenue home. They soon learned that he had a Dodge van with curtained blue windows, a houseboat, and an eight-year-old Grumman Tiger Airplane—an orange and brown four-place craft with a 180 horsepower Lycoming engine capable of flying anywhere in the United States at cruising speeds of almost 200 miles per hour. Walker was a licensed pilot and, on the surface, a successful businessman.

His pretty girlfriend, Pamela Kay "P.K." Carroll, twenty-four, looked like a blend of Grace Kelly and Faye Dunaway. She spent most of her nights with Walker, but she still maintained an apartment of her own to avoid criticism by the Norfolk Police Department. She was a policewoman trainee just three months away from becoming a permanent part of the Norfolk police force. She had worked for Walker at the detective agency. He frequently took her on expensive trips and lavished money on the excursions, renting Lincoln Continental limousines complete with chauffeurs, staying in luxury hotels, and tipping like a millionaire.

SHORTLY AFTER THE FBI launched Windflyer, Barbara Walker had second thoughts. She was haunted by the sound of John Walker's voice saying to her, "You wouldn't want your fifty-year-old husband to go to jail, would you, Barbara?"

She thought that if she warned him he might flee, but she disliked the idea of dealing with him personally. She decided to risk the FBI's wrath and call Arthur Walker. Later, when asked about this, she explained, "I called Art to tell John I had turned him in. I thought he would go to Russia. I wanted to give John a chance to run. That bond goes a lot deeper than you think." The FBI was furious, but they didn't want to do anything that would cause Barbara Walker to behave irrationally, so they concealed their anger. Later, she agreed to gloss over the incident to ease Walker's suspicions.

After Barbara's call, Art immediately telephoned John and asked to meet him. They never talked about such matters on the telephone. They tried to decide whether Barbara was bluffing. Art was worried, but John reminded him that she had made empty threats after a few drinks many times before. Art protested that she sounded serious this time. John insisted that there was no need for concern, although they should be careful for a time and try to determine whether they were under surveillance.

"No one is good enough to tap my telephones and get away with it," John boasted.

3

Who Is Johnny Walker?

To the God who gives joy to my youth.
                    —Johnny Walker, altar boy, 1947

While they staked out his home and office and monitored his telephone, the FBI—particularly agent Robert Hunter—began a thorough study of John Anthony "Johnny" Walker, Jr., and his family. Special agents of the Naval Investigative Service also began quietly gathering material on Walker. They now believed Barbara Walker's story, for they had learned just enough through initial wiretap surveillance to confirm that something was amiss. They weren't sure yet whether they had a whale or a minnow, but they were certain that the surveillance and the thorough background investigation would be worthwhile.

Walker grew up in Scranton, Pennsylvania, a former anthracite coal-mining town that managed to survive by industrial diversification after the anthracite veins were mined out. By the mid-nineteenth century, it was such a bustling town with plenty of work to be had that it attracted many immigrant settlers, including Slavic, Italian, English, Irish, and German families. One of those Irish families was the Walkers; and one of those Italian families was the Scaramuzzo family, the large family of John Walker's mother, Margaret Loretta Scaramuzzo. The Scaramuzzos owned the Boston Fish Market on Penn Avenue, a thriving concern.

Scranton is circled by mountains that take on a bluish haze in the summer and become a blaze of red and gold in the autumn. The Lackawanna River cuts through the heart of the town.

It is a Norman Rockwell kind of city mixed with industrial squalor and a bit of seediness: a miniature Pittsburgh. But it could be, despite its gray side, a good place for a child to grow up—a kind of Hannibal on the Lackawanna. There are creeks and mountains to explore within walking distance of every neighborhood. In the winter, there are plenty of good places nearby to sled and ski. And schools are lenient about absences during the hunting season, with deer abounding in the hills within easy driving distance. People are hardworking, largely blue-collar types, but friendly and generous. They are also usually very, very patriotic.

It is against this backdrop that John and Arthur Walker were formed and matured.

They both attended St. Patrick's Catholic High School, which still exists in Scranton but has been converted to a Catholic elementary school. It is a severe-looking red brick structure, constructed in 1887, that in some ways looks more like a fortress than a high school. John Walker, Sr., also attended St. Patrick's. Arthur thrived there, and Johnny hated it. John Walker, Jr., was an underachiever and the nuns gave him a rough time. Although Walker was fond in later life of depicting the nuns as cruel and overly exacting, they were described as firm but imminently fair by Arthur's classmate, Vincent Peter Tiberi. He laughed as he recalled that one of them used to throw a bucket of holy water over unruly students in the classroom, declaring "the devil is in this room."

Both Art and Johnny had been altar boys in the church where they answered the priest who said, "I will go to the altar of God," with "To the God who gives joy to my youth."

Margaret Walker, a sweet, self-sacrificing woman who held a modest-paying job in a photo studio, had a beautiful voice and enjoyed singing and playing the piano. Arthur inherited her musical talents. He was in the band, playing second trumpet alongside his best friend, Tiberi, and he lettered in baseball and football. He was handsome, with a full head of jet black hair that he kept slicked back in the fashion of the 1950s. He was a member of the drama club and acted in virtually every school play. Ironically, he usually played the hero, and Vince, the villain. John, on the other hand, tried with little success to master a variety of woodwind instruments.

Arthur caught the eye of Rita Clare Fritsch, one of the prettiest girls in his class. She made it a practice to join in the projects in which Art was involved, and soon the two became inseparable. Classmates recall that they started out almost as brother and sister, the relationship evolving to boyfriend-girlfriend. Vince had the use of a 1952 Oldsmobile 88, and he and his girlfriends and Art and Rita were frequent companions, playing miniature golf, going to drive-in movies and school functions, but mostly hanging around an ice cream parlor on Main Avenue called Pantages. At lunchtime they would sometimes walk across the street to Skettino's grocery where they bought sandwiches and soft drinks. That was a rare treat for Arthur and John, however, because the family was very poor. They usually brought a sandwich from home. It was a not very unusual teenage lifestyle in the 1950s. "We were instilled with God, country, and family," said John Tulaney, who sat across the aisle from Arthur.

The school motto was First Things First. "It meant you should put your life in perspective," Tulaney explained. "Your home and your family were very important. The Korean War was hanging over our heads then, and we wanted to serve our country." (Tulaney joined the Army and retired as a lieutenant colonel.)

It irked Johnny Walker that Arthur was held up as a model and a paragon, so Johnny became a rebel, a sullen outsider, hanging out with the seedy fringe of kids who ridiculed the kind of students Arthur ran around with, the wholesome, hardworking students who participated in sports and extracurricular activities. While Art was a good student, making Bs and As, Johnny could scarcely keep a C average.

He was a small, almost mousy youth with a weak chin, and he developed a reputation for having a sharp but nasty wit, his defense against the wholesome good students whom he secretly envied.

There was a dark side to Walker family life. According to James Walker, the youngest of the three brothers, peace at the house on Geraldine Court was often shattered by his father's drinking. Alcohol "drove us the hell out of the house."

"When Johnny drank, his whole personality changed," said Frank Malone, who worked with the elder Walker. "He became argumentative and an authority on everything. I once saw him throw a bottle through a plate glass window when a bartender refused to serve him."

John senior was a music lover and often invited musician friends to his house. They would play in jam sessions all night. Johnny Walker often told friends about his father's all-night music sessions and "having to step over drunks passed out on the floor the next morning."

John senior was the doorman-manager of the Roosevelt Theater in Scranton before becoming a disc jockey for radio station WARM and later WEJL. He became known as "Johnny Walker the Night Walker" on his nighttime radio show. This made Art more popular, but Johnny moved even further out of the mainstream of student life.

Johnny began working as an usher in the theater, constantly watching the good guy-bad guy movies of the era. He would regale shipmates years later with stories of the libidinous scenes he had witnessed—not on the screen but in the seats. He did not tell them that he was embarrassed and wounded when girls he admired in school showed up with other boys.

The steady diet of movies fed his impressionable ego. Johnny began to live in a dreamworld of heroic and daring accomplishments—the derring-do he saw on the silver screen.

"John never played sports," James Walker remembered. "He was more interested in adventures, like going for hikes, that sort of thing." Friends and relatives say he had the unique capacity for investing even the most mundane hike in the woods with adventure—making it a dangerous safari. A walk along the Lackawanna was a trip along the Amazon. His fantasy world of movies and real life began to merge. One close friend described an elaborate earth and wood fort he built to fend off an enemy attack.

All the time he was becoming increasingly resentful of authority as the family's home life deteriorated. Relations between his parents were strained. His father's drinking, a family secret for a while, soon became common knowledge in the neighborhood. Policeman Armando Allegucci recalled making trips to the Walker home to quell family disturbances. The children were often shipped off to relatives to get them away from the fireworks at home. This was when Arthur learned to mask his emotions, both at home and at school.

"It started when I was young. We three boys had one big room upstairs. My dad would come home, and I'd be the one who would have to go down and take the flak. The two younger ones would stay up there hiding and I would have to take whatever flak a drunk wants to give you, a whipping or whatever. I worked hard at masking emotions, which you learn in the Navy. It's a close life on the submarine. You can't let your emotions get the better of you, whether it is anger or sadness. You got to keep the stiff upper lip—you can't show anyone that you are afraid. It's the fear that you really have to mask, you know. You can't let anyone know about that, the fear."

Arthur appeared in the St. Patrick's yearbook more than anyone else in his class. Indeed, it was his picture that introduced the yearbook and his picture that ended it. He was shown in both his football and baseball uniform, wearing jersey No. 13 on the football team. The teams he played on had winning records against some of the toughest schools in the Catholic league. Another picture showed him acting the lead in a play called *The Blarney Stone*.

When Arthur graduated he made plans to marry Rita, and he began attending the University of Scranton. He did well there, but life at home as a day student became unbearable so he joined the Navy "to get away from our father," according to James.

Johnny Walker was never in his school yearbook, not even for routine class pictures. He had no friends to double-date with like Art had, so he spent many nights sulking and hiding from his parents in the modest home on Geraldine Court. Often he would walk down to Pantages where the other kids were hanging out, hoping for a measure of acceptance. He had a casual relationship with a couple of girls, but they never seemed to take him seriously. He used to dream of doing something dramatic that would get their attention and affection, something as dramatic and daring as the scenes in the movies he saw constantly.

It was on one of these nights in the spring of 1955 when he was hanging around aimlessly that an event occurred that revealed some of the incipient flaws in Walker's character.

He met another youth, a local tough who had a fast car. He told Walker that there was a girl in Pittston he was interested in and suggested that Walker go with him to see her.

They drove to Pittston, a small town near Scranton and en route heard the final minutes of "Johnny Walker the Night Walker" on the car radio.

When they arrived in Pittston, the girl they had driven to see was not at home. On the way back, the fellow told Walker that he often committed burglary to raise extra money, and he suggested they break into a few places. Walker agreed.

They broke into two Esso service stations, getting two tires, a few cans of motor oil, and a few dollars. Then they broke into a used-car lot's small office, where they found only a few cans of tire cleaner. It was not a very good haul. Then Walker's newfound friend suggested that Cuzzo & Gavigan's mens' clothing store at 139 Main Avenue in their own neighborhood, just down from Pantages, would certainly have some money in the cash register.

By now it was almost 4 A.M. They drove to the store and parked the car in the lot of Durkan's Funeral Home next door. Walker's buddy left the keys in the car in case they had to make a quick getaway.

They pushed open a board in a rickety clapboard fence and walked toward the store's rear door. It was dark, but nearby street lights provided some dim illumination. The lot in back of the store was strewn with junk and litter. They found to their dismay that the windows were barred. They noticed a large ventilating shaft and decided to break in by crawling down the shaft. Soon they discovered that this, too, was blocked. They decided to give up, and as they were crawling out of the shaft Johnny stepped on a loose board that plummeted to the concrete, making a loud, reverbrating noise. It was 4:05 A.M. As luck would dictate, Scranton policeman William Shygelski was walking by the front of the store. After the board dropped, the two youths were silent for a time, trying to determine whether anyone had heard the noise.

Shygelski drew his .38-caliber service revolver and raced around to the back. The youths heard his footsteps, and Walker's buddy dashed for a pile of litter and hid, correctly judging that he would not have time to reach the car.

Walker raced toward the car, clambering through the fence. Shygelski ordered him to halt, then fired one shot. Suddenly John Anthony Walker, Jr., realized that life is not the movies. That shot was for real. He started the car and raced away, heading home to Geraldine Court. Because the patrolman was on foot, Johnny did not drive fast after he got a few blocks away. But Shygelski, who had perhaps seen a few movies himself at the Roosevelt Theater, commandeered a passing car and directed the driver to give chase. Initially he lost Walker but found him stopped dutifully at a red light at North Hyde Park and Jackson Street, near both his home and St. Patrick's.

Walker looked up to see the patrolman get out of the car and approach him on foot, gun drawn. Walker sped off. Shygelski dropped to one knee and fired a careful shot at the gas tank of the vehicle and missed. He raced back to the commandeered car and gave chase. Police reports said speeds reached 95 miles per hour. Shygelski gave up the chase, and Walker continued west towards Williamsport, a two-and-a-half-hour drive. He arrived about 6:30 A.M. and, exhausted, randomly parked in a driveway. Later in the morning, when he was found sleeping in the driveway by a 22-year-old house painter who lived in the house next to the driveway, he struck up a conversation and made friends with the painter. He asked for permission to sleep in the car in the driveway, which the painter secured from his brother-in-law, who owned the house. But soon the family took pity on Walker, and they let him sleep inside the house. He gave them the two automobile tires in payment. Later in the day, aware that his mother would be alarmed when he didn't come home, he called a girlfriend and told her to tell his mother he was okay. He also told the girl that she could write to him at a greeting card and novelty shop in Williamsport where he had gotten a job.

It was true to his character that Walker called the girl and bragged that he was a fugitive. He could just as well have called his mother at her job in a photo studio or his father at the radio station. The girl turned him in, and he was arrested by the Williamsport police on June 1, 1955, and brought back to Scranton, where he was held in county jail. He promptly told the police about his buddy, and they were both brought before juvenile court Judge Otto P. Robinson, who was known as a very strict, tough judge. When they came before him, Robinson said, "I can't see anything in favor of either one of you. You are just two crooks. The only thing in your favor is that this is the first time you have been in court."

The police checked with Mother Vincent at Walker's school, and she told them that Walker's conduct was "generally fair" and that he was a "fair" student. On the other hand, the Rev. John W. Casey, pastor of St. Patrick's Church, now the pastor emeritus of Nativity of the Blessed Virgin Mary Church in Tunkhannock, Pennsylvania, appeared in court on behalf of Walker. Father Casey, always protective of his flock, exaggerated on the side of charity as he told the court, "John Walker is an exceptional student and, it is hard to say this under the circumstances, but in school he has been a fine student." Father Casey, said longtime Scranton residents, always made such appearances and always spoke highly of students in trouble.

Judge Robinson turned to Walker and said, "In church and school you are supposed to learn what is right and what is wrong."

He first sentenced them to Camp Hill Correctional Institution for an indefinite term, letting the sentence sink in a bit, then placed them on probation instead. "This is a chance for you fellows to go straight," he said. "Don't make another mistake. You've got to be honest or you go to Camp Hill. Learn the Ten Commandments and obey them and you won't be in further trouble.

"In a year or so you boys will be in the service and when you go in there, they will ask you if you have a criminal record. When they ask you if you have ever been in juvenile court, so help me, you'd better answer it correctly, for they will come up here and check your record. The officer for the Army will ask us about you, and we would like to say, 'Yes, they were in a little trouble, but since that time they were able to straighten themselves out.' The Army doesn't want crooks."

The burglary was reported in the *Scranton Times,* publicity that Margaret Walker found mortifying. Although the names were protected, in such a small town the news swept around the neigh-

borhood. The publicity also caused Walker's already poor relationship with his father to deteriorate further.

Walker dropped out of school and began a listless, meaningless
life of hanging around town, playing pinball machines, escaping
into his fantasy world, hiding from his father, staying out late. But
he had to attend Mass as one of the terms of his probation, and he
disliked this intensely.

Arthur Walker, who was stationed in New London, Connecticut, happened to be home on leave shortly after the burglary, and
he decided to talk to Judge Robinson in Johnny's behalf. He asked
Robinson if he would suspend the probation if Johnny agreed to
join the Navy. Judge Robinson agreed, and Johnny Walker began
his Navy career. He was sent to Bainbridge Naval Training Center,
glad to get out of Scranton.

Years later Walker would tell friends of the night that he "E and
E'd"—Escaped and Evaded—the Scranton police. He would depict
the event as a swashbuckling youthful adventure—like a scene
right out of the movies.

Arthur, in an interview with the *Washington Post Magazine,* had
a different recollection of those days:

> I don't know if I understand my relationship with John when I
> really think about it. It developed over a period of years, our
> upbringing, me being the oldest, and there were some bad times in
> our home. Some bad times. I remember when I was about twenty
> and was in the Navy at New London. I went home one weeknd to
> Scranton to see Rita, really, not the family, but I was sitting in the
> house and I could see that John was going under because of our
> home life. I had gotten out. I was still sending my paychecks home
> to my mother, but there was little money and my father was
> drinking heavily then, and he and Mom were fighting. It was
> before he left and it was bad, really bad.
>
> I had been in the Navy about two years, and it was a whole new
> world to me. I had seen opportunities open for someone who
> wanted to learn something, and I said to him, "Hey man, here it
> is . . ." So I took him down to the Navy recruiting office. [That's
> when Arthur spoke to Judge Robinson in Johnny's behalf.]
>
> After that I think that he knew that if he needed something, he

could ask me and I would do it for him. We got a phone call or letter once, and all he said was that he needed one hundred bucks and that was a lot of money back then . . . I wired it to him.

It wasn't always monetary. A lot of what was between us was protective feelings for one another in childhood, watching out for each other, protecting your brother, you know? It's what you did, what you were supposed to do.

The Navy paid Johnny Walker's bus fare to Bainbridge, Maryland, for basic training. As the bus slowly wound its way up into the mountains and out of Scranton, Johnny Walker said goodbye to the city of his youth. He would only come back for brief visits.

In Bainbridge, he learned to keep a neat bunk, tie bowline, square, sheet bend, and water knots, jump from a ship feet first with his head down and his arms tucked under his chest, and very basic elements of navigation and drilling. In the aptitude tests given recruits, it was determined that Walker might make a good radioman.

To his surprise, he found that he liked the Navy. Even though he resented the authority, he could work the system to suit himself far more easily than he could fool the nuns at St. Patrick's.

EARLY IN HIS Navy career, Johnny learned in a call to his mother that John senior had left his mother for a young woman named Dottie. His mother reported that he had lost his disc jockey job and had gone to another radio station in Maryland. John Walker, Sr., would later file for divorce and eventually start a new family.

4

Navy Life

Happy Birthday Chiefie Weefie.
—Inscription on a birthday cake made for John Walker
on his twenty-eighth birthday, July 28, 1965

John Walker's early career followed the standard route, but he
made the grade more rapidly than most. Those who worked with
him found him to be a quick study. After leaving the Bainbridge
Training Center in 1956, he attended Naval Schools Command in
Norfolk, Virginia, then served aboard the USS *Johnnie Hutchins,* a
destroyer escort, as a radioman until 1958. He was then sent to the
USS *Forrestal* aircraft carrier as a radioman. In 1959 he was
assigned to the Naval Amphibious Base at Little Creek, Virginia.
From 1959 to 1960, he served aboard the USS *Howard W. Gilmore,*
a submarine tender, then was transferred to the USS *Penguin,* a
submarine rescue vessel.

As always, he envied Arthur, who was actually serving on
submarines while he was relegated to submarine support vessels.
He admired Arthur's submariner emblem: a submarine prow and
conning tower flanked by dolphins. He wanted his dolphins and
applied for assignment to submarine duty, but weak eyes kept him

out. However, Arthur pulled strings and succeeded in getting his brother detailed to submarines and submarine training in 1960.

Until this time, his access to sensitive material had been random and limited. In 1960 he was assigned to the U.S. Naval Submarine Base in New London, Connecticut, where for the first time he had frequent access to sensitive manuals detailing naval equipment and how it functioned.

In 1961 he was sent as a radioman to the diesel submarine USS *Razorback,* his first submarine duty. In 1962 he was selected to serve as a radioman aboard the new SSBN *Andrew Jackson,* a nuclear ballistic missile submarine in the final stages of construction that would be commissioned the following year. It was customary to choose crews before actual sea duty began. Walker's potential for serious damage to national security began aboard this vessel.

After duty aboard the *Andrew Jackson,* he was sent in 1963 to Crypto Repair School, Naval Schools Command, in Vallejo, California. There he had unlimited access to cryptographic equipment manuals and other data that were solid gold to the Soviets. He also learned for the first time exactly how cryptographic equipment worked and became adept at repairing such equipment. All who knew him said he had an astonishing aptitude for electronics.

He was returned to the *Andrew Jackson* as chief radioman in 1963. He was on board in October 1963 when the sub fired an A-3 Polaris missile off Cape Canaveral. Rear Admiral I. J. Galantin, the Polaris program director, also was on board.

In 1965 he was transferred to the SSBN *Simon Bolivar* where he became senior chief radioman and obtained official top-secret clearance for the first time. This gave him unquestioned access to a wide range of top-secret cryptographic communications. It was here, while based in Charleston, South Carolina, that Barbara Walker said her husband began spying for the Soviets. However, some investigators wonder whether his espionage activities might have begun as early as 1965. Only after exhaustive debriefing, agents say, can they be sure of how early Walker began his espionage activities.

He served on the *Bolivar* until 1967, when he was moved to the Naval Submarine Force, Atlantic Fleet, Norfolk, Virginia. He was a communications watch officer and message center officer. Here he knew the location and mission of every U.S. attack submarine, as well as U.S. intelligence and techniques for locating every Soviet submarine and surface vessel.

Aside from the information on cryptographic equipment, information passed during this time could have been the most devastating of all, some Navy analysts say.

Arthur Walker also began his Navy career at the Bainbridge Naval Training Center, going on to Fleet Sonar School in Key West in 1953, and then to Submarine School in New London, Connecticut, in 1954.

He served on the SSN *Torsk,* a diesel sub, from 1954 to 1955 and was then sent to Naval Schools Command at the Naval Station in Norfolk. He was sent back to the *Torsk* in 1955 and served until he was again sent to Fleet Sonar School in Key West. He returned to the *Torsk* once more in 1956 and served until 1959. This submarine was converted to carry a guided missile system during this period in Charleston, South Carolina.

In 1959 he was stationed aboard the SSN *Madrigal,* a fleet snorkel submarine, and was aboard as it completed the evaluation project of the Regulus Trounce Guidance System. He returned to the Navy Submarine School in New London in 1959, then to the USS *Orion,* a repair ship. He served briefly aboard the SSN *Carp,* another diesel submarine.

In 1960 he was sent to Naval Schools Command in Newport, Rhode Island. From 1960 to 1963 he served on the USS *Corsair,* a survey ship based in New London. He was promoted to lieutenant junior grade during this time and participated in the North Atlantic Treaty Organization's "Big Game" exercises in 1962, which took him to Italy, France, Greece, and Spain.

The following year, 1963, he was assigned to the diesel submarine SSN *Callao* and participated in torpedo experiments and evaluation of sonar equipment. From 1964 to 1966 he helped train reservists aboard the USS *Manta,* a survey ship.

From 1966 to 1968 he served on board the diesel submarine *Grenadier* in a secret project not listed in the service record other than to mention that it was a classified mission. It was during this time period that he overlapped duty with John in Charleston, South Carolina. Some investigators believe that it was while both were in Charleston that the two brothers discussed for the first time the value of the secret information to which they had access. There is some indication that Arthur may have been the first to mention it.

Arthur was a lieutenant commander in the Fleet Tactical School—a training aids division officer and staff duty officer in Norfolk—until his retirement in 1973.

Arthur Walker and the *Torsk* both retired from active duty in the summer of 1973, the *Torsk* in May and Arthur in July. He spent more time on the *Torsk* than on any other vessel of his career. He knew the *Torsk* and its idiosyncracies better than he knew his children. It is an unusual submarine because it spanned events ranging from action against the Japanese during World War II to the missile age, including a role in the 1960 Lebanese crisis, the Cuban missile crisis—during which it boarded and searched Soviet ships—the Korean War, and countless training missions.

It would be tragic if the *Torsk,* the Norwegian word for codfish, is forever remembered as the submarine Arthur Walker spent so much of his Navy career aboard, because its history is distinguished. The keel was laid in Portsmouth, New Hampshire, on June 7, 1944, a time when the United States had lost almost fifty submarines. By the end of the war fifty-two submarines would be lost, including their crews of 3,505 officers and enlisted men. The *Torsk* completed training and shakedown off the Florida coast and then went through the Panama Canal. It arrived at its first battle station in the Pacific on April 15, 1945, off Honshu and Kii Stuido. She operated in a pack with the *Sandlance, Cero,* and *Guardfish.* In the waning days of the war, the *Torsk* torpedoed a cargo ship and two small coastal defense frigates. The frigates were sunk on the day of the cease-fire but before the order reached all of the armed forces.

The *Torsk,* 311 feet by 27 feet across the beam, carried six torpedo tubes forward and four aft. Fourteen spares were carried, and many of them did double duty as bunk platforms for the *Torsk*'s complement of seventy-four enlisted men and eight officers. Torpedoes used by the *Torsk* in World War II weighed 3,000 pounds each and carried a warhead of about 500 pounds of TNT. By the end of the war, improved warheads carried 668 pounds of an improved explosive called torpex. Each "fish" cost about 10,000 dollars.

Like most World War II vintage subs, the *Torsk* had two battery rooms with 126 cells in each one. Each cell weighed 2,000 pounds with an overall weight for the batteries of 250 tons. Each cell held 31 gallons of battery acid mixture (compare that to about 2 quarts for an automobile battery). The *Torsk,* as did all diesels, had to run on the surface at night to power generators for the batteries, using four monster Fairbanks-Morse diesels (the connecting rods were almost too heavy to pick up). Each engine produced 1600 horsepower and could drive the boat at 20 knots on the surface; two large 2700-horsepower electric motors drove twin screws to make about 8 or 9 knots while submerged. It was a Model-T compared to nuclear submarines.

The *Torsk* had a Kleinschmidt Evaporator on board that converted 1000 gallons of seawater per day into fresh water. Under the galley was a freezer locker that held twelve beef carcasses, for the Navy always stressed the quality of food on board submarines, even during the diesel era. The submarine also had its own ice cream-making machine.

The *Torsk* was assigned to the U.S. Naval Reserve as a training submarine in 1967 at the age of twenty-three. She established a record of 11,884 dives, a record that will never be broken because modern submarines stay down for the duration of a cruise and don't dive so often.

The *Torsk* today is open to the public in Baltimore Harbor, Pier 4. It is owned by the State of Maryland and maintained by the City of Baltimore. Officials expect that tourism will increase once it becomes known that this was Arthur Walker's submarine.

WHEN JOHN WALKER was assigned to the *Razorback,* he struck up a friendship with fellow radioman Don "Cleve" Clevenger, a big, burly man with a teddy-bear personality. The two men soon developed a Johnny Carson/Ed McMahon relationship, with John Walker as the cutup, the comic, the personality on center stage and Clevenger ready to laugh and admire the little guy.

After Walker's arrest a number of FBI agents traveled to Odessa, Texas, a dusty, hot, flat former cow town—now oil rich— to talk to Clevenger. They found the retired radioman, by then divorced, working as a cashier in a grocery chain and drawing a Navy pension. In the early days of the investigation, the FBI and

Naval Investigative Service treated everyone who had ever known Walker as a suspect. But they soon learned that Clevenger had never had the slightest idea that his good friend had a secret life. He seemed almost bewildered and hurt by the revelations about Johnny Walker.

According to Clevenger, Walker had a flair for the theatrical, usually wore a beret and an ascot at parties, and liked being the center of attention. They were constant companions.

"Johnny loved to have parties. I remember at my aloha party when I was transferred to Hawaii, we played a trick on him. The captain of our sub asked if he could bring his date inside after he had been at the party for about an hour. He told Johnny she had been sitting out in the car. Johnny said by all means, and the captain brought in a female clothes mannequin. We were always doing things like that."

Once the two of them were in Hong Kong with two hookers they had met while on liberty. The women invited them back to their place and as the four of them were walking along a corridor during the early morning hours the women began tiptoeing. Walker asked why they were tiptoeing, and one of the women said, "Because we don't want to wake up our husbands." He and Clevenger looked at each other, then beat a hasty retreat.

The devil-may-care spirit extended to all aspects of submarine life. One day they decided to play a joke on a new ensign who took himself entirely too seriously. The ensign was all starch and spit and polish, the kind of officer who could make a long submarine cruise very unpleasant, and they decided to break him in quickly. One of the men made a concoction, the main ingredient of which was peanut butter, but formed so carefully that it looked exactly like a coil of human excrement. It was placed on a piece of paper on the ensign's desk when the ensign stepped away. When the officer returned, he was furious, thinking that the men were trying to send him a message in Caine Mutiny fashion. He demanded that a nearby enlisted man step up to his desk and tell him what the material on his desk was. The enlisted man, in on the joke as were they all, suddenly scooped a bit of the material with his finger and said, "Tastes like shit, sir." The humorless ensign became even more furious and gave everyone an immediate work detail.

The most pleasant duty that he and Walker shared together was when the *Razorback* was stationed at the Seattle World's Fair in 1962 as a public exhibit. Walker was showing a middle-aged group of civilian visitors the submarine when one of them asked about a certain sign that read, Flood Safety. (The sign is actually an innocuous indicator of whether a ballast tank, used to keep the vessel in trim, is full or empty.)

Walker told them that when the sign was illuminated it meant that the submarine was about to sink and that there would be just five minutes to get out. Walker then surreptitiously flipped a switch that caused the sign to flash, and he shouted "Oh my God, that's it!" and started running. The flock of tourists fell over one another getting out of the submarine, chasing Walker through hatchways and up ladders. This was vintage Walker, the kind of antics for which he was noted.

During one of his nightly liberties in Seattle, Walker was returning to the submarine when he spotted a blimp tethered nearby. "Hey, let's go cut her loose," he told his companions, who had all been drinking heavily. Walker had actually begun cutting the tether with his clasp knife when a policeman showed up and shouted a warning, then fired a warning shot. At the sound of the shot, they ran away. It became part of Walker's daredevil legend, a legend he enjoyed fostering among submates.

It was all theater performed for the eyes of his fellow crewmen. He spent much of his time trying to dream of ways to impress them. But the humor always seemed to have a touch of cruelty to it. For instance, he tied a young sailor he found sleeping to a ladder, abandoned him there, and reported him to the captain. Another time, when Clevenger was at sea and his wife, Kathy, was staying with the Walkers, Walker sent him a "familygram" wireless message, purportedly from Kathy, that said, "Having a wonderful time—Johnny letting me use his organ while you are at sea." The humor of the message was lost on Clevenger at the moment because he and his wife were actually having marital problems.

The *Andrew Jackson*'s number was 619 and Walker joked that he liked the number because it looked the same to him upside down— even when he returned to the submarine after getting drunk.

Most submariners are noted for having a wild sense of humor. When they would find the underwater sound detectors of the Soviet trawlers, the submarine would drift quietly up to the listening device, then blast the William Tell Overture as loudly as possible directly into the undersea microphones in an attempt to deafen the Soviet sonar operators. And on the surface "we would moon the Soviets as they waited for us at the mouth of a harbor as we went by," Clevenger said.

A group of Hong Kong bar girls once began calling Walker, then a chief petty officer, Chiefie Weefie, and the moniker stuck. So at a surprise twenty-eighth birthday party for Walker given by Barbara Walker the inscription on the cake said, "Happy Birthday Chiefie Weefie." The Walkers seemed, at least on the surface, to be very happy then.

Walker had a way of winning over anyone he wanted as friend, but Clevenger recalled that he was tough and even bullying to new recruits. He would chew them out for making sloppy mistakes, then, when they appeared to buckle under the chastisement, would snarl, "What's the matter—can't you take it?" He was careful to keep his bully tactics confined to those of lesser rank.

When he and Clevenger were stationed together aboard the nuclear submarine *Andrew Jackson,* the routine cruise for the vessel was the Mediterranean Sea, their duty station. "We would make the loop around the perimeter of the Mediterranean traveling very, very slowly—just fast enough to maintain depth."

Walker seemed to enjoy the prolonged cruises, but some of his fellow crewmen did not. Once one of the crewmen suddenly snapped, and the submarine was forced to surface to allow the man to be picked up by helicopter and taken to a Navy hospital. But seconds later, the submarine dove deep and went approximately one hundred miles at high speed before resuming its quiet vigil. Normally, anytime a submarine surfaced it meant that the cruise was aborted, but this time the submarine remained on station because it had surfaced only briefly and at night.

Because of the confined spaces and the tedium, submarine crews planned events like holidays far in advance, purchasing Christmas gifts before leaving, or Halloween masks or costumes for skits that were held to mark the halfway point in a cruise. One reason the officers liked Walker was because he helped alleviate the boredom and tedium of the long cruises with his constant jokes and pranks.

Walker and some of the crew "borrowed" a handsome potted

plant at a submarine base in Rota, Spain, that belonged to a high-ranking Spanish official. It was placed atop the fins that controlled the submarine's depth as it left the harbor. The original plan had been to leave it there to wash into the sea when the vessel dived. But at the last second, one crewman rescued the plant and took it below, where it remained in the radio shack. From that moment on, Walker dictated phony Associated Press stories, inserted in the daily submarine newspaper, detailing how Spanish dictator Francisco Franco was searching for the thieves who stole the plant. Clevenger thought the stories were brilliant: they were highly believable, yet humorous, and the entire crew was caught up in the running account. The officers were so impressed that Walker was given a special commendation for helping maintain morale. "Some of the officers would even come by and say, 'Well, Johnny, how are you going to resolve the plant thing today?'"

To help morale, the submarine occasionally would go to periscope depth at night, and the captain would allow the crew to look in turn through the periscopes at the bright lights shining in the Mediterranean sky of some of the world's most glittering playgrounds.

The big locker above the radio shack desk, 3 feet high, 3 feet wide and 6 feet long, was normally used to store documents that were to be burned. Walker once got the idea that it would be fun to smuggle a prostitute on board and keep her in this locker during the day and bring her out for enjoyment during the night.

They searched Charleston and found a pretty but handicapped prostitute named Pegleg, who did indeed have but one leg, and asked her if she would be willing to make the cruise, staying in the locker. She not only agreed but was enthusiastic about the idea of changing her routine.

Walker tried to figure out how he could get her on board past security checks, in a large duffel bag. Dry runs were made with large, unusually wrapped duffels, but each time guards asked to inspect it, "so we finally abandond the idea," Walker's friend Billy Wilkinson said.

Lighthearted good humor was a vital ingredient for making life on a submarine bearable. Those chosen for submarine duty had to take a barrage of psychological tests, and even then, more were weeded out after short cruises. The fun and humor were counterpoint to deadly missions, missions viewed as vital to U.S. security in a nuclear world.

Walker was present at an incident in the Strait of Gibraltar that could have been the start of a serious conflict between the United States and the Soviets, an incident the Navy has never made public and won't even acknowledge. But every crewman aboard the *Andrew Jackson* knows it happened.

The *Andrew Jackson* was headed toward its duty station in the Mediterranean from its home port of Charleston, South Carolina. The Navy's rotation for the Mediterranean included two submarines on constant Mediterranan patrol, two in the harbor preparing for Mediterranean duty, and one en route at any given moment. American methodology for entering the Strait involved running the submarine at its top speed, nearly 40 knots submerged, then coasting past any possible Soviet sentinel submarine or listening device, props scarcely rotating.

The passage through the fifty-mile-long Strait was usually made without incident, but on one occasion the *Andrew Jackson* came very close to fighting it out undersea with a Soviet submarine. As the *Andrew Jackson* started the silent-running part of its gliding entrance near the narrowest part of the Strait, the sonarmen heard sonar pinging from a Soviet submarine stationed at the entrance. (There are two types of sonar, active and passive: active is a kind of undersea radar that causes a pinging sound the crewmen can hear without sonar listening devices; passive sonar is electronically enhanced listening.) The pinging was not unusual, but what happened next was. As the sonarmen listened, they heard the sounds that they had been trained to detect but never thought they would: the Soviet submarine opened its forward torpedo tubes. The sonarmen quickly reported this to the captain. Then they heard other sounds that indicated the torpedoes were being readied for firing.

"The captain announced to the crew that we were about to be involved in the start of World War Three," Clevenger remembered, "and he was serious." The captain gave orders to man battle stations and present the smallest possible head-on profile to the Soviet submarine and continue on course. The American torpedo tubes were opened. Soviet sonarmen no doubt heard this response. The tension on board was palpable. Men could hear one another breathing. The slightest metallic sounds and clicks of routine equipment on board sounded like cymbals clashing. The captain had ordered the sub rigged for "ultra quiet" or "damned quiet" running. In this mode, if a crewman was not on battle station, he was to get in his bunk. No talking was allowed.

"We were all convinced that the firing was about to begin," Clevenger said.

The submarine continued its glide path toward its Soviet adversary. It was a deadly game. If either sonar crew heard the pneumatic whoooosh and the follow-up turning screws of a torpedo, it would trigger an instant response.

The eerie tension mounted as the sonar blips showed the vessels nearing one another. The pinging of the Soviet radar was increasing in intensity as the range closed to several hundred yards. Gradually, the U.S. submarine passed the other vessel. Crewmen smiled broadly as it became clear that there would be no undersea duel. It was over. The Navy never reports such incidents to the public and when an incident leaks to the press, the official response has always been, "It didn't happen."

"But this happened and everyone on board knew it happened," Clevenger insists.

On another cruise, a Russian submarine, probably one of the exceptionally fast Alfa class (260 feet long with a diameter of 32 feet, propelled by a 24,000-horsepower nuclear reactor), picked up the *Bolivar* on radar and began following it. This was no game. "Everyone on board knew that the Russians would not hesitate to sink an American sub caught far from its home port," Wilkinson said. (The United States has since signed an international agreement with the Soviets designed to lessen the danger of such underwater brinksmanship although some incidents still occur.) Everyone manned battle stations. The captain ordered the *Bolivar* to accelerate to near maximum speed, and he put the submarine through evasive maneuvers to try to get enough lead to rig for silent running. The Russian sub could not be outrun, but after hours of evasive maneuvers and the sound of the Soviet radar pinging in relentless pursuit, the *Bolivar* escaped. Later, when some crewmen tried to leak the story to the press, the Navy's official response—as always—was that they were unaware of any such incident.

The *Bolivar* may have escaped because of its ability to descend to greater depths or its silent running capacity; or it may have escaped because of the superior knowledge of undersea terrain that allowed the U.S. submarine to "jink" through undersea canyons—or take sudden evasive maneuvers. Mapping the undersea terrain with the help of sonar was often part of a submarine's mission and was once part of a mission assigned to the *Bolivar* crew.

5

Submarine Life—
The Deepest Cover

You could hear the pressure hull groan and creak. We thought that was it.   —Don Clevenger, Odessa, Texas

In 1870, when Jules Verne wrote *Twenty Thousand Leagues Under the Sea,* he probably thought he was allowing free rein to flights of fancy that could never be matched in human experience. Even the *Torsk* or the *Razorback* would have been an incredible marvel to him. But he would have been astounded at the capabilities of the modern nuclear-powered submarine, with its inertial guidance systems, precise navigation, gourmet restaurant-quality food, ballistic nuclear missiles accurate, after streaking four and five thousand miles, to within a few feet of a target despite being fired from a moving vessel under water, and sonar that can differentiate between a few shrimp and every single Soviet vessel by "acoustic signature."

Modern nuclear submarines, moving at speeds up to 40 knots and at depths down to 3,000 feet, are greater engineering marvels than jet aircraft. There are few environments more hostile than the ocean depths, where the hull of a submarine must bear 145 pounds per square inch pressure for each 100 feet of depth while maintaining an equable temperature, even keel, speed, and clean air. The nuclear submarine is capable of traversing deep ocean canyons at high speed while seeing and hearing with its sonar eyes and ears. The firepower on one nuclear submarine is greater than all of the explosives detonated during World War II, including the atomic bombs that ended the war. Former President Jimmy Carter said that the missiles carried by one nuclear submarine could "destroy every large- and medium-sized city in the Soviet Union." And Carter made that observation before the U.S. Trident program was completed, a new class of missiles with multi-targeted warheads of even more devastating power.

There is an élan among submariners that is akin to the camaraderie among fighter pilots or Green Berets. The submariners were, and are, a tough and proud group of men. John Walker seemed to fit in as his career straddled the diesel and nuclear submarine eras. He particularly seemed to like the danger. He was no longer the kid who had to fabricate adventures in Scranton; he was living them.

Both Walkers began their submarine service on diesel-powered submarines, but Arthur never made it to a "boomer" as Navy jargon refers to nuclear-powered submarines carrying intercontinental ballistic missiles. However, the Navy thought enough of Art's ability to assign him as an instructor of Antisubmarine Warfare (ASW) techniques.

Diesel submarines give one the feeling of walking around inside a giant metal pipe about the size of a big-city sewer drain. They are a kind of time machine allowing those aboard to step back into World War II when captains scanned the gray-green horizon through periscopes, looking for the Japanese Rising Sun or a German battleship.

There were amenities aboard diesels, to be sure, but they were spartan. Even the captain's quarters were smaller than a jail cell—about the width of a closet and just long enough for his bunk, with a telephone over his head for he was never really off duty. That is true today even on nuclear subs.

The officer's mess or ward room on a diesel submarine was one of the most open spaces on the vessel, and even it could barely accommodate the eight men at a Formica-topped, stainless steel picnic table. Each compartment, of which there usually were eight or nine, could be sealed off so that in the event of an accident, some men could perhaps be saved. The officers also had a small pantry and a fold-down sink. Every inch of space on the old submarines was used for something, whether it was wiring, piping, or storage, all coated thickly with gray enamel. Navigation charts were sandwiched between plastic, and an excellent nautical chart of the world for the navigator formed the top of a table in the area below the conning tower. There were many passageways where two men could not pass at the same time, yet eighty lived and worked, and often died, in this confined area.

Life aboard a diesel submarine, versus life on a nuclear one, could be compared to life in a dormitory room versus life in a mansion. Diesel submarines were hot, the dirty air filled with a mixture of sweat and diesel oil. They were not for anyone with even mildly claustrophobic tendencies. There were usually just two tiny showers aboard. One of them was often filled with potatoes for the cook's use and the other was used only by food handlers. Although officers had the right to use one of the showers, they rarely did, preferring to set an example for the men. Everyone soon began to smell goatish. Indeed, one small ward room was known as the "goat locker."

After the clean clothes were used up, sailors stopped wearing socks and underwear and usually wore only light khaki pants, a T-shirt, and sneakers. Rank was not discernible by dress—or smell. The temperature, particularly during hot weather or tropical cruises, could reach 130 degrees in diesel submarines. Those who served aboard such submarines said it was not unusual during some maneuvers and war games for matches and cigarette lighters not to ignite for want of oxygen. It was very rough duty and required a certain kind of man to cope with it.

Clevenger recalled one incident when the snorkel device, used for bringing fresh air into the submarine for the men and the diesel engines, malfunctioned because of a heavy storm on the surface. The diesels kept running, using up the air inside the submarine, and a severe vacuum was created. The crew worked frantically to repair the sensors, and the snorkel opened up suddenly. The sudden change in atmospheric pressure within the submarine popped sailors' eardrums and caused many of them to have bloody noses.

He also remembered another incident "when Johnny Walker

told me, 'If you believe in The One Above, then you better start praying.' We had gone beyond our safety depth." Diesel submarines had a maximum safe depth of 412 feet (the general rule of thumb was that they should not be taken down much deeper than their length) and a safety margin of another 400 feet if they were lucky. The *Razorback* had somehow exceeded its cruising depth, and everyone aboard thought the hull would soon split open, just as with the *Thresher* in 1963. The submarine—as it was later theorized—had entered a large freshwater bubble from the Columbia River not far away. Because salt water is far more bouyant than fresh water, the ballast of the *Razorback* was wrong for the sudden freshwater pocket of several hundred feet. The twin shallow-depth gauges soon maxed out at 165 feet, and the other deep gauges spun toward 412 feet, then beyond.

"You could hear the pressure hull groan and creak. We thought that was it," Clevenger said. A taut string fastened horizontally between the round steel ribs as an impromptu pressure gauge sagged as the millions of tons of water pressed in on the submarine. When the string sagged, indicating the tremendous force, men looked at each other, too choked with fear to speak, as tense as the creaking and groaning steel hull that contained them. But just as the submarine exceeded its normal safety margin, the crew managed to get it headed upward. The collective sigh of relief was audible throughout the submarine. Men talked and laughed again; some cheered. But sweat drenched every forehead.

The words of Samuel Johnson that a ship was like "being in jail with the chance of being drowned" could apply even better to submarine duty.

Walker's friend Bill Wilkinson (who became a Grand Dragon of the Ku Klux Klan after he left the Navy) recalled that once, during a war games maneuver and diving exercise, the panic of a crewman almost cost the lives of every crew member. There had been a high-speed dive after sighting an "enemy ship" on the horizon. The dive was at more than 20 knots surface speed, and the crewman operating the diving planes, for some unaccountable reason, could not bring the submarine out of its 30-degree dive. Needles on depth gauges spun past the danger mark. Several crewmen grabbed the controls of the diving planes from the white-faced, fear-frozen sailor and wrested the submarine's nose up. Again, the pressure hull creaked and groaned and came near cracking under the tremendous sea pressure.

The crew was so angry that the offending crewman was put ashore on a Carribean island and flown back to the U.S. mainland where he completed his career on dry land. He would never be allowed to set foot inside a submarine again. He had betrayed the "family" that every submarine crew considers itself.

The seriousness of the mission was illustrated by the death from natural causes of one crew member aboard a nuclear submarine. The body was placed in a rubber bag and put into the freezer locker where beef carcasses and other perishable foods were stored. The cruise continued and the body was not turned over to the family for many weeks.

Arthur was once at a considerable depth aboard a submarine when a pinhole leak began spewing seawater, soaking the compartment. The submarine moved to a shallow depth, and a penny was hastily spot-welded over the hole. It proved so seaworthy that it was left in place for the life of the submarine.

DIESEL SUBMARINE DUTY was so hard that those who went from diesels to nuclear-powered subs said it was "like dying and going to heaven." They could not believe the difference. The "boomers" carried 300 tons of air-conditioning equipment and air scrubbers that filtered the air through racks of charcoal granules, at the same time adding pure oxygen. The air on nuclear submarines was better than you could find in a Wyoming forest. The passageways and quarters were spacious. Bunks, instead of being tucked into niches of machinery, were bigger and more comfortable, with thick foam mattresses. Food was better because of the increased storage and freezer capacity. There was a well-stocked library, comparable to that of a small school, a cafeteria, ward room, yeoman's shack (ship's office), first-run movies, a recreation room, and three levels in "which we could work and play," Clevenger said. There also were frequent showers. The radio shack, where John Walker worked as a radioman supervisor, was bigger and far more sophisticated. The chief's quarters, where he lived when off duty, were spacious and allowed some privacy.

The *Andrew Jackson* carried a variety of torpedoes and sixteen Polaris nuclear missiles with a range of 2,500 miles. It was 425 feet long by 33 feet in diameter, although its hull bulged on top to allow for missiles. It had a submerged speed in excess of 30 knots.

It was this submarine and the other thirty-one in her class that struck fear in the hearts of Kremlin strategists. When commissioned, it was the largest submarine ever built. Its speed was awe inspiring, and its ability to travel silently at great depths (its hull and an inner hull sandwiched thick rock-wool insulation that deadened sound as well as shielded the crew from the cold ocean depths) made the submarine leg of the U.S. Triad, which included the Strategic Air Command's B-52 bombers, ground-based missiles and the nuclear submarine fleet, the most feared of all by the Soviets. Its torpedoes were wire and acoustically guided, deadly undersea fish that homed-in on and chased their target.

The *Andrew Jackson,* was, in short, the most awesome fighting machine the world had ever known. This class of submarine is still the backbone of the American submarine fleet although the new Ohio class will eventually replace it. The Ohio class, of which there are three, with eight to sixteen more projected for construction, is 560 feet in length and 42 feet in diameter. Only the Russian *Typhoon* is larger. The Ohio class sub carries twenty-four Trident missiles and is propelled by a 60,000 horsepower nuclear reactor. Its speed is classified but believed to be in excess of 40 knots. Its maximum depth is classified but believed to be in excess of 3,000 feet.

The Soviets believed they might conceivably cope with SAC and possibly target U.S. ground missiles, but they could not keep track of the proliferating state-of-the-art U.S. nuclear submarines in the early 1960s. Their own technology was abysmal by comparison. The United States, which had 150 nuclear submarines in seaworthy condition by 1985 (all nuclear with the exception of four or five special-duty diesels), produced submarines of exceptionally sophisticated technology. (The exact number deployed is a secret but it is thought to be in the neighborhood of forty to fifty at any given time.) Thanks to the undisputed leadership and genius of Admiral Hyman Rickover, who conceived of and shepherded the nuclear submarine into existence by persuading the Atomic Energy Commission to cooperate with the Navy, the United States enjoyed a major margin (estimated at five years) over the Soviets in nuclear submarine technology. This was accomplished at a time when nuclear reactors occupied whole city blocks, and few in the 1950s believed they could be built small enough to be enclosed in a submarine 33 feet in diameter.

Inertial guidance systems on nuclear subs used advanced electronics that were (then) beyond the capacity of the Soviets. The navigation systems (SINS) used computers that were constantly fed such factors as true speed, ship movement and direction, true north as determined by a sensitive gradiometer that took into account changes in the magnetic errors generated by the earth, and other factors. This information was also constantly fed into the guidance systems of the missiles so that the missile guidance systems "knew" at any given second where their targets were in relation to the sub. Tests showed that the subs could surface within a few yards of any destination after cruising submerged, with only occasional celestial input (via periscope), for seventy to ninety days, the length of a cruise patrol. Cruising beneath the North Pole became routine.

The SSBN *Simon Bolivar,* on which Walker served as a radioman, was the class of submarine the Soviets most feared. The *Simon Bolivar* had everything the *Andrew Jackson* had with several major advantages, chief among them that engineers had learned to make its machinery and prop wash even quieter. Silent running technology was one of the most sought after by both sides.

Because of the loss of the nuclear submarine *Thresher* in April of 1963, the United States learned the hard way the necessity of making their deep-diving submarines incredibly resistant to the pressure of great depths. Lessons learned from the *Thresher,* along with advances in metallurgy, helped improve emergency ballast procedures and welding and brazing techniques, checked by X ray.

The *Thresher* had lost power for a time, and by the time the reactor was cranked up again the submarine had glided below 1,000 feet and its hull imploded. The sudden increase in air pressure killed every man aboard before they were touched by one drop of seawater.

Despite the lessons of the *Thresher,* Clevenger recalled that a spanking new nuclear submarine was just hours from its first sea test when crewmen found hull plates that had not been welded but simply covered by masking tape and then painted over. The theory in the hushed-up incident was that welders, working on the hull in wintertime, had taped over a joint to keep out the cold and forgotten to remove the tape later and weld it. And most any submariner had heard stories that circulated about the many malfunctioning parts of the *Thresher* even before the submarine went "gray lady down." There was a widely circulated story that on sea trials the controls operating her periscopes had been switched, so that those that would normally operate one of them actually operated the other.

But technology on the Soviet side was worse. The crudity of Russian electronics, for example, was brought home when a Soviet pilot defected, flying his MIG to Japan. American technologists swarmed over the aircraft and were startled to find wiring, vacuum tubes, and coarse technology not much advanced from the electronics of the post-World War II era. It was this kind of technology gap that the Soviets hoped to overcome through espionage.

It was during this time, in the KGB planning facilities located in a forest near Moscow, that U.S. intelligence experts believe the order went out to concentrate on obtaining communications and nuclear submarine technology. A good start on sophisticated radio technology had been provided by technical manuals found on the *Pueblo,* the U.S. Navy spy ship seized off the coast of North Korea on January 23, 1968, but these soon became out of date as the United States rushed to change their communications technology. The Soviets also found an intact set of radio receivers on the *Pueblo* that used spinning high-tech plastic rotors to decode messages.

It was during this period, also, that Admiral Rickover complained that some of the private defense contractors, proud of their sleek and advanced submarines, handed out scale models of the latest U.S. submarines. Rickover said the models were so exact in scale that the Soviets would benefit from our years of exhaustive testing to determine the most slippery conformity of hull design simply by photographing or obtaining one of the many models in circulation. Although his warnings weren't taken seriously by many of the defense contractors, later Soviet submarines were found to be virtually exact copies of the American Ethan Allen class.

But the weaponry and electronics, the guidance systems, the sonar listening devices, and the top-secret radio equipment would have to be obtained through espionage. For despite the easy target that the American defense industry provided critics who were disturbed by the fat defense budget, there was no comparable research and development available to the Soviets. Without a profit incentive, love of Mother Russia alone had not been enough to keep pace.

The Soviets knew that the United States had found ways to harness computers to virtually all submarine technology. For example, every propeller picked up on U.S. sonar was tape-recorded and the tape subjected to immediate computer analysis. The computer searched its memory bank for just such a sound and its variables—variables not discernible to the human ear—and helped the Americans make great leaps in "acoustic signature" technology. It is now believed that not even a Soviet garbage scow can move without being identified in this fashion.

THE U.S. HAS, and Walker was very familiar with, a vast sonar net, called SOSUS, that uses stationary undersea relay points in the Atlantic, Pacific, Gulf, and other strategic areas. (The very name SOSUS was once classified.) This is part of the elaborate methodology, along with satellite infrared photography and other still-classified techniques, that allows the United States to keep far better track of Soviet submarines than they can keep of ours.

The top thirty-six American nuclear submarines, the heart of the fleet, include five Trident-class subs carrying twenty-four ballistic missiles with a range of over 5,000 miles. Each missile carries eight independently targeted warheads, a total of 192 per submarine. Each warhead is eight times more powerful than the atomic bomb dropped on Hiroshima in 1945.

The rest of the latest-model submarines carry Poseidon missiles, each with ten independently targeted warheads. The Tridents and their increased range give the submarines more ocean in which to hide, causing problems in detection for the Soviets. The United States is also converting about seven more *Bolivar*-type submarines to carry the Trident.

Walker was able to keep the Soviets supplied with this kind of low-level information along with the more sought-after cryptographic data, also keeping them completely up to date on all submarine-related technology.

Walker may have left the Navy before getting a chance to obtain much information on the Trident, although there is a chance he could have obtained some information in the last year or two of his career.

The Trident is currently state-of-the-art: a 34-foot-long missile that weighs 70,000 pounds. It is far more complex but just as reliable as the Polaris missile. It has three tandem stages of propulsion, with a guidance system supposedly more accurate and reliable than that of the Polaris missiles. Each propulsion stage uses solid fuel and employs rotating nozzles linked to its inertial guidance system to keep the missile on target.

THE SOVIETS SENT agents (in the era before travel restrictions) to operate covertly around the major submarine bases at San Diego and Mare Island in California; Norfolk, Virginia; Charleston, South Carolina; Bangor, Washington; Kings Bay, Georgia; and Holy Loch, Scotland. The KGB had an acronym, MICE, that is used in searching out possible American agents. Former KGB Major Stanislav Levchenko, who revealed the acronym, said it stands for Money, Ideology, Compromise, and Ego. A high-ranking American intelligence official reported that the KGB particularly sought out communications specialists who were at the nerve centers of land and sea operations and had access to codes and a host of other data without arousing "need-to-know" suspicions. They looked for braggarts and heavy drinkers, men who were susceptible to women, men with grudges against their service or their country, men with nihilistic and amoral views, men vulnerable to flattery, men who had an exaggerated view of their own importance, and men with money or drug problems.

The standard recruiting technique involved feigning friendship, then seeking innocuous documents such as base telephone lists, ship repair records, or information so available that much of it could be found in *Jane's Fighting Ships,* the standard publicly available reference book on ships of the world. After such information was passed, the Soviets would reward the "friend" with as much as 10,000 dollars. The target agent would then justify this to himself by thinking that the joke was on the Soviets. Why not make a little money with this simple information? What had the Navy done for him but keep him submerged at sea for seventy days at a time away from his wife and children, make him work long hours for low pay, and allow smart-alecky U.S. Naval Academy graduates to boss him around?

This was what they were looking for, and this is what they found in John Walker. He was almost the perfect MICE profile with one exception: he cared nothing for ideology. The Soviet agent who "turned" Johnny Walker—if he was not a "walk in" as he claims—is no doubt a candidate for the Lenin Medal. When they found Walker, they struck pure gold.

Although Arthur Walker told the FBI that John Walker approached the Soviets by parking near their embassy on 16th Street in Washington, American intelligence authorities say that Walker would have to have had a generous amount of luck if that was, indeed, the way he linked up with them. He has steadfastedly stuck to a version of this during his debriefing, but there are numerous stories of Americans who inadvertently walked into the Soviet Embassy (it has long been next door to the University Club, and some people walk in by mistake) being questioned and placed under surveillance by the FBI. In short, the direct approach, for various classified reasons, probably would not have worked. More likely, some intelligence experts speculated, John Walker was ashamed to tell his brother that he had been hooked in the standard KGB fashion. Walker, in fact, first told FBI agents that he had been recruited. Later he changed his story.

6

Crypto

It makes my skin crawl to think of the things Johnny had access to and saw every day. He even saw top secret war plans. I know because I saw them myself.
— Bill Wilkinson, former radioman aboard the
SSBN *Simon Bolivar,* nuclear submarine,
Denham Springs, Louisiana, September 1985

The use of rotors to encrypt messages had its beginning when Thomas Jefferson invented a wheel cipher sometime between 1790 and 1793. Jefferson was disturbed by the British practice of intercepting and reading mail to foreign consulates and diplomats. He devised a plan for a wooden device using thirty-six round wafers on whose perimeters each letter of the alphabet and the numbers zero through nine were imprinted.

Contemporary American submarines use a highly evolved electronic version of Jefferson's idea. To crack the U.S. code, the Soviet technicians created a battery-operated testing implement dubbed the "rotor decryption device."

"Perhaps the most intriguing and revealing device found in Walker's home was a rotor decryption device," said Michael Schatzow, the Assistant U.S. attorney in Baltimore, Maryland, who prepared the evidence that was to have been used to prosecute John Walker. "Detailed instructions for the device were found with it. This small instrument, which can be folded to fit within the palm of one's hand, is not commercially available anywhere in the world. It was obviously made by the Soviets for one purpose. The device is a sophisticated continuity tester, which is designed to test the wiring circuitry for rotors that were used by the United States Navy for secure communications during the period that John Anthony Walker, Jr., was on active duty. These rotors were used to both encrypt and decrypt Naval messages. It was essential to know the wiring of each individual rotor if one were to attempt to intercept the messages and have a chance of decoding them."

The rotors are small, Bakelite plastic devices with pins and sockets. All spin at different rates of speed in a wire basket, the spinning speed depending on circuitry. The idea is to create billions of mathematical possibilities for a code, making it impossible to decipher it. The radioman must set up the rotors in a certain way in addition to putting them in the correct sequence.

The device that Walker used for the Russians, under the noses of his fellow crewmen (there were always supposed to be two men in the radio shack for security purposes when the submarine was at sea), allowed the Soviets to duplicate the rotors and then use computer technology in the absence of key lists to break the code of the KL-47 cryptographic machine. Naval authorities estimated that computers, rapidly working out variables based on the known information provided by the rotor circuitry, probably gave the Soviets a 60 percent chance of cracking the code, even when the key lists, or rotor sequence, were not immediately available. However, when Walker came ashore, he gave the Soviets the key lists saved from his cruise so that they could easily reconstruct the messages they had recorded in undeciphered form.

Walker's submates recalled that the Navy was very lax about changing the key lists and did not change the circuitry of the rotors at all. The biggest change in the rotor circuitry and other electronic changes, which are secret, came after the capture of the *Pueblo* and its crytographic equipment.

"Of all of the intelligence passed on," Schatzow said, "the cryptographic information was undoubtedly the most valuable to the Soviets. Walker had access to the rotors throughout his Navy career and, with the device, which had a round dial similar to a telephone, he could in essence provide the Soviets with the wiring circuitry for each rotor."

With that information, the Soviets could keep abreast of any changes simply by having Walker make routine checks from time to time.

According to Schatzow, the device worked so fast that Walker could easily have tested every rotor while the other radioman was grabbing a snack or taking a trip to the head. It would test one rotor in about ninety seconds, or allow testing of all of them in just twelve minutes.

The rotor decryption device was probably given to Walker during one of his face-to-face meetings with the Soviets in Vienna or Mexico City. The FBI found that he traveled to Vienna many times. They fixed dates for these trips on ten occasions and admitted that there probably were a number of others they didn't know about. Walker also had traveled to Mexico City. Both cities are known as nests of KGB activity.

Walker admitted during preliminary debriefing that he carried the device on board the *Bolivar* and used it in behalf of the Soviets. He kept it hidden away in his locker in the chief's quarters and probably used the device mainly when the submarine was in port because there was no requirement for two men to be on duty in the radio shack then.

Why was Walker—an enlisted man—so valuable to the Soviets?

"There is very little that goes on in a submarine that the radioman doesn't know about," said Bill Wilkinson, who served for three years with Walker and who was a close friend for twenty years. "Most every message with the exception of two or three 'eyes-only' messages for the captain, decoded by the captain, came through the radioman.

"Despite the Navy's effort to compartmentalize, we even saw plenty of stuff involving the Pacific Fleet. And I saw maps of our hydrophone net, so I know Walker saw them too. In fact, I have no doubt that he copied them for the Soviets."

Clevenger agreed with Wilkinson. Crewmen were not supposed to know the mission or position of the submarine unless it was part of their job, and that included radiomen; but radiomen always knew from the message traffic where the submarine's mission would take it and what it was hoped it would accomplish.

Walker knew the exact speed of the submarine, its maximum

depth capacity, and he knew how it received its top-secret low-frequency messages via a trailed surface antenna and how photo-voltaic cells were able to absorb compressed messages so that much information could be transmitted in seconds. But he provided the Soviets much more valuable information than this.

"It makes my skin crawl to think of the things Johnny had access to and saw every day. He even saw top-secret war plans. I know because I saw them myself," Wilkinson said. "And they weren't just plans that involved the role of submarines. They were far more elaborate than that. We weren't even supposed to have that stuff."

But how did Walker provide other classified material to the Soviets without arousing suspicion, particularly when copies of documents must be accounted for?

At the urging of his Soviet contacts, Walker became known as extremely ambitious. He began taking every available Navy correspondence course, supposedly in order to move up in grade. To better grasp the wealth of material available to him, he even took a speed-reading course. He was known as the kind of seaman who was interested in everything—everyone else's job, the equipment they used, and how that equipment worked. Walker's ambition and apparent anxiousness to move up was a perfect cover for a seemingly insatiable curiosity about every part of a nuclear submarine.

Walker spent much of his off-duty time poring over tech manuals. This was not viewed as sinister at the time—merely another sign of his ambition to move up in the ranks. His brother had been selected as an enlisted man for Officer's Candidate School, and it was assumed that he hoped he would be, too. But Arthur had completed almost two years of college, and John was a high-school dropout with a burglary conviction on his record. He was never going to be an officer, and this fostered an already smoldering resentment. He also resented the fact that he would never have been assigned to submarine duty if Arthur had not pulled strings in his behalf.

Anything that needed copying could be copied during Walker's night watch in the radio shack. There was a copying machine a few feet down a passageway in the yeoman's shack, or ship's office. Although most big industries—particularly defense industries—have counters and locks on duplicating machines, including paper accountability, incredibly, there was no such safeguard on board the *Bolivar*. Nor was there on any nuclear submarine.

"Anybody could photocopy anything any time and nobody would care," Wilkinson reported. "And normally no one ever checked your duffel when you finished a cruise and went ashore. I guess the Navy figured if you had a top-secret clearance they didn't have to bother." (The Navy is now taking steps to tighten security on submarines, account for copying machine use, and make random checks of duffel bags, all lessons learned from Walker.)

Clevenger and Walker were in charge of accounting for and logging secret documents when they served together aboard the *Andrew Jackson* from 1964 to 1965. According to Clevenger, they "never came up short" in logging the documents. He had never observed Walker making copies of secret material, but he acknowledged that it could have been done easily.

"Johnny always had to be in the center of everything that was going on in the sub," Clevenger said. Although the "need to know" required that sailors aboard a submarine stay out of sensitive areas, long cruises, boredom, and confined quarters caused most captains to relax such rules. Because of this, there were few if any parts of a submarine that Walker did not study, including the reactor area and "Sherwood Forest." Sherwood Forest was the area behind the conning tower where missile silos stand vertically like the trunks of large trees, a deadly nuclear-age forest. Crewmen recall that to combat boredom, one sailor skateboarded around the submarine, including the long straightaway between the missiles in Sherwood Forest.

There was also a "Christmas Tree" on board, a control panel that showed a variety of information, including what ballast tanks were full or empty or what hatches were open or shut.

Security on submarines was so laughable, noted Clevenger, that he and a friend used to carry .22 automatics on board for target shooting in Spain. And although they had a wholesome interest in target shooting, the ease with which they brought the pistols on board raised the specter of what a couple of psychotic sailors could do.

Clevenger and Wilkinson recalled that Walker always had his nose in a book or Navy manual or some sort. "And these were not lightweight books he read but heavy stuff. Whatever Johnny was, he was not dumb," Wilkinson said. "That's one reason he got away with it for twenty years." Clevenger agreed that he was a very bright and capable person. According to his friends and family, Walker considered himself to be more intelligent than most of the officers with whom he dealt on a daily basis.

"In most ways, he was not as smart as he thought he was," U.S. Attorney Michael Schatzow said, "but when it came to Navy electronics, he could converse on an equal plane with virtually anyone."

"I would guess his I.Q. was in the near genius range—130 or more at least," Clevenger said. "The officers liked him because he was intelligent. You just don't go from seaman to officer-one status unless you are bright. And Johnny Walker was bright."

SKITS WERE PERFORMED to while away the time, and during one of them Johnny Walker wore a blond wig, a sarong, and fake breasts. He played the part of a seductress, and the script required that he sit on the lap of a Navy chief. Fellow crewmen said he played the part of a woman very well.

Walker constantly played practical jokes. Once, when he knew that a fellow crewman was scheduled for a proctoscopic examination, he painted eyes and a face on the sailor's buttocks to the amusement of everyone but the sub's doctor, who wound up staring into the impromptu "face."

Walker also had jokes played on him. Crewmen decided on revenge and told the doctor that Walker was having severe problems with his elbow but was afraid to talk to the doctor. When the doctor repeatedly asked him about it, Walker became snappy and resentful. So the doctor snuck up on him while he was asleep in the chief's quarters and began examining his elbow, which woke him and caused him to fly into a rage, to the amusement of those who had plotted it all.

At the beginning of a cruise, Walker would take a roll of toilet paper and mark off the days on each square, then roll it back. He kept this on a roller at his radio supervisor's desk and tore off a sheet as each day and night in the sunless depths rolled by.

"One time I took this roll and tossed it in the trash, and he was furious—he went bananas," Wilkinson said. "He yelled at me, 'You're not relieved until you put that back!'"

"You couldn't help but like the guy. He was the kind of guy that you envied in some ways, but you didn't envy him and dislike him. You envied him and he made you like him."

According to Wilkinson, Walker had a warm and friendly personality that he could turn on and off at will, almost as if it were electronic.

Walker was known to have a greater repertoire of bawdy drinking songs—some of them very obscene even by sailor standards—than anyone on board the sub.

"We once emptied a bar filled with pretty tough types down at Cocoa Beach [Florida] while we were ashore after testing missiles on the missile range," Wilkinson said. "It was pretty raunchy stuff, so a lot of people just got up and left." Walker seemed to enjoy shocking people, and one of his favorite curses both aboard and off the submarine was "God sucks!"

Walker was a conspirator in unofficial procurement when the sub was being loaded. A box of grain alcohol used for cleaning electronic equipment was shunted to a hiding place in the radio room along with a box of chocolate chips destined to be used by the cooks for chocolate chip cookies. Throughout the remainder of this cruise, the cookies were without chocolate chips while Walker and a few of his friends ate the hoard and drank the alcohol mixed with fruit juice.

Walker had learned long ago at St. Patrick's High School that because of his size his best tactic was to talk his way out of any difficulty, and his friends said he was a master of defusing tense situations, usually with a light comment or joke.

According to Wilkinson, "You couldn't get mad at Johnny, no matter what. That's the kind of guy he was. People liked him—officers and enlisted men. And he seemed to like his work. He did more than he had to do at his job, and it was exemplary. He was very ambitious. We knew he was a lifer—that's somebody who wanted to stay in and make a career out of the Navy."

Walker spent most of his time while on duty undersea wearing a blue jumpsuit and sitting at a fold-down desk in the radio shack on a padded secretary's swivel chair. Every other hour, messages would come in. Much of the time they were routine NINK messages, which simply meant "all submarines copy this message." NINKS were usually innocuous. All radiomen know Morse code and any emergency messages were prefixed by the audible *da da dit dit,* the Morse code for the letter *Z.*

Walker always had to be alert for a WSRT—Weapons System Readiness Test—which could come at any time. As soon as such a test began, computer monitors would come on automatically to determine the speed and efficiency of the submarine crew, particularly the radiomen. No one knew until the last minute whether such tests were real—the start of a nuclear duel between the superpowers—or mere tests. The crew was told to assume the worst and act accordingly during each WSRT.

One radio operator took messages while another decoded them. When a WSRT came in, Walker would immediately notify an officer in the conning tower and that officer would announce over the 7-MC internal speaker system that all crewmen were to man their battle stations.

Within seconds, the captain and the executive officer would sprint to the radio shack. Each had memorized a safe combination. There were two safes, one within the other. The captain would operate the combination to his double-door safe out of sight of the other crewmen, then the executive officer would open his safe. They would rip open envelopes and compare code words inside with the code word sent by message.

If the code words matched, the process would begin for firing the ballistic missiles and World War III would be underway. The captain would go to the conning tower and insert a key he carried around his neck at all times, and the weapons officer would go to the Missile Control Center and insert his key, which he also carried around his neck at all times, in another console. A secret number of other crewmen (believed to be three) would have to operate various switches in a given sequence before the missiles could be fired from about 100 feet below the surface of the sea.

The entire process could be completed in a few minutes. It was this procedure that would be followed in the event of a retaliatory strike.

And in such an emergency, Pentagon planners have always thought that the most effective and massive retaliation the United States could inflict would come from the nuclear submarine fleet, with fifty or more of the vessels spurting twenty missiles each through the surface of the sea from strategic locations around the world. From Walker's duty station in the Mediterranean, for examples, missiles could streak to Soviet city targets in minutes. Other missiles would head to targets from the Indian Ocean, the North Sea, Aegean Sea, and even the Baltic Sea and the Gulf of Finland, virtually in the backyard of the Soviet Union. One reason the Finns are constantly finding Soviet submarine activity in the Gulf of Finland is the Soviets abiding fear of U.S. nuclear submarines. The United States is just as concerned with Soviet submarines based in Cuba.

One bit of top-secret data normally found in the radio shack was target data, or information about the targets in the Soviet Union of each missile on board and very often of other submarines as well. Confidential information was on green paper, secret on yellow, and top-secret on pink. Nonclassified material was on regular white paper. Target data was usually on pink paper. Wilkinson felt certain that Walker furnished such target data to the Soviets.

Wilkinson and Walker used to while away free time talking of what they wanted to do ashore to make money. Wilkinson dreamed of opening a mobile-home park and spent hours drawing diagrams of where the trailors and landscaping would be.

"Johnny wanted to open a bar in the worst way. He asked me to go in business with him. I agreed, but I just couldn't raise the cash for my part. We went so far as to open a joint checking account, but just couldn't swing it. That's when he started that bar, 'The House of Bamboo' I think it was, in Ladson [South Carolina]. I picked out the name of the bar."

One of Walker's main characteristics was a deep and abiding resentment of authority. It was a smoldering emotion that he buried, but it evinced itself in many ways, principally in the desire to get even. He had a book of dirty tricks that he had ordered from a magazine specializing in survivalist gear. The tricks included putting epoxy glue into locks of cars and homes. (His daughter Laura said he had a number of books on revenge. "It's really cruelty. It scares me. If he thinks like that, imagine what he's got plotted for me.")

Walker was getting even every time he passed information to the Soviets. They valued him. It was balm to his injured ego. The Ego part of the KGB acronym MICE.

Walker fought a constant but losing battle to control the resistance to authority that began with his anger at the nuns of St. Patrick's High School in Scranton, the anger and resentment he felt toward his father, the local celebrity disc jockey who had left his mother for a younger woman, the resentment of his older brother's more successful Navy career, the anger and resentment toward Otto Robinson, the judge who had called him a punk crook after the burglary conviction.

Walker not only read all of the "familygrams" sent to his submarine but also, out of curiosity, all of the familygrams sent to the entire Atlantic fleet. Each crewman was allowed to receive three during the cruise, with "babygrams" an extra bonus. "He enjoyed being a step ahead of everybody else and knowing something they didn't," Barbara Walker said.

During bull sessions, Walker often bragged about his sexual exploits. He amused crewmen by telling them that he would tell his wife that he was going on a "secret mission" whenever he planned a stolen weekend with a girl. He bragged that while ashore, he had had a secret sexual relationship with the beautiful blond wife of another seaman, a friend who was away on a cruise. He described the alleged seduction in great detail. Walker boasted so often about his sexual conquests that many of those on board began to doubt his sexual prowess. They also wondered why this strutting, garrulous little man tried so hard to project the image of masculine womanizer.

Walker was an almost excessively clean, neat man. He recoiled at even the smallest bit of dirt or clutter on his desk, even coffee rings. A fanatical nonsmoker, he was given to lecturing the smokers on board. "Don't you guys know what you're doing to your health?" he would rant. "Don't you know that they have proved that smoking causes lung cancer?" He was particularly bothered when men came into the radio shack smoking cigarettes, often chasing them away if they did not outrank him. But Walker was not disliked despite his reputation for being a fussbudget.

The best evidence of Walker's perfectionism, Clevenger reported, was the way he cut teletype messages. Prior to Walker, the standard practice in the radio shack was to tear them off a teletype and put them on a clipboard. "But Johnny would tear them off very carefully, then square them with a paper cutter, then crease them over carefully and cut holes for them in a paper punch. That's how much of a perfectionist he was. He was like that in everything he did." (The FBI found evidence of this same perfection in the way packets of top-secret material were wrapped and sealed in plastic with corners neatly folded. This is something the Soviets ask agents to do to guard against the opening of documents by anyone of lower rank in the Soviet delivery chain.)

Throughout his submarine duty, Walker was known as violently anti-Communist. He never passed up a chance to curse the Communists around his shipmates.

"I remember once when we were leaving Charleston Harbor on the *Bolivar,* and we saw the Russian trawlers waiting to pick us up," Wilkinson said. "It was back in the days of only the three-mile limit. Johnny said, 'Look at those SOBs,' and started cussing them for all he was worth."

He had an inordinate interest in the macho stories veterans in the crew told about combat aboard diesel submarines during World War II, stories of being depth-charged or stalking enemy shipping, of the thrill of running silent to avoid detection by enemy destroyers, of the hunt for Japanese and German vessels. He loved the endless stories that began, "You think this is something, back on the WWII diesels we . . ."

Walker occasionally wrote for the newspaper on the *Bolivar* as he had done for the *Old Hickory News* aboard the *Andrew Jackson* when he fabricated the Spanish potted-plant stories. The news for the paper was gleaned from radio reports they picked up. He and Wilkinson had some nudie magazines and began routinely placing a photo of a nude woman in the newspaper. When the communications officer issued a directive that there would be "no more nude women" depicted in the newspaper, they substituted a nude man instead.

Walker seemed to enjoy the long submerged cruises. While other men pined away for wives or girlfriends, he appeared to thrive in the submarine environment. But any submariner—even those who loved the duty, like Walker—will say that there is no feeling quite like that when the submarine surfaces near its home port for the first time during daylight at the end of a seventy- to ninety-day cruise. The sun is blinding. Fresh air, compared to the well-scrubbed air of the submarine, smells strange. And within minutes, the algae that collected on the sub's hull during the long cruise begins to stink in the sun and fresh air. Despite this, it is an exhilarating feeling of rebirth and renewal. The sight of sea gulls wheeling in the blindingly bright sky, the feel of wind, and the sight of land combine to thrill even the most jaded of seamen.

Had the Navy conducted a spot check of Walker's duffel after a cruise they would have found it crammed with key lists for the cryptograph machines of the Soviets, the rotor decryption device, photocopies of material from the burn bin, top-secret technical manuals and schematics.

Instead, Barbara would be waiting in the MG; Walker would toss his duffel in the trunk and head for home. Within days he would be off to deliver the results of his espionage to a drop site in northern Virginia, sometimes as a stopover before driving to Scranton to big-time it around his family. During these trips home he would grandly slip his mother a couple of hundred dollar bills, a small part of his payoff. He would sit down to Italian dinners of pasta and regale his mother and younger brother with tales of high adventure on the submarine, and he would get his kid brother off to one side and tell him of his many sexual conquests.

It was part of his fantasy: hometown boy makes good.

7

The Bamboo Snack Bar

You have no idea how ironic it is that I own a VFW bar.
                                            —John Walker

For a time, the Walkers lived in Navy housing in Charleston as he served aboard the SSBN *Andrew Jackson* and later the SSBN *Simon Bolivar*. They stayed in a development known as "Men-Riv," named after South Carolina's powerful chairman of the House Armed Services Committee, Representative Mendel Rivers.

After returning from a seventy-day cruise aboard the *Bolivar*, Walker decided that Navy housing was too institutional. And he was ready to start the bar that he and his friend Bill Wilkinson dreamed about. Because Charleston is a historic city with rigid zoning laws, most growth has occurred west and north of the city. The North Charleston area was growing rapidly, but there were still places a person could buy for a reasonable amount with commercial/residential zoning. He hoped to find something that could easily convert to a bar, a place he could live in or near at the same time.

After weeks of looking, he and Barbara found an old concrete-block house on four and a half acres in a small town called Ladson, just north of Charleston. They bought a used house-trailer and moved the family into it while Walker set about renovating the house and furnishing it with a pizza oven and gas grill for making hamburgers and grilled sandwiches, drink coolers, a bar, and tables and chairs. He borrowed 16,000 dollars in 1965 to make the purchase, which he repaid in monthly installments of $160.

Walker talked several local teenagers into helping him renovate the house, knock out partitions, build the bar area, and turn it into what Walker hoped would be a popular and moneymaking neighborhood bar like the one around the corner from his home in Scranton. He remembered that bar as always being full of local people spending money and watching TV, the cash register ringing a steady counterpoint to conversation and good times. It was a bar that his father had frequented. He wanted his bar to be like that—the kind of place his father would enjoy.

Donnie Filyaw was one of the teenagers who helped Walker. He recalled that Walker worked alongside the rest of them, putting up 4-by-4 supports to keep the ceiling up after the interior walls were knocked down. Walker paid the teenagers with cheeseburgers, beer, and a steady line of chatter about Navy life. He had a way of talking and kidding and generating enthusiasm among his young helpers, whom he treated like adults. They worked hard to help him. "He was just a likable guy, so we decided to help him out."

Walker realized that because he was away on cruises much of the time and Barbara had to watch the children, they would need help running the place. Barbara could not do it alone, particularly since the business was steadily improving. So they hired a next-door neighbor, Nora Moody, as cook and part-time barmaid at three dollars per hour. Aunt Nora, as everyone knew her, and Barbara soon became a personable duo who attracted customers.

"The place made money from day one," Nora Moody remembered. "All this stuff about him becoming a spy because the business failed—well I don't understand that. It always did well."

"Johnny wanted to open the bar because he heard a big plant was going to open nearby," Clevenger thought. "It was a calculated business venture on his part. But Nora was wrong about making money from the beginning. I can remember when Kathy and I and Johnny and Barbara would be the only ones in the place in the early days. Nora didn't start right away."

Nora Moody and Barbara became good friends and spent a lot of time in the bar, even when it was closed on Sundays, drinking and talking. They were once charged by a South Carolina law enforcement agent with operating a bar on Sunday and were fined.

They also became involved in a feud with the president of a local Baptist College, who complained to local authorities that some of the students were drinking in the place. He once paid a visit to the bar and had an angry confrontation with Barbara.

"All it says on my license is that I can't serve people under age. It doesn't say anything about whether I can serve college students if they are old enough," she told the man in no uncertain terms. He beat a hasty retreat.

When Walker was ashore, he spent a lot of time in the bar. He was a big talker and kept up a constant chatter with his customers, many of whom were Navy men and Navy friends. Although his father had had a drinking problem, Walker was a moderate drinker who would sip a beer but rarely drink a lot of hard liquor.

Nora Moody recalled that he seemed to be a physical coward. Whenever a fight started, even if between young men who would have been in awe of an older man like Walker, "Johnny would slip into the kitchen or out the back door after telling Barbara to break it up."

But Barbara was up to the task. "She was tough but real nice and kind. She would break up a fight in a second, and they respected her. She was firm, and they knew she meant business. She would step right in there and break it up in a hurry. She wasn't afraid of anything. Barbara was a mighty fine lady, and I think about her a lot even to this day."

The early days of the bar project may have been the happiest period for the Walkers. He had advanced rapidly in grade to chief petty officer. They had a wide circle of Navy friends, which included Wilkinson and his wife, who lived on the Isle of Palms, and Clevenger and his wife. The Walkers and the Wilkinsons or the Clevengers would play canasta until 3 A.M. Or have a Navy party. Kathy Clevenger stayed with the Walkers while Don was at sea, and when the Clevengers first arrived in Charleston from San Diego, the Walkers put them up while they looked for housing. The Walker children called Donald Clevenger "Daddy Don." Faded photographs show Clevenger with Michael in his arms and the three small girls standing at his feet, varying in height like steps. (Don remained Walker's only friend after his arrest, writing several sympathetic but unanswered letters.)

And Nora not only was cook and chief bottle washer but a family friend who helped look after the Walker children, including the toddler, Michael. "He was such a sweet little boy then. And the girls were nice, Margaret, Laura, and Cindy. It sure seemed like a happy family."

John Walker acquired an orange-red MG sportscar and soon became a familiar sight in the neighborhood as he drove around with the top down in the Carolina sun, wearing his blue Navy baseball-style cap with SSBN *Simon Bolivar* in yellow lettering on the front. The family took no vacations during this time although they took frequent day trips to the beach on the Isle of Palms with the children.

Yet it was during this idyllic time that two things happened: the marriage began to go sour and John Walker became a Soviet agent.

Some intelligence experts believe that Walker may first have made contact with the Soviets at the Bamboo Snack Bar. It wouldn't take long for anyone frequenting the Navy bars in the area to wind up there and learn that the owner was a radioman aboard the nuclear submarine *Simon Bolivar*.

On the other hand, "If I had to bet my nickel on it," said former CIA official and author Robert Crowley, "I would bet that Walker got the idea from the Navy, when they got all of the men together as they do from time to time and warned them that there were people hovering about who were willing to pay for classified material. They may have even dispatched him to talk to a suspicious person to check him out. That may be how he first established contact."

Clevenger believes that "Johnny was recruited when he was having trouble with the Bamboo Snack Bar. He was the kind of guy who hated to give up on anything—to admit defeat with that bar. And they didn't build the plant there like he thought they would, and the property was not worth anything. I think that's the way it happened."

Walker would occasionally disappear and use as his excuse that he was going on a "secret mission for the Navy." One of those "secret missions" apparently was his first prolonged face-to-face meeting with a Soviet contact. But his "secret missions" usually were stolen days with various girls he met in the Charleston area. With a newfound source of income, he found it easier to woo the kind of women who are in plentiful supply around any naval installation.

It was also during this time that he began to covet the property next to his—the property owned by Nora Moody and a relative. There were rumors that a shopping center would soon be built in the area, and John Walker wanted to be in on the North Charleston real estate boom. He began badgering Nora to sell her small piece of property and house to him. But she refused. She had never told him that she did not own it outright, so he thought she did.

One evening she had the night off, and she left her home unattended. When she returned she found it surrounded by fire trucks; it had burned to the ground. Walker did not wait for the ashes to cool to renew his attempts to purchase the place, pointing out to her that it would be of little value now. She refused to discuss it.

It was during this time that Clevenger's wife came to him in tears and said Walker had tried to persuade her to have sex with him. "I didn't hold it against him because I just thought he was drunk and didn't know what he was doing," Clevenger said.

One casualty of his new occupation was his relationship with Barbara. The "secret missions" soon deteriorated into unexplained absences. He began to treat her and the children with more abruptness and less attention. He spent less time in the bar, turning it over to Barbara as a virtually full-time project. He also became crueler to the children.

Barbara Walker recalled that it reached a point where "the children would run and hide when they heard his car" arrive outside. In Walker's skewed perception, it was no doubt a chore to return from his free-spending playboy life-style to a house trailer overflowing with four children and a wife. It was probably difficult to return from Charleston's famous Henry's restaurant, or the Mills Hyatt House and chateaubriand for two and the company of a lovely younger women, to "the rug rats and the drunken bitch," as he referred to them.

The Soviets, if true to form, probably insisted that he do as little as possible to change his overt style of living. So Walker was caught in a vise of his own making. He had money to spend but one leg was shackled to the house trailer, the bar, and the wife and children. He took out his anger and frustration on them. Barbara Walker told FBI agents that they had no idea how difficult he was to live with, how demanding of attention, of homage.

The day trips with the family to the Isle of Palms stopped. Johnny Walker the friendly man behind the bar stopped. Barbara Walker had to make her own life. She became friends with a woman named Joan Adlet who lived nearby, Kathy Clevenger, and a few other Navy wives. According to Arthur, Walker soon began neglecting the children.

Kathy Clevenger thought Barbara seemed to be much happier when Walker was at sea than when he was at home. She and Barbara became fast friends. One of their hobbies was shooting. They enjoyed getting in a small boat and taking trips on the waterways and rivers that lace the Charleston area and shooting the heads off snakes.

Throughout this time, the children became more and more afraid of their father. "Johnny believed that children should be seen and not heard." Kathy said the three girls "would sit at the table like little zombies, afraid to utter a sound. If they did, he would shout at them to shut up or give them a beating with his belt.

"Once we kept the girls and it took about a week before they would say anything because John had them so afraid to talk."

When Walker tried to seduce Kathy—"he thought he was God's gift to women"—she rebuffed him in no uncertain terms. She debated whether she should tell Barbara about it and finally decided that it would hurt her. "I didn't want to do anything to hurt Barbara. She was wonderful."

One Monday Barbara found that John had cleaned out the cash register and disappeared, leaving her to scramble to pay the regular Monday morning deliverymen for the week's supply of beer and wine, snacks and food. There was no note in the cash register, and Barbara at first thought it had been robbed.

Such surprises caused bitter arguments. When she told Rita Walker that during one such argument John told her she should sleep with customers to raise extra money for the bar, it led to a permanent breach between Rita and John Walker.

Walker enjoyed "pretending he was something he wasn't," Kathy said. He would give a big party attended mostly by enlisted men of lesser rank than he so that he could enjoy playing big shot before a command audience.

The Clevengers were transferred to San Diego before Walker. When the Walkers arrived about a year later, in 1969, the Clevengers were surprised to see them drive up towing a big, expensive looking sailboat. Its name was *The Dirty Old Man.*

John Walker liked Charleston, the old antebellum homes, the seashore at the Isle of Palms and Sullivan's Island, and the feeling of place and belonging of the people. Even after he left Charleston he came back frequently, usually flying into Summerville Airport.

Curly Houck, the bartender at Ladson Post No. 3433 of the Veterans of Foreign Wars, who took over Walker's bar for the VFW Post, recalled Walker's last visit in 1983. Walker flew into Summerville with his girlfriend, P.K. Carroll. Houck and other members of the Post had asked for a talk to try to buy the building from Walker.

"I would never sell one of the few investments I've made that has worked out well," Walker said.

Then Walker did something that Houck recalled may have had more significance than he realized at the time. He spent a long time looking over the trails and paths on the brushy lot behind the bar. He seemed almost too fascinated with the trails. Houck speculates that he might have been looking for either drop sites or a place to bury money or precious metals. But the FBI had yet to go over the property with a metal detector.

P.K. Carroll later said John told her he was looking over the area with a view toward possible construction of a trailer park. This had been Wilkinson's ambition.

Walker told a group in the bar, "You have no idea how ironic it is that I own a VFW bar," a remark that made more sense later.

"We had a party for him," Houck said. Walker showed up wearing an expensive-looking yellow shirt and tailored brown trousers. He began expounding on an invention he said he had perfected, an electronic device that could be used to make much better high-fidelity sound by altering the equalizers.

"If it works out like I think it will, it will make me a millionaire," Walker bragged to those in the bar. "I'm getting a patent on it right now."

Several attractive women at the party, believing they were in the presence of an electronics genius and future millionaire, took his shirt off and fluttered around him, caressing him and flirting with him the rest of the night while P.K. tolerantly looked on. Walker loved the attention and expansively discussed his genius for electronics and real estate deals. He seemed particularly happy to learn that a big shopping center was finally going up nearby as he had always hoped.

Walker also flew into the area a number of times during the 1980s without surfacing at the bar, which interested the FBI.

IN 1967 WALKER was transferred to Norfolk. He arranged for Barbara to remain in South Carolina and take care of the bar while he commuted on weekends. He moved into a luxury high-rise, the Algonquin House, got a taste of the dashing, bachelor life-style, and began to skip the weekend commute. The marriage became more and more strained. He bought two new sailboats and for a time concealed these purchases from Barbara. While she was toiling in the grungy little bar trying to keep it afloat, he would enjoy sailing in the Hampton Roads area with a date, pretending to be a single Navy chief.

It was in Norfolk that Barbara found the tin box and confronted Walker.

He was away often during this time. He had a succession of girlfriends on whom he lavished money and expensive dinners. He told them that he owned a bar in Charleston that was a virtual gold mine. In actual fact, the succession of lessees who operated the bar after Barbara left Charleston could scarcely do enough business to pay Walker his 200-dollar-per-month rent. Walker was making his extra money from the Soviet Union.

He had been made a communications watch officer for the Naval Submarine Force, Atlantic Fleet. For the first time in his Navy career, he was at the nerve center of communications for the entire Atlantic submarine fleet. He knew at any given moment where all U.S. submarines were deployed. He knew where U.S. intelligence said the Soviet submarines were deployed. He knew where all of the U.S. surface ships were and their destinations.

In short, had the Soviets been allowed to choose where to place Walker themselves, they could scarcely have chosen a better slot. They could determine from contact with Walker on a regular basis how effective they were at avoiding the SOSUS net; they could listen in on all Atlantic and probably a good part of the Pacific Fleet communications as Walker supplied them with key lists or rotor sequences on a daily basis, and he could tell them precisely where American subs were cruising.

The United States was then at war with North Vietnam, which was supplied and informed by the Soviet Union. According to Navy Secretary John Lehman, there is every evidence that Walker's espionage activity cost American lives because of intercepted radio traffic during this time. The radio traffic dealt with the time and place of Naval air strikes and their coordination with Air Force land strikes based in Thailand. When American pilots continually found themselves flying into an enemy prepared with Surface-to-Air Missiles (SAM) and heavily clustered anti-aircraft missiles, it had to be more than coincidence.

The Soviets did not break our code—they bought it. While John Walker was indulging his playboy tastes in pretty women and expensive meals, American servicemen were dying, in many instances, because of his treason.

A clearly angry Lehman said Soviet eavesdropping evidently had "devastating consequences" for American troops and fliers in Vietnam. The code-breaking assistance Walker gave to the Soviets could only be compared in damage to the help provided by the Poles in 1939 when they gave the British and French the German code machine, Enigma.

"Had we been engaged in any conflict with the Soviets while the Walker ring flourished," Lehman said, "it could have had the devastating consequences that Ultra was to the Germans."

During much of the Vietnam War the Soviets were decoding U.S. messages on ship movements, troop movements, and where U.S. bombers were going to strike next. The intercepted messages also told the Soviets at what ranges the United States could detect Soviet submarines. Lehman added:

"This enabled them to speed up the development of submarines with capabilities to beat the capabilities they knew we had."

Much of the collective American military frustration over the effectiveness of the North Vietnamese during the Vietnam War can now be seen in clearer focus. The coordination of sea forces with land troops in Vietnam was a daily and routine matter of message traffic, virtually all of it in code. Few major or minor offensives were initiated without generating such traffic, often to the Joint Chiefs of Staff on a high-priority basis.

The Soviets often had to restrain the North Vietnamese from being too obvious in their ambush or preparations for an offensive for fear of tipping off U.S. intelligence operatives. This also would explain how a small, low-tech country could shoot down so many American aircraft, avoid detection themselves in troop movements, and ferret out American weakness for exploitation.

Intelligence officials say it would no doubt have been far worse had not the Soviets, fearful that they might waste this secret jewel by helping the North Vietnamese too much, exercised a lot of selectivity in the information parceled out to the North Vietnamese. The Soviets also were concerned that there might be a security leak in the North Vietnamese government of Ho Chi Minh.

Purchase of the U.S. code can be superimposed on a number of other events in retrospect. For example, could this explain the dilatory tactics of the North Vietnamese delegation during the Paris Peace Talks that began in 1968? Why would they be in a hurry to reach an accord when they could play the chess game with an opponent who was signaling his moves in advance?

And how the Soviets must have enjoyed the American show of force in various parts of the world when they could intercept messages that informed them precisely of what the limits of action were. They knew just how far they could go without starting a serious conflict. It gave them a power card in the cold war brinksmanship of the late 1960s.

It was during this time that Walker's Soviet contacts told him he was considered a hero of the Soviet Union by its military establishment. They made him an admiral and promised to provide him with a uniform when he came to Vienna. The idea of being decked out in a Russian admiral's uniform had to have appealed to his histrionic nature.

The Soviets must have groaned when Walker was transferred from Norfolk to San Diego to teach cryptography in 1969. It was in

San Diego on this tour that he was destined to meet Jerry Whitworth and recruit him as a spy specializing in the Pacific Fleet, stepping through the door of compartmentalization that the Navy hoped would make espionage more difficult.

8

Johnny Walker Red

He was a fun guy to be around, but now I realize that maybe he was a scumbag—that the man I knew was a very carefully constructed image.
—Ted Uhlrich, Norfolk, Virginia, September 1985

After leaving San Diego, Walker was sent in 1941 to the USS *Niagara Falls,* a combat store ship that serviced Navy vessels off the coast of Vietnam. During part of this time, Walker was a Navy courier, carrying messages too involved and "hot" to send by radio, as he told friends. Debriefers are trying to determine whether Walker somehow copied any of this sealed courier material and handed it over to the Soviets during leave time in Hong Kong.

By this time John Walker had become a very unpleasant man. He cursed in every sentence, no matter to whom he was talking. He frequented pornographic movies and enjoyed telling friends about them in detail. He had a collection of pornographic video cassettes at his home, and he bragged about keeping a drawer next to his bed full of exotic sexual implements. He bragged of having sexual relations with one girlfriend in his airplane. He was prone to giggling wickedly about dirty tricks and deceptions. Although P.K.

was his steady girlfriend, he lost few opportunities to see other women.

He was sent back to Norfolk in 1974 where he bought a house. The shaky marriage steadily deteriorated. He fought, not just with Barbara, but with his daughters as well. He began staying away nights. He and Barbara were divorced the following year. Walker at first turned the house over to Barbara, but when she fell behind in property taxes, he demanded it back. It was then that she moved to Skowhegan, Maine, and he took over the house.

After his retirement from the Navy in 1976, Walker failed in a car radio business with his brother Arthur and in an effort to set up an association for professional salesmen. Charlie Smith was John Walker's partner in The American Association of Professional Salespersons.

Smith said Walker often talked to him about the bar in South Carolina and his family. "There was a load of friction in his home. He had a wife and family to support, and another apartment and a girlfriend. The wife knew about the girlfriend, and the girlfriend knew about the wife.

"Barbara was hostile to him from the start. She was a frustrated woman. I think that when she left Tidewater she felt her Wheaties had been pissed in.

"Johnny seemed fairly well read. He had opinions about politics. He was outspoken. I never heard him use any racial terms and didn't know anything about any Klan connection. I thought he was very squared away, very organized, a good citizen.

"Art was—I don't think he was bright businesswise. Johnny backed him in Walker Enterprises. The company sold car radios and stuff like that to auto dealerships. I didn't give him much credit for being able to know the day of the week or anything. Johnny was bright.

"Johnny took people with talent and bled the talent from them, and then when they were used up, he'd leave them. I never got friendship from him, but I can't say anything bad about him. I don't know anybody he was close to.

"What he told me about his business in South Carolina was that as an enlisted man he had opened a bar. He said that one day beer was delivered to the place by mistake and he paid for it and took it to the bar where it should have been delivered and gave it to the guy.

"As a reward, the guy thought he was so swell he got involved in a vending machine business. He used to take trips down to South Carolina and come back with cash. Charleston is where he said he was going."

In 1979 Walker got a job in Norfolk with Wackenhut Security, a large security firm in the same league as the Pinkerton Agency. The company has contracts with Los Alamos and the Savannah River Plant, where nuclear warheads are manufactured. It was from Los Alamos that atomic bomb secrets were slipped to Julius and Ethel Rosenberg. The FBI would like to know whether the Soviets asked Walker to try to insinuate himself into this big security firm.

Phil Prince was working for Wackenhut when Walker showed up one day to ask for a job. If opposites attract, then Phil Prince and John Walker are perfect examples. Prince had had three tours of duty in Vietnam—and he had to wrangle the last tour. He was wounded three times and received the Silver Star for valor in combat in 1968. He won a battlefield commission that cited his "outstanding combat leadership." Prince is a big, open, direct kind of guy—he reminds people of a young John Wayne. Most people like him instantly. There is no doubt that John Walker saw in Phil Prince all of the real qualities of character that he could only feign at best. They became good friends and business partners.

"I met Johnny when I was director of investigations for the Wackenhut Corporation," Prince recalled. "Johnny came in and wanted to know what it took to become a private investigator. I don't know whether at the time this was something he really wanted to do or whether he thought it might have made a good cover.

"I looked at his intelligence background. He said he had worked in Naval intelligence as a courier. He said he had been in South Vietnam off the coast either on subs or destroyers, I don't remember which. He said he would drop off courier packages with confidential information.

"He wore a full beard, moustache, wire-rimmed glasses, and a toupee. It was the kind with an adhesive. It was a while before I knew he wore it. I never saw him without it in three years. Because of his ego, I am sure he would be devastated without it.

"John was pretty deep. He had a good mind. He was not dumb by any stretch of the imagination. He could always support his arguments. And it was usually through his reading. If you got him in a discussion, say about the John Birch Society, he could support his arguments. He thought the Holocaust was an absolute myth.

"John was very patriotic. It was a beautiful cover that he had when he first interviewed for the job. He only wanted a part-time job. He said, 'I only need to make 5,000 dollars a year because of Uncle Sam—my Navy pension—and I've had some good investments.' A lot of the investments he had were with the bar and restaurant in Charleston. And he had made a killing—about 50,000 dollars—on the silver market. And he said he had pinball machines in restaurants and bars. Some of his investments were on the West Coast. He said he was in with a group. He said he had to leave once every six months for a meeting either on the West Coast or the East Coast.

"So I sent him to Thomas Nelson Junior College to get his private investigator's license. I had retired [from the Marine Corps] August first in 1979 and had gone to work for Wackenhut in October. In December of 1979 I was made director of investigations. It was sometime shortly after that John came in and then picked up his P.I. license. He told me he had a van he could use for surveillance, several different kinds of cameras and several different kinds of lenses.

"He seemed perfect for me. The guy didn't want to make very much money, he was enthusiastic, intelligent. It seemed like he would make a pretty good investigator. I monitored him pretty closely his first two or three cases, and his writing when he wrote up the cases was very good. So after the first few cases I more or less let him go on his own. He did a fine job. His specialty was the workman's compensation case.

"But he did get himself in trouble one time when he disguised himself as a priest. At that particular time I was working for a good client. I turned John over to our investigative supervisor. It was only when the [trespassing] charges came up that I learned that he had gone into this place disguised as a priest. He had gotten this card out of the Universal Life Church in California that identified him as a minister. He thought perhaps that could be done legally with this as his credentials. He was very innovative.

"I remember he talked a man into letting him into his house across the street from a suspected workman's compensation [fraud] case. Johnny used the front window of the man's home to film the man changing tires."

A woman who suspected her husband of adultery but was not sure came to Walker. Walker proposed a raffle, the winning prize for which would be a weekend in a luxury Atlanta hotel. He would arrange for the husband to win the raffle. Walker was sure that the husband would take his girlfriend on the trip. He would have the room wired and install a video camera in a vent. This way they could get the goods on the husband.

The client agreed and Walker had 2,400 raffle tickets printed and sold them all for a dollar, pocketing the money and not telling his client that he had really conducted a raffle. He charged her, in addition to the fee, the cost of the setup hotel room in Atlanta.

Walker managed to talk the husband into purchasing a raffle ticket, and later he grandly announced to the husband at his office that he had won a trip for two to Atlanta. When the appointed weekend came, Walker was ready with his electronic gear, including video camera. But to his and his client's chagrin, the husband took an old buddy with him, and he and his male friend simply went out on the town and got drunk, stumbling back to the room and passing out.

Did Prince ever sense there was something strange about Walker or some facet of his personality that didn't ring true?

"The only thing I thought was strange about Johnny was his connection with women. Johnny had a very difficult time holding a conversation with an intelligent woman. For example, he did not like my wife. My wife did not like him. Art's wife did not like him. You'll find a lot of the wives—it was an innate sense among intelligent women—there was something about him they did not like. He was very good to the girls that he dated. He took them to parties, out on his houseboat, up in his plane, nice dinners. He could pretty much overwhelm them. John also always carried around a couple of hundred dollars in folding money. But he didn't throw it around. He didn't spend it lavishly."

Prince left Wackenhut to form Confidential Reports. A short time later, Walker showed up offering to help.

"After I left to start my own business Johnny knocked on my door and said he wasn't getting along very well with my replacement at Wackenhut and wanted to know if he could work with me.

Johnny had a lot of assets that I could use, including a copying machine, the airplane, the van, the houseboat, all of his cameras and lenses."

Prince gave Walker a third of the business.

"We started getting busy so we rented an office on South Parliament Drive. Johnny was never interested in any great remuneration. Just expenses. So we started out with an excellent relationship. We had a lot of business—attorneys, insurance companies. Then toward the end he was just so darn difficult to get along with."

It appeared to Prince that Walker, when he reminisced about his past, wanted to blank out certain aspects of his life.

"I think his father was one of them. I went over on two occasions on the Eastern Shore to see his father in Temperanceville. I enjoyed his company. But John didn't want to talk about that." Prince had the feeling that Walker came from a rough family background.

"Because of being Italian, he had this family thing—the family image—that he would always protect his brothers and son and that they would always protect him, that this was the only true allegiance. He mentioned this to me on a couple of occasions."

Walker did not believe in confrontation. "He used to say 'You never confront a person face to face. You get even. Maybe three years from now.' Call and have the guy's electricity turned off. The dirty tricks department.

"Despite his life-style, John worked very hard at his job. He was in every morning, and he worked late. The cases took priority. But I noticed toward the end, when I decided to sell Confidential Reports, he reminded me of an old woman in many respects."

John's son, Michael, respected him and admired his playboy life-style, and, according to Prince, they had an agreement: "As long as he stayed in school he could do anything he wanted to do—bring his girlfriend over to the house or the houseboat. Anything that he wanted to do. John always referred to his daughters as 'the bitches.' It was part of his strange relationship with women.

"He had a mouth that could embarrass any sailor in the world, and he was very free with his language, and he used it around children, women. It's something I think the women didn't like—like my wife for example. I don't know whether he believed that was just free expression or showing that he was somewhat of a free spirit.

"He loved to carry that pistol wherever he went, a two-inch .38 Smith & Wesson. My wife was a travel agent in Virginia Beach, and John went one time to make reservations. To show everyone he took off his coat so they could see his pistol. He carried it [in a holster] on his side. I always thought that was a little strange."

To Prince, John and Art seemed very close, but they were very different. "I think Art was a little bit envious of Johnny's life-style. Art used to come up and spend a lot of time at Confidential Reports."

Prince didn't suspect that John had covert sources of income because his explanations seemed logical. "He told me he came by the van when he made the 50,000 dollars. And he said the airplane was a good tax write-off. And at the time he owned a two- or three-story apartment building with eight or ten renters.

"During my interviews with the bureau [FBI], [I learned] that he had my telephone and my office bugged. I had no idea. Even though we were in that kind of business, he was the last person in the world I would suspect. The FBI thought that he was probably trying to find out how much I knew—if I had stumbled onto anything at all, because he made several of these 'business trips' while he was with me.

"Johnny started Electronic Counterspy [another detective agency specializing in searching for electronic bugs]. It came under the umbrella of Confidential Reports. We even flew in his plane down to Savannah and took a whole day's course in how [specialized equipment] operates detecting bugs and taps. And John got a couple of good contracts. Newport News Shipyard was one of them. I went over there on two occasions when we made the sweeps and looked for any clandestine transmitters.

"He said all of this equipment, which cost about twenty- to twenty-five thousand dollars came from an uncle. I never believed that. I thought it came from his own personal assets."

Prince never worried about flying with Walker, whom he described as a very careful pilot. Walker often acted as copilot in ferrying twin-engined aircraft overseas. Prince wondered if Walker used this as a cover to go to Europe for contacts with the Soviets.

Prince is bitter about Walker. "You have to understand that after twenty-two years in the Marine Corps, three tours in Vietnam, three Purple Hearts, the Silver Star, I put my time in. I lost a lot of kids. I am a little sentimental about that. I think about that a lot.

"One, I am incredulous. Two, I feel a sense of personal betrayal. And three, I would like to wrap his glasses around my fist. I was in a state of shock for a couple of weeks because all of these things were going through my mind. I tried to think, did I ever unwittingly help him? I provided him with cover."

After Walker's arrest the FBI asked Prince to take a polygraph, which he considered an insult. "There were five basic questions about espionage and my loyalty to my country. The last one was 'Are you a loyal citizen of the United States?'"

The forty-six-year-old Prince found it hard to stop thinking about Walker. "It's something I'll probably remember the rest of my life. What makes me angrier than anything are his motives— just for his ego and money. That puts him way, way down. If he was doing it out of ideology and he actually believed in what he was doing—you can give a person a certain respect for putting his life on the line for what he actually believed in. I suppose that bothers me more than anything."

WALKER ENJOYED ELABORATE disguises. But one time—when he misrepresented himself as a reporter—it backfired. A black woman had brought a suit against a contractor for shoddy workmanship. Walker was hired by the contractor and decided to try to get the contract back from the woman by pretending to be a reporter who was interested in preventing abuses by contractors. Walker told the woman he was working closely with Fred Talbot, a reporter with the Norfolk *Ledger-Star,* whom he actually had never met. Talbot had done some news stories on contractors and their problems.

The woman called Talbot to complain that Walker kept showing up at her home. They arranged for Talbot and a *Ledger-Star* photographer to eavesdrop on a meeting with Walker.

"We sat on the floor behind the bar. Walker introduced himself as a news reporter with Universal Life Press of California. He said he was writing a story about home repair rip-offs and problems that blacks were suffering.

"And he said he was writing for *The Christian Science Monitor* and that the story might also be used by a publication of the Reverend Jerry Falwell of Lynchburg, Virginia. He said he was sharing information with and working closely with Bob Geske of the *Virginia Pilot* newspaper. He also said he knew me, Fred Talbot, of the *Ledger-Star*. He said Geske was working on a similar story, and he said he was doing everything possible to help the people in the black community.

"Walker repeatedly asked Miss Alexander to go and find her original contract with the contractor. He also asked that he be allowed to take the original contracts ... photocopy them and bring them back. ... She continually grilled him and asked him for proof of who he was.

"After about twenty minutes John Shealy and I stepped out from behind the bar and introduced ourselves, Shealy popping photographs all the way. I walked over to Walker and asked to see his identification. It was really amusing because Walker was taken by surprise, his eyes getting like saucers. His neck seemed to bulge a little bit.

"Walker handed me a large object which said Press Card or Press and it was from Universal Life Press. It had his photograph along with a fingerprint and his name. I then asked for his driver's license. The name on the driver's license was John Anthony Walker of the Ocean View area of Norfolk. I decided to check this out in his presence. I called Universal Life. I heard a recording which said they sell preacher's licenses for 50 dollars. I then remembered that the group also sells press IDs. I called Universal Press and the people there said they'd never heard of him. I also called *The Christian Science Monitor* in his presence, and they also said they had never heard of him. I called Geske and he said the guy used to work for Wackenhut Security. . . .

"Geske said Walker was a 'creep.' Walker refused to say whom he was working for. He kept saying he was a reporter 'just like you.' Miss Alexander, by now fearful of the man and in tears, called the police. . . .

"While I continued to question Walker, Shealy went out front and examined Walker's camper. Without entering the locked cab,

Shealy noticed a business card on the floor. Shealy photographed the card. It read, 'John Anthony Walker, Jr., Confidential Reports, Inc., Manager and Investigator, Virginia Beach, Virginia.'"

MIKE BELL, ONE of Walker's superiors at Wackenhut, did not like or trust Walker from the first second he met him, and he told everyone around him as much.

"I would catch him in lies about where he had been and what he had been doing. There was something about him that was untrustworthy. People like Phil (Prince) would say, 'Aw, Mike, you're being too hard on Johnny.'"

Bell said that aside from the furtive, sneaky qualities he alone seemed to see in Walker, there was something else about him.

"I know he really doubted his masculinity. That's why he was always bragging about his sexual conquests, or trying to act tough.

"He once said, 'I may not be very good with my fists, but I'm pretty good with a knife.' He carried this big switchblade with him.

"And he had a crossbow. He said he liked crossbows because they killed silently. I always thought that he wanted to kill someone. I think he thought of himself as a hit man or something.

"We rarely carried our pistols. There might be one or two times a year when we'd have occasion to carry our pistols, but Johnny took his with him everywhere he went. He made a big deal out of carrying it.

"He talked big, but when it came to action he was a coward. We were in a bar once when this guy started a few words with us. Johnny got real quiet. He was the kind of a guy who would watch while some guy hit a woman and then walk up afterward and say 'It's a good thing he left when he did or I would have knocked his block off.'

"I could never understand why other people couldn't see what he really was like. I'd say, 'Look, this guy is crazy. Get rid of him. He's going to get us in trouble.' But the other people in the office liked him and thought he was the best thing since ice cream."

One of the things that most disturbed Bell was the contract Walker had with the shipyard. It called for quarterly sweeps to detect bugs, or more often if there was to be a high-level meeting of Navy brass. "I would be willing to bet anything that Johnny placed bugs in the meeting rooms before those meetings, and no telling what he got out of the place other than that."

Bell was quite certain that Walker went after the shipyard contract for his agency, Electronic Counterspy, as a means of getting back into higher quality espionage on his own, rather than having to depend on Arthur, Michael, and Whitworth.

Bell discovered that Walker had a habit of destroying files that made him look inept or ignorant or that involved questionable methods of investigation. "I called Walker in one time and asked him what happened to some files. He said, 'Well, you don't put everything in writing, Mike.' I lost my temper. I told him, 'Bullshit. That's not how you were trained. That's not the policy of this company.'

"I thought he was a manipulator and a liar. He wanted to control you and make you a puppet. Johnny would sit back and observe people. He would watch the people at a lounge or disco or something. The first time out he wouldn't contribute a lot. The next time out he would be an authority on everything, trying to impress you that he was wealthy and had this and had that. And he would constantly want to pick up checks and flaunt it.

"I came from a military family. My father spent thirty years in the Navy. I knew he couldn't have that much money. I questioned him about it one time. He said he was going to Carolina or California or someplace—that he had successful businesses. I had a problem with the money. He said he was into video and pinball machines. I let that go. I wasn't being paid to investigate Walker. Then he started buying all of this equipment. He said he bought sixty to seventy thousand dollars' worth of equipment. And he was going back and forth to New York, where he said he was going to electronics school.

"And we had a lot of problems on how to conduct an investigation. Johnny went after people with a vengeance. He would receive a relatively small assignment and build it way out of proportion in his mind, with all sorts of people being in collusion with this or that person."

Walker would sometimes suspect respected and wealthy people in the Norfolk area of scams that were patently absurd and later proved to be nonexistent.

"He had a funny look in his eyes. He would make eye contact

with you, and it was like his mind was thinking about something else. It got to the point where I couldn't even be civil with him anymore.

"He was a wimp and he was always trying to impress everyone else that he was bad. He was the kind who would waylay you. But I don't think he would have had the guts to get close to you, face to face. That's what used to tickle me about the knives and [sword] canes. But he knew no one would believe he could do anything with his fists. I think you could smack Johnny in the mouth and he would not come back at you. He wasn't the type."

Bell and Phil Prince were close friends until they differed over Walker. "I told Phil, 'I'm just not having anything to do with him—the guy's nuts.' But Phil liked his military background. He was a gofer for Phil, and Johnny led him to believe that he idolized him."

According to Bell, who now owns his own private investigation company headquartered in Richmond, Virginia, Walker plainly thought that being a private investigator "was like Magnum P.I. or Burt Reynolds, running around, chasing cars, and all of that baloney. That's the type person Johnny would hire for his company because Johnny thought that way himself. Private investigation is not glamor. It's a business just like any other business."

Walker never talked about anything personal to Bell, outside of sexual exploits.

"Johnny would come back and tell me about his sexual conquests and go into detail—I mean explicit detail. I thought it was immature on his part, the locker room talk that I always thought most guys dropped in high school. Then I had an opportunity to meet some of the girls he would surround himself with. They were the type that you could literally sell the Brooklyn Bridge to. For lack of a better term, they were airheads.

"He boasted a lot about how good he was at picking up women, but if you went into a place, he turned into a quiet, shy type. And if he did meet someone, it had to be someone he could con—like I said, airheads. But that type of person will do whatever you want them to.

"Although I didn't know he was a spy, of course, I just knew he was associated with something strange. I knew something wasn't right. I can't understand why no one in the military could spot this—especially with a person with clearances and access to this classified material. Phil's a smart man—I don't understand why he didn't see it.

"You know, Johnny lied so much I think he sometimes believed what he was saying. It was so transparent, yet he kept on lying and lying—about everything. I have no doubt whatsoever that he would lie under oath and commit perjury.

"One time he went out on a case involving this girl who allegedly had a back injury, and he ended up seducing her. This is the most unprofessional thing you can do. I advised the client not to go to hearing with it. I told them what had happened. Can you imagine how embarrassing that was?

"Basically, he wanted to be this now guy—the kind of guy that when he walked through the door everybody would say, 'Hey, Johnny Walker's here.' But in essence, no one did. He was just a sleaze with no ethics."

TED UHLRICH ALSO worked as an investigator with John Walker at Wackenhut. He had admired him until he found out about the espionage. Walker was an innovative detective with good ideas, in Uhlrich's opinion, particularly ideas that would catch people who were pretending to have disabilities for insurance purposes.

"I remember we had a guy that Johnny and I decided to use the cement drop on. He was supposed to be in bad shape and wasn't supposed to be able to do any work. He was slick. He was building an addition onto the back of his house but we could never catch him. So we dropped two fifty-pound bags of cement on his lawn early one morning—about four A.M. We made it look like they had dropped off a truck. When he came out to get his paper he noticed them. We hid in the bushes across the street. He threw the bags over his shoulder and walked off" while they photographed him.

There was almost admiration in Uhlrich's voice as he described one of Walker's most successful scams for catching people who insurance companies believed were faking injuries that prevented their working. "Johnny came up with the great grocery giveaway. He would get the secretary to call this guy up and say, 'Mr. Johnson, do you own a 1978 Cadillac Seville, license plate so and so? Well, congratulations, you are our WPIC pick of the week. You have won a free bag of groceries worth fifty dollars. You can pick them up at the Bi-Lo market at such and such address. There are no strings attached whatsoever. All you have to do is show up and show your driver's license and pick them up. Be at the market at such and such a time.' Then Johnny Walker would be parked in his van with a movie camera. We would put hams and turkeys and potatoes and heavy stuff in the bag. We had one instance where a man showed up with his son and his son loaded the groceries. But most of the time it worked.

"Johnny was innovative, he was brilliant, he had chutzpah, he had charm. He liked disguises. He could adapt and blend very well. Johnny was the kind of a guy—he had very strong feelings about religion. He thought it was a ridiculous waste of time. He thought it was a lot of mumbo jumbo. His view toward nuns was less than circumspect.

"He was an ordained minister in the Universal Life Church. He said everybody knows it's a big scam, but he said it gives you a little bit of legitimacy. It was his way of satirizing organized religion. He would expound about these TV evangelists and all the money they're making and all the rest of it. He saw religion as the ultimate sting or scam operation—all ministers were corrupt, all priests were corrupt, all nuns were corrupt. They were only in it for money—they were either crooked or dumb. He said if some of the nuns were really dedicated to helping people, then they were dumb."

Uhlrich thought that this was Walker's "way of getting even with the church. I'm sure he was into this spy business because of the money and the glamor involved, but I think in his deep subconscious it might have been his way of getting back at a society that failed to recognize him."

He also thought that Walker might have had a subconscious desire to get caught. That could explain his apparent cheerfulness since his arrest.

"But I just don't understand the man getting his family involved—why he would use his children, his mother, everyone? The only reason Michael got involved in all of this was to gain acceptance by his dad.

"'PM Magazine' did a piece called 'Superspy,' an ironic title. He [Walker] was shown checking his gun. But he was inordinately naive about weapons. He has a real lack of basic knowledge about guns. Johnny would come over while we were looking at weapons and he was mystified. He knew very little about guns, although he tried to pretend he did. He didn't know anything about them."

Uhlrich once called Walker "Johnny Walker Red" in jest, after the well-known Scotch, but Walker was not amused. He became furious, shouting, "Don't ever call me that again!" Obviously it was too close to the truth to be funny.

Uhlrich once asked Walker where he got the money for his airplane, camper van, car, pickup truck, house, and houseboat. Walker replied, "Well my motor home is not that big a deal—it's used, the houseboat is an unpretentious thing, my airplane I have to charter out to pay the maintenance. I'm not living high on the hog."

"He didn't want anybody to think he had any money," Uhlrich continued. "The FBI told me that they think Johnny has hidden a million dollars—probably in the Bahamas. They have reason to think the money may be sitting in an account in the Cayman Islands or someplace.

"In a sense I envied him. It was more than just his swinging life-style. He was an easygoing guy. Nothing ever seemed to bother him. I only saw him angry once and that was when he had to make a trip to California. He said a business partner out there was ripping him off." Uhlrich learned later that there was no such business partner—Walker was simply creating the cover for a trip to pick up classified materials from Jerry Whitworth, who was living in Davis, California.

The sophisticated electronic equipment owned by Walker was puzzling to Uhlrich. "I couldn't figure out where he got the money for all of it. It was not the kind of stuff you buy at Radio Shack. Some of the stuff must have cost fifty to sixty thousand dollars. He was proud of the fact that it was state-of-the-art and very expensive. He had shelves and shelves full of it."

Walker's anti-Semitic, anti-black racist views and his alleged connection with the Ku Klux Klan did not ring true to Uhlrich. "I got the feeling he was just mouthing the words. I am convinced in my mind that it was a cover, including the super-patriotism. He never went around with us espousing the ideology of the Klan. When he appeared on a local broadcast as a representative of the

Klan, he was investigated by the Anti-Defamation League. And the thing that they were impressed with was that he was very knowledgeable about the Klan, but very unemotional and detached. They said he was not a zealot."

Walker took his job seriously and worked hard. "I was in it to make a living," Uhlrich said, "and he was in it to have fun. It used to amuse me—here's an idiot who even enjoys stakeouts. Stakeouts are the most boring aspect of investigative work."

Uhlrich believed Walker had a real distaste for kids. "He called them rug rats and just didn't like them. He hated kids. But he seemed like a normal father when his son was around. He didn't talk about his parents or his family background much."

Although Barbara Walker went to Skowhegan in poverty with her children, and Walker managed to keep all of the assets, he seemed to enjoy telling colleagues, "That drunken bitch really took me to the cleaners. Cleaned me out for nearly everything."

"Obviously this didn't happen," Uhlrich said.

Walker "had an eye for women," Uhlrich continued. "He dated some very good-looking women. He owned some apartment buildings near the Virginia Beach strand, and one of his girlfriends, Roberta Puma, ran them for him. It was not unlike Johnny to meet some girl and say 'I'm glad to meet you. Do you screw around? How about my place tonight?' He didn't care. And he used the same kind of language around everyone. His attitude was if they don't like it, they don't have to listen to it or they can leave. He didn't modify his language because of social pressure.

"People either liked Johnny very much or didn't care for him at all. But most people liked him.

"I realize now that I didn't know the real Johnny. But from the very beginning, I believed the accusations. They fit. He had the opportunity, the motive—everything. He was a fun guy to be around, but now I realize that maybe he was a scumbag—that the man I knew was a very carefully constructed image."

9

Operation Windflyer

I was looking at his eyes and his trigger finger. If there had been any indication that he was going to pull the trigger, I would have fired. —FBI agent Robert W. Hunter

A simple telephone conversation signaled the moment the FBI had waited for with catlike patience during the previous five months. One mistake now would ruin everything. The ball was in the court of the FBI's Foreign Intelligence Squad, operating out of Norfolk but working closely with the Bureau's Washington field office.

The case was a daily concern of FBI Director William Webster, who kept on top of it through Deputy Director Philip Parker. Memorandums marked "Windflyer" had top priority throughout the bureau.

The task was far more difficult than surveillance of a man with little knowledge of electronic devices. In some ways, John Walker was as experienced as many FBI agents, and he had had similar training in firearms use and surveillance techniques. Although he was not the firearms expert that Ted Uhlrich was, he was known as a good shot with a pistol. And agents were sure he had received training by the Soviets during trips to Mexico City and Vienna.

All of the waiting and watching and listening culminated in May 1985 when Walker was seen almost jauntily loading a brand new Chevy van, a van he had bought secure in the knowledge that he would soon be about 50,000 dollars richer. He had also promised to buy P.K. a new Chevy Blazer when he returned.

ROBERT W. HUNTER, a nineteen-year FBI veteran, was in the midst of a divorce after twenty-three years of marriage. He had been trying to hold the marriage together, but he knew that being the wife of an FBI agent was not easy. He was gone odd hours, and most of the time he could not, as a specialist in counterintelligence, tell his family what he was working on.

At the same time that his marriage failed, the Washington and Norfolk offices decided to place him in direct, day-to-day charge of the Walker case. He threw himself into it to the exclusion of everything else. An ardent freshwater fisherman, he let his fishing tackle get dusty. He spent hours listening to Walker's telephone conversations. He and the other agents under his control, and his bosses, Wagner and Wolfinger, held many brainstorming sessions about the Walker case.

Hunter argued that close, daily surveillance would be too risky for someone with Walker's training. "But I also said if we couldn't do this job on a so-called detective, then we should hang it up."

Sometimes Hunter would drive by Walker's house in the early hours of the morning, always in a different car, and think about the strange man who lived there. He tried to see inside the soul of John Walker, to understand what made him betray his country, and he had many long conversations with Barbara and Laura to try to get a handle on Walker, to learn what he might expect.

He rarely got to see his children: Robin, twenty; Robert, eighteen; Susan, sixteen; and Grady, his youngest, at ten. And he couldn't tell them why. He hoped they wouldn't assume that it was because he didn't want to see them more often.

His son Robert asked him to speak to his government class at First Colonial Beach High School on May 17, 1985. By that time, Hunter knew that Walker planned a trip on the coming weekend, but he couldn't say no to his son. He closed his speech to the students by telling them that he might have something more interesting to talk to them about later.

110

It turned out that he was right.

The FBI had overheard John Walker planning a trip. He had told Art and several friends, "I'm going to do something that only I can do." He said he was going to Charlotte on business. The FBI telephone surveillance crew reported the conversations, and Hunter decided that this might be a trip to make a drop even though Charlotte was an unlikely place to go for that purpose. Hunter placed Walker's home under full-time visual surveillance starting May 18. And it paid off.

On Sunday, he saw Walker get in his new van and drive to a McDonald's on Tidewater Drive near Walker's home. Hunter had never seen him up close so he decided to get a cup of coffee at McDonald's, too. Walker was eating his breakfast just minutes after the McDonald's opened at 7 A.M., when Hunter walked past him and sat nearby. Walker had no reason to suspect the man who was dressed in almost preppy fashion, with loafers, casual slacks, and a sports shirt. Hunter, a handsome man with gray hair and blue eyes, five feet ten and 185 pounds, tried to be inconspicuous—just another person grabbing a quick Sunday morning breakfast at McDonald's.

He was excited by the prospect that the case might be ready to break open. He had spent months learning submarine lore and trying to decipher the strangely self-content man who sat 12 feet away eating scrambled eggs and sausage. Walker didn't look up once. He was plainly preoccupied with his thoughts and plans.

When Walker finished breakfast and returned to his van, Hunter remained seated for a time to avoid suspicion. There were many other agents poised and waiting.

It was still early in the morning when Walker got back to his home and began packing a duffel bag. Before he left, he called Michael's wife, Rachel. She had just graduated from Old Dominion College, and he congratulated her and promised he would get her a gift later. He told her, too, that he was making a business trip to Charlotte and would be back on Monday.

Meanwhile, agents in a variety of automobiles and disguises were stationed throughout the area, waiting. Hunter got in his Chevrolet Cherokee, provided by the Bureau, and drove around Walker's neighborhood waiting for word. Soon, on a secret channel, he heard what he was waiting for. According to FBI aerial surveillance, Walker was leaving.

Pilot John W. Hodges, a twelve-year FBI veteran and member of the Bureau's Foreign Counterintelligence Squad, based in Norfolk, banked the single-engine aircraft and squinted through sunglasses at the highway below. Automobiles appeared to be crawling bugs from his altitude of 4,000 feet. But it was terrain he knew well. He saw the silver and blue 1985 Chevrolet Astro van as it left the driveway of 8524 Old Ocean View Road and began threading its way through Norfolk, Virginia, traffic. It was a beautiful Sunday afternoon, May 19, shortly before 2 P.M. The first hopeful sign came when Walker—even before he left Norfolk—began circling blocks, cutting down side streets, and doubling back on his trail. He was plainly trying to determine whether he was being followed.

He looked everywhere but up.

Soon Hodges and the ground surveillance agents realized that Walker had no intention of going to Charlotte. The van headed to Interstate Highway 64, toward Richmond. Part of the ground crew remained a few miles behind Walker, only occasionally closing to within visual range of binoculars. But other agents drove alongside him for part of the trip, not looking at him but talking among themselves to avoid suspicion. Hunter passed Walker and raced to beat him to Washington to arrange final details with the Washington field office, which had prearranged surveillance arrangements worked out with the Norfolk office in the event that Windflyer came to Washington.

Walker drove about 60 miles per hour. Hodges tried to keep the aircraft high and in Walker's blind spot, directly behind at about a 50-degree angle. Because of the slow speed of the van, Hodges had to vector from time to time, picking up the vehicle often enough to give the ground crews a fix.

This was a tense time for all of the agents. Extreme care had to be taken to avoid being seen by someone who was alert and well-schooled himself in the surveillance business. If Walker was indeed headed for a drop, this was going to be the best chance to date to make an arrest and, with any luck, grab his Soviet contact. But if Walker spotted any one of them, he would destroy any classified material he had with him and stop all espionage activity. This would leave the federal prosecutors with tainted testimony from a disgruntled wife, and little more.

Walker took the U.S. 295 bypass around the northeastern quadrant of Richmond and headed north on Interstate 95 instead of south. The agents were heartened by this.

Once on the interstate, Walker stopped maneuvering to detect whether he was being followed. When he arrived in the Washington area he took the Beltway around the city and entered Montgomery County, Maryland, crossing the Potomac River over the Cabin John Bridge. Here he began his "dry-cleaning" run, a convoluted path designed to detect a tail or surveillance. The route was laid out by KGB agents attached to the Washington embassy. It was perfectly designed to detect surveillance. And it worked—at least for Soviet Vice-Consul Aleksey Gavrilovich Tkachenko.

The "dry-cleaning zone" was a maze of country roads in some of Washington's most pleasant suburbs. The route followed old wagon trail roads that dipped and curved through horse country, gentleman farming country, and huge mansions, doubling back near the Potomac River and traversing such roads as Clopper Road, White's Ferry Road, Quince Orchard Road, Query Mill Road, Piney Meetinghouse Road, and Old Buckridge Lane.

It was brilliantly laid out, allowing the prey to double back on his trail, take abrupt turns that would be made far too soon to be seen by anyone not very close. Some sections crested hills that allowed a long stretch of clear visibility in a rearview mirror. Other parts swooped down and crossed quaint bridges over sparkling brooks that could have graced a picture postcard. Agents noted that one of the bridges was a narrow, one-way bridge that could easily be blocked to traffic in an emergency.

The way that the FBI communicated from air to ground and among each other during this crucial time is a secret that no one at any level will discuss. The Soviets have what CIA personnel term a "roof garden" array of scanners and electronic detectors of varying degrees of sophistication in Washington that could detect transceivers in use in the drop zone. Had there been any unusual traffic, the operation would have been called off immediately. The Soviets, according to one high-ranking CIA source, can even detect when transceivers are on but not in active use. The Soviets have been known to communicate with their own transceivers by using the on-off buttons to make coded clicks.

From time to time, Walker got out of the van and looked back at his trail. He was like a fox trying to shake a relentless, invisible hound. Agents backed off and let him run. Hodges had by then relinquished the air surveillance to another agent-pilot, who tried to keep the aircraft at a sufficient distance so as to be unobtrusive yet still keep Walker's van in sight. There were several other small aircraft joyriding in the area, which would serve to lessen any possible suspicions. But at 4:45 P.M., the agents lost Walker.

Norfolk FBI Supervisor Joseph R. Wolfinger noted, "At that time Walker was observed making U-turns, driving circuitous routes, and stopping at the side of the road, all in a manner calculated to detect if he was being followed. This activity was observed for approximately one hour, at which time surveillance contact with Walker was lost. The . . . surveillance detection activity is a known method of operation of trained espionage agents and is known to occur prior to and after espionage activity."

The FBI "had to assume" that dotted at strategic points throughout the area were KGB personnel, a high-ranking FBI official said. Their job was to watch for vehicles taking the same route Walker took. If they saw indications of surveillance, they were to warn Tkachenko.

Ironically, the FBI inadvertently avoided this early warning system when they lost Walker. They would not spot him again until 7:48 P.M. But they weren't concerned. Better to lose him temporarily than be "made" by him.

Walker spotted a soft drink can at the first place listed by the Soviets as a signal that they were ready to pick up his drop. The signal was at a bend in part of the route. When Walker saw it, he left an empty 7-Up can with an orange dot on it, per Soviet instructions, as his signal that he planned to make a drop.

It was at this point that the FBI made an unavoidable mistake that may have cost them the chance to arrest Soviet Vice-Consul Tkachenko. They could not have kept him, but they could have expelled him with enough publicity to be embarrassing to the Soviets and make propaganda points to a world that constantly uses the CIA as a whipping boy.

An agent, deciding that Walker might have dropped a container of microfilm, microdots, or other information, retrieved the can a short time after Walker drove on. High-ranking officials say the FBI had no choice: they had to assume that the can itself might be

Walker's drop, and they did not want any further information to be passed to the Soviets.

It probably will never be known whether Tkachenko decided to leave the area because the signal can was missing or because he and other KGB agents had spotted the FBI activity in the area or were actually watching Walker's signal location and saw the FBI retrieve the can.

Walker did not see any of the FBI. He dropped the 7-Up can as he was supposed to at Prince Orchard Road and Tavilah Road and continued to follow Soviet instructions. The next move would be the drop of classified information at a point near the intersection of White's Ferry Road and Partnership Road. The drop and pickup sites had been photographed by the Soviets and marked with arrows and written instructions, printed out simply and clearly in English. Each was in a place that could be observed from a distance by someone with binoculars.

About 8:20 P.M. FBI agents Ralph Harp, Charles Turner, and Mary Ann Sheehy were waiting to make a left-hand turn off Dufief Mill Road onto Darnestown Road when they saw a blue Chevrolet Malibu with tags DSX-144. Driving the car, according to a positive identification by Sheehy, was Soviet Vice-Consul Aleksey Tkachenko. He had his wife and child with him so that it would seem to be a Sunday outing. He apparently was on the way out of the drop area when he was spotted. The FBI decided not to stop him in the hope that there were other KGB agents in the area.

Tkachenko went into hiding so fast that he abandoned all of his household goods. There was even meat left in a pot on the kitchen range in his luxury apartment in Alexandria, Virginia. It had apparently just been readied for cooking. The manager of the building said the apartment looked as if the family had packed hastily and left. (Three days later, FBI agents watched as Tkachenko and his wife, Ulga, two daughters, Maria and Exsona, and four beefy bodyguards slipped to National Airport and boarded a flight to New York and thence to Moscow.)

A short time before Tkachenko was spotted in the area, Walker stopped his van, looked around, then placed his paper shopping bag filled with 129 classified documents at the base of a pole that had a

No Hunting sign on it. It, in turn, was next to a large tree with one very heavy curved branch, just as depicted in the KGB's photographs. It was an easily identifiable drop site, and the grass at the base of the pole was high enough so that passersby would not see the bag.

Unfortunately, ground agents were too far back to see this, but they could discern from Walker's behavior that he was about to make a drop. One agent said he could "smell" it coming.

Around 9 P.M., agent Bruce Brahe, a twelve-year veteran with the FBI, George Perkins, and Douglas Stauffer went to an area near the intersection of White's Ferry Road and Partnership Road, where earlier Walker had been seen from a distance. It seemed to be a likely site for a drop. The search had to be conducted quickly for fear that Walker would return. Part of standard Soviet instructions were that if there should be a mix-up, they could use the drop site instead of the agreed-upon site to leave money and instructions.

"Special Agent Perkins dropped us off," said Brahe. "It was dark, and Special Agent Stauffer and I then conducted the search of that area. . . .

"We began to scour the area and went directly toward what was the major landmark in the area, a large tree approximately three hundred yards south on Partnership Road, south of a triangular intersection near White's Ferry Road. Prior search teams had also searched that tree but were always under time pressure because of the proximity of Walker and had to therefore vacate the area quickly.

"We began to expand the search and to do it in fairly scientific squares of six feet. We began to look visually and kick through the grass and—when we felt it was safe—to use the aid of a flashlight. Approximately thirty feet north from the tree, toward the triangular intersection, and fourteen feet from the macadam, was a telephone pole. There was a No Hunting sign on it. I got a feeling that's where it was going to be and I began to walk toward it.

"As I kept looking around the back of the pole, I saw a small, what appeared to be brown, paper bag crumpled at the base of the pole and I kicked it. It had a crumply, dry sound. Most of the bags we had found and the various paraphernalia—the Coke bottles, the beer cans, various and sundry litter—were insect-infested and damp from dew or moisture. This was not. And when I suddenly realized it was not, I got excited, and I reached down and touched it. I opened it. As I looked inside I found what I thought was a peculiar thing—the contents were dry both on the outside and inside, and in addition to that, there was trash inside the bag, which appeared, for want of a better term, to be clean trash. The caps were placed on the bottles. The bottles were rinsed out. There was no residue of liquid in the bottles.

"I immediately knew this was the package. I couldn't believe that it wasn't. And as I began to go deeper into the bag, I then found a package, approximately nine inches by eleven inches, standard bond paper size, about an inch thick, and it was wrapped in what appeared to be white plastic garbage wrapping. It was neatly wrapped. I don't recall whether or not it in fact had hospital corners, but it was well done and it was well taped. It was obvious that someone had taken some due care, and it was obvious to me, too, that it had some weight. And as I began to flex it, it appeared to have what I thought might be documents in it.

"We didn't know whether we were going to be looking for secret writing—so-called SW, or microdots. We didn't know what sort of—the term is *tradecraft*—he would be using. I called Doug over."

"Are you sure?" Stauffer asked.

"I'm damned sure," Brahe said.

"Because we were close to the road and didn't want to use the flashlights to excess, I grabbed the bag and ran at a dead run into a cornfield, perhaps some hundred yards deep into concealment and cover, where we could inspect the bag in a little more safety, which we did."

They decided that they might destroy prints or other evidence if they opened it in the cornfield, so Stauffer took the package via backwoods trails to an "outdoor command post" nearby. It was 9:24 P.M. After Stauffer delivered the package, he and Brahe returned to the drop site and concealed themselves in the light underbrush, hoping that a Soviet agent would show up to pick up Walker's package. They waited patiently for an hour and twenty-five minutes. Then at 10:49 P.M. John Walker reappeared.

"A blue and white van with temporary tags came south on Partnership Road, past that drop site, moving at a fairly high rate of speed and continued on. Forty minutes later the same van returned, moving slower this time. The driver got out. He walked around to the base of that pole, both front and rear, and inspected it for several seconds." Brahe and Stauffer held their breath, grateful for the moonless darkness.

Walker stood just ten feet away, scratching and poking around, trying to determine whether the Soviets had picked up his package.

"We were surprised to see him. We expected to see the Soviet and not him and, of course, at 11:05 he realized the package was gone. We felt that he felt safe and was simply checking to make sure that the Soviets had picked up the drop he had put down. At 11:30 he came back again, driving south."

Walker again got out and probed the area. The scene was repeated, and again he failed to see Brahe and Stauffer, whose camouflaged outfits were superb for the purpose of blending into the foliage. (Some of that foliage was poison ivy, it turned out, and they both developed bad rashes.) Meanwhile, the package left by Walker was being examined at a safe place some distance away.

"The manila package was opened and found to contain a white plastic trash bag sealed with masking tape," Joseph Wolfinger said. Affixed by cellophane tape to the exterior of the white plastic film bag was a packet containing three documents consisting of six pages. Among these documents was a message addressed "Dear Friend," consisting of three pages printed on a daisy wheel computer printer. this note said:

> This delivery consists of materials from *S* and is similar to the previously supplied materials. The quantity is limited, unfortunately, due to his operating schedule and increased security prior to deployment. His ship departs in early March and they operate extensively just prior to deployment. The situation around him looks very good and he is amassing a vast amount of material right now. His last correspondence indicated that he now has material that will fill two large grocery bags. Storage is becoming a problem. As is obvious, I did not make a trip to Europe to pick up material for this delivery.
>
> His schedule does fit fairly well with our meeting and I plan to meet him during a port call which will give me two days to make it to our meeting. I will arrange to pick up the best of his material and

deliver it in bulk; photographing it while on the road does not seem practical. Also, the entire amount he has would be impossible to safely transport and I plan to deliver that at the schedule you will provide. I hope his ship doesn't experience a schedule change which will put me in the same situation we once faced in Hong Kong. . . .

I did not make the primary date and we met on the alternate. So I have to make a decision and here it is: If his schedule changes and I cannot make the primary date, I will collect the material and make the Secondary date.

D continues to be a puzzle. He is not happy, but is still not ready to continue our "cooperation." Rather than try to analyze him for you, I have simply enclosed portions of two letters I've received. My guess? . . . He is going to flop in the stockbroker field and can probably make a modest living in computer sales. He has become accustomed to the big-spending life-style and I don't believe he will adjust to living off his wife's income. He will attempt to renew cooperation within 2 years.

F has been transferred and is in a temporary situation giving him no access at all. He is having difficulty in making a career decision in the Navy. He is not happy and is experiencing family pressures with our father who is 73 and in poor health.

F feels obligated to support them. He may come around and good access is possible.

K and I have discussed your proposal and I will pass on some extensive details when we meet. Briefly, he is involved in carrier and amphibious ship-maintenance planning. He would instantly recognise [sic] unrealistic repair schedules and see that ships were "off their normal schedules." This may provide a basis for the information we seek. Otherwise, he has no useful material.

So I will see you as scheduled and hope I will make the Primary date with no problem. I'm sure you have access to *S*'s port schedule and can anticipate my moves in advance. I am not providing his schedule in this note for obvious reasons.

Good luck . . .

The package also contained two letters from *D* that began "Dear Johnny."

The letters said that he—*D*—wanted to try to make a go of it as a stockbroker.

Among the 129 documents, said the FBI, was an executive order identified only as Executive Order 12065, "the disclosure of which would cause serious damage to the national security."

Although the FBI had a rough idea who *S* and *D* might be, the rest of the letter codes would await the discovery of a notebook page and index card hidden in Walker's house that would prove to be the Rosetta Stone that made it all snap into focus.

While experts in what the FBI and CIA term *tradecraft,* or espionage methodology, analyzed the documents, Walker continued to dash about in the van, looking for his money and rechecking the drop site where he had left the information.

At one point during his shuttling about, Walker drove to the parking lot of the Quince Orchard Shopping Center and looked nervously at his watch and around the lot. It is possible that at this time he was under surveillance not only by the FBI but also by KGB agents watching at considerable distance through binoculars, intelligence sources said. At another time he parked in an abandoned service station next to a car containing agent James McLay and investigative specialist Katie Southern, who pretended to be boyfriend and girlfriend.

Walker again doubled back on his trail and drove to the site where he expected to find his usual payoff, about 5 miles farther on still another road, near the intersection of White Grounds Road and Old Bucklodge Lane. He parked his van about 10 yards from the intersection and shone his flashlight around the base of a forked tree in the woods.

He got out of the van and made another search. The money still was not there. He seemed puzzled and frustrated. During this foray, Walker unknowingly came within yards of another FBI agent. He then returned to his own drop site for a third time and Brahe and Stauffer again flattened themselves in the underbrush while he looked around. Again they escaped detection.

He drove to the Ramada Inn in Rockville and checked into a seventh-floor room, Number 765, at 12:17 A.M. as "John Johnson." He had decided that perhaps the Soviets had been spooked and would leave his money later. They had never double-crossed him before.

The FBI by this time realized, after a quick analysis of the contents of the bag, that they had enough evidence to arrest John Walker and secure a court order for the search of his home. Hope was growing faint that he would meet with a KGB agent. It was decided by the early morning hours that Tkachenko had probably been warned or frightened in some manner and that no one would come to the drop site.

The decision was made to arrest Walker when he left his room again. The agents realized that he might leave with a group of other guests, and innocent people could be hurt if there was an exchange of gunshots. So they approached the desk and identified themselves. "We told them that it was a matter of utmost urgency and we sought their cooperation," Hunter explained. "They were very good about cooperating with us."

The decision was made to have William Wang, an agent of Chinese-American descent, impersonate the hotel desk clerk. The FBI took over the desk and Wang called Walker at 3:30 A.M.

"Hello, Mr. Johnson," he said.

"Yes, what is it?" Walker snapped.

"Is that your Chevrolet van, the blue and white one with temporary tags, number X076-291?"

"That's right. What's the matter?"

"A gentleman ran into it. I'm afraid he has done some damage to it. He is down here at the desk now, and he wants to make sure you have his insurance information. Can you come down?"

"Yeah, I'll be down," Walker said.

The FBI was aware that this was a somewhat crude ruse. But they also knew that—like a threatening chess move—the opponent could not ignore it.

Walker did begin to wonder if it was a trap of some kind. He grabbed his .38 Smith & Wesson revolver, stuck it into his belt holster, and opened the door to the hallway. He saw no one. He left the door to his room open and cautiously walked to the stairwell and looked down. It appeared empty. He thought if he were to be ambushed, that would be where it would come from. Had he looked farther down in the stairwell, he would, indeed, have found waiting agents. Other agents watched him from a nearby room.

Walker returned to his room and looked out of the window. Unfortunately, he could not see his van from where he was. But it seemed quiet outside. He decided that his suspicions were for nothing. Then again, could it be the Soviets trying to make emergency contact?

He determined to chance it. More than likely it was simply an accident. After all, he had spent eighteen years being hyper about things that turned out to be nothing at all. At 3:45 A.M., Walker, wearing old clothes, running shoes, and his hairpiece, padded softly down the carpeted hallway to the elevators. His pistol was on his hip. He walked to the elevator, and then he saw two men, Agents James L. Kolouch and Hunter. Alarm bells sounded in his head: there shouldn't be two men standing at an elevator at this time of the morning.

"FBI. Freeze," Kolouch said.

Almost at the same time Walker pulled his .38. But it was too late. He was looking down two pistol barrels.

"Hold it! Drop the weapon. FBI," Hunter and Kolouch shouted in unison, standing just 5 feet away.

Walker did not drop the pistol. He had it pointed at the men, but they held their fire although no one would have faulted them had they shot him. They took the calculated risk that Walker would be intelligent enough to know that where there were two agents, there would be more, and that he might kill one of them but the other would kill him.

"I was looking at his eyes and his trigger finger," Hunter said. "If there had been any indication that he was going to pull the trigger, I would have fired. But from all that we had learned about him—particularly how long the espionage had lasted—we knew he was too valuable to shoot unless we had to." If Walker had been a drug dealer or petty hoodlum pointing the pistol at them, "there's no doubt we would have fired," Hunter said. They depended on his ultimate rationality at that moment. "It was only a few seconds, but it sure seemed a lot longer. We were just a few feet apart, Kolouch and I, and I saw him looking back and forth at us."

After again ordering him to drop the pistol, Kolouch and Hunter were on the verge of opening fire when he dropped it. He also dropped a manila envelope that would prove to be interesting to the FBI. The agents kicked the pistol away and slammed his small body against the wall.

"I held my gun on him while Kolouch searched him," Hunter said.

"We rushed up to him, put him against the wall, and started a search," Kolouch explained. "We were joined by several other agents. We started from the top down, taking everything off that could come off. I ripped off his toupee and came down, emptied out his pockets. His shoes were padded running-type shoes. We took those off."

The agents then led Walker to a room they had reserved for processing. As they marched him down the hall, he flippantly observed that it had been "one of the oldest tricks in the book."

"It worked, didn't it?" Hunter snapped.

"I have friends in the FBI," Walker said nervously. "I have a great deal of respect for the FBI."

Walker had been so sure that he was not under surveillance that he had carried the Soviet instructions and photographs and other material with him in the manila envelope. He had decided that after working out details with the man who ran into his car, he would make another trip back to the drop site, and he wanted to avoid having to go back to his room for the instructions.

Once in the room down the hall, Hunter pulled out a card and read from it to Walker:

> Mr. Walker, you are being placed under arrest on suspicion of espionage and conspiracy to commit espionage. You have the right to remain silent. Anything you say may be used against you in a court of law. You have the right to have an attorney present, now or any time during questioning. If you can't afford a lawyer, one will be appointed for you at no cost. Do you understand the rights as I've explained them to you?

Walker nodded in affirmation. He giggled as if at some secret joke on himself. The agents found out later that it was a nervous habit.

"I want an attorney," he said.

10

The Pack Rat

*It is certainly the biggest and most damaging espionage case
in this century.*
              —Assistant U.S. Attorney Michael Schatzow

Within hours after his arrest, thirty agents (including special
agents from the Naval Investigative Service) were making a thorough search of Walker's home in Norfolk, his houseboat, his office,
his airplane, and his two vans. They hit the jackpot.

Hidden in a book on his bookshelf was a notebook page that
stated simply: *D*—Jerry. *K*—Art. *S*—Mike. *F*—Gary.

An *A* was mentioned in another instance, but it was later found
that *A* was Walker's method of referring to himself. Letters in his
home pointed toward his son, Michael, and the documents Walker
left at the drop site were determined to be from the aircraft carrier
Nimitz. Other letters in his computer were for or about Jerry
Whitworth.

The FBI concluded that Walker had been trying to mislead the
Soviets into thinking that his young half brother, Gary, was part of
his operation in order to obtain more money for payoffs. There was
also a theory that he had begun a long-term effort to persuade Gary
Walker to start stealing secret information. (Gary Walker later
passed a polygraph examination and was completely exonerated.)

They found deeds to property in Florida and two lots valued at 6,000 dollars and 7,500 dollars on Great Exuma Island in the Bahamas. This land was not on the beach and was zoned for commercial use. They also found a sword cane, a cane that concealed a pistol, two small bags of marijuana and a marijuana pipe, other weapons, including a crossbow, a variety of disguises and costumes, and maps of various overseas destinations.

After the contents of the house were inspected and classified, the FBI began work with wrecking bars and sledge hammers. They found 6,000 dollars' worth of silver bars hidden beneath the floorboards in Walker's home. And an Austrian map was found in his den, hidden in a phony electrical wall socket by his desk.

It showed a section of Vienna. With it was a letter entitled *The Vienna Procedure,* which detailed how to make face-to-face meetings.

"As a rule they try to do this as little as possible," agent Gerald B. Richards, an FBI counterintelligence expert explained.

"Of course they do not want to expose themselves any more than necessary. So the use of dead drops is much more prevalent and much more common, but on occasion they have to meet to iron out problems that may be occurring as far as maybe financial payments—the agent may not consider he's getting enough money or vice versa. Or the handler feels that the materials he's getting don't have enough substance."

One document showed he had flown to Casablanca for one of his face-to-face meetings with the Soviets.

An envelope from the Hotel Intercontinental in Vienna included a letter printed in ink stating, *Procedure for summoning me to an exchange.* Another letter was headed *Procedure for a face-to-face meeting outside the country.* The next heading stated, *Procedure for an extraordinary face-to-face meeting in the country.* Each detailed the procedures that Walker was to follow when meeting Soviet agents.

Within days, agents were sent to Vienna to check out the Vienna Procedure firsthand and walk the anti-surveillance, or drycleaning, route. They found it every bit as clever and carefully laid out as the Maryland route had been, only compressed for walking purposes.

As we have already seen, by far the most startling discovery in

Walker's home—one that was reported directly to President Reagan—was the small, round, Bakelite plastic device, made in the Soviet Union, that allowed Walker to keep track of the wiring pattern of rotors used in top-secret American cryptographic decoders. The rotor decryption device was sent to FBI laboratories for analysis. Naval Intelligence, with sinking hearts, realized that Walker had kept track of changes in the rotors over the years. And even after he retired, he had not discarded the device, perhaps hoping to pass it on to his son or someone else when the need arose. FBI scientists placed batteries in it and found that it worked perfectly.

Incredibly, Walker seemed to enjoy collecting the memorabilia of previous dead drops. Numerous photographs were found similar to the ones in the manila envelope Walker had on him when he was arrested. Most of these were in the northern Virginia area. They came complete with arrows and handwritten instructions on the backs, some with drawings of certain intersections. The find gave the agents invaluable insight into tradecraft used by the Soviets in the Washington area.

There also was a stockpile of classified material indicating that Walker may have been holding some back for later drops to make more money. The FBI decided not to disclose the nature of this classified material. They also decided not to release the content of much of the correspondence involving Whitworth.

Walker's methodical nature helped tighten the noose on the whole operation. For example, there was one particular symbol on his calendars that puzzled agents until they found that the symbol coincided with dates of previous dead drops and face-to-face meetings with the Soviets. The same symbol had been prematurely placed on his calendar for May 19, the day of his last drop.

Fortunately for the FBI, Walker was a veritable pack rat when it came to saving even the most minute form of records, whether they were movie ticket stubs or airplane ticket carbons. This information, cross-referenced with what was known, enabled the FBI to construct a solid record of trips, dead drops, and world travel. They superimposed this on the port calls of Michael's carrier and the ships on which Jerry Whitworth had served, and a pattern snapped into vivid focus.

Among the strangest documents found was one in which

Walker obviously was trying to justify to the Soviets a raise of one million dollars for himself. There were random notes about his spy organization, for example:

> Spent over sixty thousand to build up organization to allow safe travel, handle funds. Can make forty-five thousand at regular job—why make less with danger involved? D (and) wife make one hundred thousand; D fifty thousand . . . what advantage?
>
> Can get D to commit with I only; intended to ask for one million at 83 meet, but instead found myself on the defensive. Request 1 (million dollars). Guarantee 6,000 for A as long as organization producing.
>
> Realization that no one should expect less than 4,000 monthly if producing good yellow. For K, eight to nine thousand monthly (100,000 annual).
>
> No member of organization or prospective has any of the classic problems that plague so many in this business. I have no drug users, alcoholics, homosexuals. All are psychologically well adjusted and mature. Organization launder funds.

Another note from the Soviets apologized for a payoff of only 24,500 dollars, noting that it was "half the usual amount" because they were concerned about airport customs finding too much unexplained cash.

This note had been written before the end of the flush times, when Walker himself was delivering a steady stream of classified material. He apparently was reduced to less after he became merely the conduit for three others. Although he was giving Arthur and Michael very little money, Whitworth continued to receive substantial sums, leaving less for Walker. That was the reason he was jotting down notes about his spy ring.

IN AN OPEN society in which there is freedom of the press as a constitutional guarantee, the FBI's arrest became a matter of public record the same day it occurred. The national press pounced on the story like a starving man devouring a prime rib steak. Although the FBI had intended to keep the identities of their tipsters, Barbara Walker and Laura Walker Snyder, hidden, within hours reporters were tracking down family members, old

friends, acquaintances, swarming over Cape Cod, West Dennis, Hyannis, Scranton, San Diego, San Francisco, Charleston, and Norfolk.

"I'm a celebrity," John Walker crowed to a Norfolk newspaper the day after his arrest, adding incongruously, "things are going good."

Before realizing that the FBI would establish links between him and three accomplices, he announced that he hoped his arrest would not damage the careers of his son and brother. (He had hastily written his brother Arthur to reassure him that he would not talk to the FBI about Art's role in the spy ring. Arthur later turned the letter over to the FBI.)

When asked about details of his espionage, he said, "I can't think of anything I could say without getting my ass in trouble with my attorney."

Agents had questioned him for two hours after his arrest, and he would not say if there had been other questioning sessions. "I expect to be indicted any day now," he said. "So far I don't have any timetables."

He had seen "bits and pieces" of stories about himself on a television in his cell in the Montgomery County Detention Center, where he was being kept alone. He indicated that he enjoyed the publicity. "I feel like [Adolf] Eichman or someone."

He was worried about the FBI questioning his friends. "They come after all of your acquaintances, and I'm worried about bad publicity and guilt by association."

When Walker found out that it was, indeed, Barbara Walker who had turned him in, he said not very originally, "What is it they say—hell hath no fury like a woman scorned?" In each court appearance, he smiled and waved cheerfully to reporters and seemed to be enjoying himself immensely.

After the arrest, his girlfriend, P.K., who had just been promoted to the plainclothes division of the Norfolk Police Department and seemed to have a promising career ahead of her, was fired. No explanation was necessary because she was still in the probationary period.

The arrest jogged the memory of Roberta K. Puma, Walker's old girlfriend, who recalled that he had used her to make a drop in the Rockville area years earlier. Unwittingly, she said, she drove a similar route and dropped a garbage bag that contained what she thought was trash

Walker made a game out of it and communicated with her by use of a shortwave radio.

Puma, who had managed an apartment complex owned by Walker a few years earlier, said she had agreed to accompany Walker on the bizarre trip in the spring of 1977. Walker had often tried to impress her, and when he suggested they go on a "sleuth-type operation," she dismissed it as "one of the goofiest kinds of come-ons that I had ever heard."

Afterward, Walker asked her to spend the night with him in the same Ramada Inn in which he would be arrested eight years later. But she said she refused, and they drove back to Norfolk.

In retrospect, she realized that Walker was either using her to make the drop so that should she be arrested, he could escape, or using her to make a trial run on a drop route. She had saved the photographs with the instructions written on them, which the FBI immediately confiscated.

This incident later became part of the indictment against John Walker.

Some agents argued that Puma may have come forward with her story as a clever way of covering herself. A polygraph test, however, cleared her.

Former friends and co-workers were stunned by the arrest. Could it be true that the happy-go-lucky Johnny Walker, given to practical jokes and an eye for beautiful women, had deceived them? Behind that facade of prankster and super patriot, member of the John Birch Society and Ku Klux Klan recruiter, was there a traitor who had betrayed his country for two decades? Was he really a person with no higher motivation than simple greed?

Phil Prince was sitting in his office at the Tandy Corporation in Rockville when a reporter from the Norfolk *Virginian-Pilot* called him and asked him numerous questions about Walker before telling him about Walker's arrest.

Prince immediately telephoned the FBI.

"You'll probably want to talk to me," he said.

They did, said the FBI. One of Nora Moody's children called her to tell her to turn on the television set and determine whether the John Walker who was arrested was the Johnny Walker they used to know, the man for whom she was the cook at the Bamboo Snack Bar. Laura also found out about the arrest from television. She was "hurt and upset but not shocked" by her brother's arrest. "I took it rough. I heard about both of the arrests from the news." Michael's arrest "was the toughest. I really regret that he agreed to do it."

Walker's mother, Margaret, had just returned from a funeral in Maine when she was told about the arrest by her youngest son, James, who had already talked to reporters from the *Scranton Times*. James had learned when his wife, Tina, called and said, "They've arrested your brother Johnny for being a spy."

He had always envied Art and Johnny and had felt left out of their world. He was impressed by Johnny's airplane, his boats and high living, but now he was glad that he was not part of that life. His telephone began ringing incessantly. He had to have the number changed to avoid the horde of reporters who descended upon Scranton, knocking on his door at all hours of the day and night, leaving notes, begging and pleading for interviews.

Margaret Scaramuzzo Walker continued to work in the photo studio where she had worked since her children were small. She continued to say the Rosary every day. But she stopped reading newspapers or watching television, and she became reclusive, depending more and more on her youngest son, James, for solace and comfort. It was just too painful for her.

"Mom doesn't want to talk about it, to think about it," said James Walker, who did his best to shield her from reporters. "She just sits there every night and lets the phone ring." Soon she had the number unlisted, but a continuous parade of people drove by Geraldine Court just to look at her house.

And even as the FBI completed the thorough search of John Walker's house in Norfolk, the curious began a steady stream of automobiles down Old Ocean View Avenue to stare at Walker's two-story brick and clapboard house.

The FBI locked P.K.'s and some of P.K.'s mother's clothes in the house, and six months later P.K. was still pleading with the government to let her retrieve her belongings.

P.K. told her friends that she would write a book about what it was like being the girlfriend of spy John Walker, but later she abondoned the idea and sold her photos and a brief interview to *People* magazine for 10,000 dollars. Federal authorities said Laura and Barbara Walker began trying to secure book contracts, and Walker himself tried to sell the movie rights to his life story. Later Walker asked P.K. to send him the files from the detective agency so he could write a book he said he would entitle *Johnny Walker, P.I.* And Margaret sent word to an author that she might talk for the right amount of money. Federal authorities were disgusted by the family's rush to make money from the crime.

Clevenger learned about the arrest from the 6:00 evening news, and he blinked his eyes in disbelief. "That was Johnny all right. But could it be true about the spying?" In a flash, Clevenger knew it was true. "Somehow it all fit." A puzzle of many year's duration had fallen into place.

Clevenger contacted *Life* magazine to see if he could sell his story.

Ted Uhlrich thought there had to be some mistake. "This couldn't be the Johnny I knew." But soon he changed his mind. "I believed the charges because everything fit—the trips to the West Coast—everything."

Rachel Walker's mother telephoned her and asked her to turn on the television set. "You won't believe this," she said. "They've arrested Mike's dad, John, for being a spy."

The news shot through the Navy town of Norfolk like a lightning bolt. John Walker had crossed the path of hundreds of people in the city, which has more than 100,000 Navy men or Navy civilian personnel living there. He had appeared on a magazine-format local television program, spotlighted as the successful head of a detective agency. "It's damned glamorous work," he told the TV reporter as he showed the pistol he wore and climbed into the cockpit of his airplane while the cameras whirred.

The national press, which had been in a lull for the few days since Klaus von Bulow was found innocent of two attempted murder counts in the alleged insulin poisoning of his wife, Martha "Sunny" von Bulow, jumped into high gear again in going after the Walker story. Speculation was rampant, and there were numerous errors and incorrect stories. The *Washington Post* reported that Barbara and Cindy had turned in John Walker. A woman in Maine said Barbara had made the decision based on a session with tarot cards. (Barbara Walker's sister, Anne, said this was nonsense, that her sister, an ardent Catholic, did not believe in anything remotely smacking of the occult.) An editor with *The New York Times* was arrested for trespassing as he sought to corner Barbara Walker on Cape Cod.

It was during this time, in the aftermath of the arrests, that P.K. was told by law enforcement officials that word had leaked out of the Norfolk underworld that Walker had offered two men 100,000 dollars each to break him out of the Montgomery County Detention Center before he was salted away in a maximum security federal prison. Laurie Robinson later said Walker had asked her to be his contact for the escape plan, which he code-named "The System." She refused.

John Walker's assets were soon attached by the Internal Revenue Service and he was charged with failure to pay taxes on income derived from spying. An IRS lien for 252,487.66 dollars was placed on his property. It was not the first such lien he had faced. The IRS had placed a lien for 28,207.51 dollars on Walker Enterprises, the car-radio shop he had started with Arthur, on July 20, 1981. Court records also show that Walker was sued three times for a total of 1.6 million dollars because of claims stemming from private detective work he did. Two of the suits were pending at the time of his arrest. One of them was filed by the wife of a wealthy developer, who claimed that she was harassed by Walker as he disguised himself variously as a Catholic priest, a Boy Scout leader, and a bird watcher in a workman's compensation case, repeatedly trespassing on her property.

Because he could no longer afford an attorney, most of whom wanted large cash retainers, the court appointed Frederick Warren Bennett of Baltimore, head of the Baltimore Public Defender's Office, as his counsel.

Bennett moved quickly to quell the publicity. He asked U.S. District Judge Alexander Harvey in Baltimore federal court to issue a gag order. It was granted, and a judicial curtain descended over the case, stifling press coverage.

Laura Walker Snyder made an appearance on the Christian Broadcast Network and told of her father's attempt to recruit her and said, "People meet him and think, 'Oh, he's a wonderful person,' but he's not." She added that her father always referred to the children "by very vulgar names. He calls us his little bastards."

"Why did he spy?"

"Money, greed, selfishness. He wanted to live in the greatest country in the world and to have all the benefits and the freedom of living in this great country, but he didn't want to be loyal to it. He'd rather sell it."

After her appearance, which infuriated her sister Margaret, still loyal to her father, she retreated into an Adirondacks hideaway with the assistance of the Christian Broadcast Network.

Mark Snyder, Laura Walker's ex-husband, called Laura's story about his threatening to inform on her father "garbage—hogwash." He had vaguely felt that John Walker was doing something illegal, but he didn't know what.

When John Walker flew to Baton Rouge in 1979—when Laura said he tried to recruit her as a spy—he had tried to recruit both of them as members of the Ku Klux Klan. Bill Wilkinson, a former Klan Wizard, was visited by Walker at the same time, he told the FBI. Wilkinson has refused to say whether Walker was a member of the Klan. "If Johnny gives me the go ahead, then I can talk about it. But if he doesn't I can't say anything."

Laura Walker Snyder moved quickly after the arrest to get her son back again. She drove to the apartment complex where Mark Snyder lived and waited with a friend. When her son came out in the yard to play, she drove up, hugged the boy, and took him to the car. She and the friend drove away quickly. She told friends that she wanted her son raised in a Christian home. Mark Snyder was furious.

INVESTIGATORS ALSO LOOKED into the possibility that Walker was involved in two Norfolk area deaths. One was Carol Ann Molnar, a young woman who had worked at the Armed Forces Staff College in the same office with Pat Marsee, a Walker girlfriend. Investigators learned that Miss Molnar also danced at night in a number of go-go bars—bars Walker had been known to frequent.

Agents questioned Daniel Rivas, who had worked part-time for Walker's detective agency. Rivas recalled that Walker had assigned him to follow Ms. Molnar for a time, telling him that she was in danger from a pimp. He remembered seeing Walker and Molnar deep in conversation at a bar on one occasion. Rivas identified as his a black ski mask found in the back of Molnar's car after she disappeared. He said he and Walker had occasionally used the ski mask during surveillance work.

Among the bars Molner danced in were the Galleon, the Wayside, and Bob's Runway, the NIS said. She had been seen alive last at the Galleon around 3:00 A.M. on February 6, 1983. Her body later washed up in the sea a few hundred yards from Walker's houseboat. She had been shot.

In another case, a Chesapeake policeman, Detective Garland L. Joyner, 39, was found dead on March 18, 1984, in Warwick Creek in North Carolina. Although it was ruled a suicide, investigators found that Joyner—who was right-handed—held the .38-caliber pistol in his left hand.

There were three links in the case to Walker: one was that Laurie Robinson, who was Walker's ex-partner in the agency, recalled that Walker kept a file on Joyner. Also, a Confidential Reports business card was found near the body. The third was more complex: Joyner had been investigating a gun smuggling ring. And Rivas remembered that Walker, about this time, had approached him about a scheme to smuggle 300,000 dollars worth of Uzi automatic rifles into Latin America via Mexico. Rivas turned him down.

The Justice Department and the NIS, however, said the evidence in both cases was tenuous, and a spokesman added that "everyone seems to want to link Walker with a murder somewhere." Nonetheless, investigators said the file on both was open, and a third, they said, was being checked out. They would not give details of the third case.

WAS JOHN WALKER an idealogue or an opportunist? Was he a race baiter, a Klansman? Was he a super patriot gone sour? There was even speculation that he might have been a double agent and that the entire episode, arrests and all, was part of an elaborate disinformation plan by the United States designed to mislead the Soviets.

Clevenger considered the possibility that Walker was a double agent. "I thought it would be wonderful if it were true." And Barbara Walker at times had hoped against hope that it was.

The effort to find the real John Walker was frustrating for all concerned. The John Walker who was a roué and rake to some women was a perfect gentleman around others. Some friends could only call him John and others knew him only as Johnny. The John Walker who played Klansman with Bill Wilkinson never mentioned it to Phil Prince. The beer-swilling John Walker who tried to cut the blimp loose at the Seattle World's Fair could quietly sip Scotch and discuss philosophy in another environment. The John Walker who helped Donnie Filyaw repair his car seemed mechanically inept around Ted Uhlrich. The John Walker who smoked at some cocktail parties ranted at others about the dangers of smoking. The John Walker who urged Don Clevenger to study and further his education (and Clevenger said it was this encouragement that led to his getting a master's degree from Pepperdine University) would disparage the educational and self-help efforts of his own children.

Wherever John Walker was, there was general agreement on one point, "It is certainly the biggest and most damaging espionage case in this century," said attorney Michael Schatzow, echoing FBI Deputy Director Philip Parker.

11

Michael and Rachel

I took the stacks of documents off the ship in my duffel and gave them to my father at his house . . . my father was pleased and said it looked like we were on a roll.   —Michael Walker

Rachel Walker will always remember Michael, with his coarse brown hair wet and bleached almost blond in places by the sun, crouched atop his surfboard and darting inside the curl of a wave on Virginia Beach. It was the endless summer—the sun-drenched summer when they met after graduating from high school.

She had first become friendly with John Walker and P.K., who dined frequently at the Lone Pine Restaurant where Rachel was the hostess. Walker always made small talk with her. One night he invited her to go boating on the weekend with him, P.K., and others, including Michael. Until that point, Michael "always brought a different girl on the boat," P.K. said. "But then we started seeing him with Rachel more and more." Soon he was dating Rachel exclusively. Rachel had a spectacular figure, and she and P.K. together on the houseboat frequently drew stares and whistles.

It was a sensuous summer of days in the sun, the briny smell of the sea, of white sea gulls wheeling and turning in the sky, of beer and wine, of making love.

It was the summer of 1982 when they fell in love. He brought her one long-stemmed red rose on every date. He had enlisted in the Navy on a deferred basis while he was still a senior in high school, and he wound up in boot camp in December, six months after meeting Rachel.

According to Rachel, "After he met me and we established our relationship, he didn't want to go into the Navy. He tried his best to get out. To this day he wishes he never would've gone in."

Before he shipped out, she and Michael and their dog spent every moment together. "We had a good time. We were in love. We were making plans. He wanted to get this sea time out of the way. He wanted to relocate in California. He's a surfer. He wanted to go where the waves are."

At the time of his arrest at the age of twenty-two, Michael Walker looked more like fourteen. He has a bland, country-boy look. The adjective female friends use to describe him most often is "sweet."

Rachel and Michael spent little time with John Walker—the last time they had seen him was Christmas, when they met to exchange gifts, but friends said he idolized his father.

John Walker "has a very strong personality," and he used that Rasputin-like personality to brainwash Michael into spying, according to Laura Walker Snyder. He tried to make it seem that spying was "almost expected." His attitude was "This is the way countries are run."

"He'd drag you down and make you feel like the lowest form of life. He'd say, 'You know you're never going to be successful and you know you can't do anything with your life. You're not a very bright person. Why don't you let me help you make a lot of money?'"

Rachel believed that Michael had never really felt the stability of family life, "and when I came along I gave him something he couldn't get from either one of the other half of the family. It was just somebody he could talk to, spend his time with, he could trust. I was his best friend, something his mother and father probably never were to him. He didn't know where he was going from the Navy. He wished he would have gone to college, but he really didn't know what he was doing."

She and Michael used to talk about his family background and how he felt he had no parents, how he didn't like leaving Norfolk to go with his mother to Skowhegan.

"He didn't like Maine. It was cold. This is a small town that he lived in and he was used to living in San Francisco, San Diego, Norfolk—all the big Navy port towns where his father was. He wasn't used to living in a small town where there wasn't any ocean or any sea or he didn't have a lot of friends."

When he joined his father in Norfolk, one friend recalled that "Mike went to bars a lot earlier and had more access to beer and liquor. He had a lot of money to spend. He spent money on girls. They fell all over him. He liked to hang out at Virginia Beach. He hung around with long-hair, hippie-type kids."

A teacher at Ryan School, a private school where he was enrolled by his father, said, "He was very much left alone at home. He did a great job raising himself. He took care of all the housework. He was constantly working around the house."

Kitty Baker, another of Michael's teachers, reported that he was not much of a student, struggling between Ds and Cs. "He was not a particularly profound thinker. He was more of a follower than a leader. He was eager to please."

When he first left for boot camp it was very hard to be separated. "I told him, 'I can't guarantee you that I'm going to follow you.' We weren't married at the time."

Michael then gave her the promise ring and told her, "I don't want to see anyone else. It's up to you if you want to see anyone else."

"I told him I didn't want to see anyone else. We'd seen each other religiously for six months." They eloped to Virginia Beach a year later, the week before Christmas 1983. They were so inseparable that she went surfing with him even in January.

"He treated me like a lady and not just another girl," Rachel said. "At nineteen, guys are—I'll be honest with you—just out for whatever. Our relationship was not based on that. We dated. We were friends before we became lovers. We enjoyed each other's company. We both enjoyed the sea. Everything we made plans for revolved around surfing. He was a surfing nut."

Rachel Walker graduated on May 18 from Old Dominion University. It was Saturday. Michael was at sea aboard an aircraft

carrier, but they were reasonably certain that this would be his
last sea duty before they settled down in a new assignment in San
Francisco.

Rachel looked forward to a long tour of shore duty to give them
some time together; they had had very little since they were
married. Michael had been at sea most of the time.

The first hint of her husband's trouble came when her mother
called her and told her to turn on the television news right away.
The newsman was reporting that Michael's father had been
arrested and charged with spying for the Soviets—and that
Michael was a suspect in the case.

"That's how I found out. No one called me. No one told me
anything." When it was reported that some of the documents came
from the *Nimitz* and that her husband may have been involved, she
was stunned beyond belief. "I just about passed out."

She was glued to the TV set during the following days, the only
way she could keep up with the rapidly unfolding developments.

"Oh my God. Oh my God," Rachel said over and over again when
the TV anchorman intoned, "Twenty-two-year-old Michael Lance
Walker has been arrested and charged with espionage and placed
in the brig of the aircraft carrier *Nimitz*."

She watched transfixed as a television newsman read off a list of
charges and discussed letters from Michael to his father boasting
of how much classified information he had filched, how he hated
the *Nimitz*, and how many pounds of classified material had been
found near Michael's bunk.

She told friends her life was unraveling. She couldn't handle the
strain of the revelations about her husband. "I don't know . . . I
don't know what to believe anymore. All I want to do is close my
front door and not open it until this is all over. This is half of me.
This isn't somebody down the street. This is my husband, my
future . . . this is me, this is home base."

She insisted for public consumption that she was unable to
believe the charges against Michael, that he never seemed secret
around her. She controlled the family finances, and she could not
recall Michael ever having any unexplained extra cash. "There
were no large sums of money deposited in our account. Like other
couples, we lived paycheck to paycheck."

She lamented that her mother-in-law had not turned in John

Walker much sooner. "There would not have been as much pain as there is now."

She talked to Barbara Walker, who expressed her deep regret. She would never have gone to the FBI had she known that her son was involved. "I never could have brought myself to do it if I had known he was part of this thing. I only hope my son can forgive me."

"She was sorry. She said she didn't know Michael was involved. She said she felt really bad because she knew I was going through a lot of pain. I don't know how I would have reacted in her situation."

John Walker told P.K. that Barbara should have known about Michael—because she knew he had tried to recruit Laura and Michael, and Michael told Rachel that "Dad framed me to get back at Mom."

"My emotions are gone haywire. Sometimes I'm bummed out," Rachel said, still sounding like a teenager. "Sometimes I'm so silly and giggly about things that are stupid, but I think it's just a way to relieve pressure. Sometimes I want to sleep and can't sleep. Sometimes I'm so sleepy, but it's the wrong time. I'm at work. I guess that's a form of depression."

She spends many nights sitting in the living room of her apartment in the dark, drinking a glass of wine or a bottle of beer without anything on her mind. "I feel like I'm in a vacuum. I don't have any control over what I thought used to be my emotions and my thoughts. Fatigue eventually takes over and I fall asleep, but it's not restful sleep.

"I love Michael and I want to stand by him. But there were times when I was just so tired of the telephone ringing, reporters wanting to talk to me, the FBI questioning me—everyone calling and demanding on me—that I just didn't want to be here. I feel like just getting in the car with Sparky [her dalmatian dog] and driving away from here. But I'm not that kind of person. I have a level head. I don't do something irrationally. I'd think about it but when I wake up in the morning, I realize what good is running away. It's not going to make the problem go away.

"I can see something on TV that will remind me of something, and I could start crying. I could see something on TV that would remind me of something and would make me start laughing, and I don't know what I'm laughing at.

"People who you thought were your friends and who said they would stand by you through thick and thin treat you like you had the plague." She and Margaret Walker remain close friends and provide each other with mutual support, sticking together during court appearances by the Walker men.

For weeks the authorities would not tell Rachel where Michael was held. Finally they allowed her to visit him in a federal jail near Baltimore. He was on the other side of a thick glass pane. There could be no handholding, no embracing. Tears moistened her eyes as they talked.

She told reporters she could never bring herself to ask him, "Did you do it?" (Federal officials said she didn't have to ask; she knew.) "He can't tell me because the walls have ears, and he might hurt himself and hurt me. And so we talk about little things like the dog." Michael repeatedly offered to allow a divorce. "He didn't want me to have to go through all of this." At his arraignment, she whispered to him, "I love you." He repeated the whisper back to her.

She has visited him in jail on every visiting day. And she spends a prearranged hour at home every night on the chance he might be allowed to call her. She and her mother have spent several afternoons crying together, and her father accompanied her to some of Michael's court appearances to help fend off reporters.

At first Michael's friends stuck by him, saying publicly that they doubted he could be involved. The support gradually faded as the FBI released parts of letters he had written to his father from the *Nimitz*.

In a March 6, 1985, letter, Michael wrote to his dad, whom he called JAWS:

> I have been taking a few shots here and there. I have a lot of miscellaneous bullshit. I am just a little worried about the quantity. Storing it is becoming a problem. I will look for other methods.

In an April 23rd letter, he wrote,

> I don't know. I asked you in my previous letter what I should do about the increasing amounts of photos I have been acquiring. Do you have any suggestions? At the rate I am going I will have over

100 pounds of sovenirs [sic]. I have run out of space and sooner or later I will have to weed out the ones that are not so important to me.

He kept many pounds of stolen classified material in a box hidden behind an air-conditioning duct near his bunk. It made him nervous. If any of his shipmates had noticed it, the Walker case might first have broken aboard the aircraft carrier *Nimitz*.

In another letter, Michael wrote about his job performance on board the carrier:

Enclosed is a copy of my latest evaluation. Not bad, is it? That is just a little proof of my performance as a sailor. If they only knew how much I hate this carrier. Also enclosed is a copy of the letter the Operations Officer sent to Rachel designating me Sailor of the Month. Can you believe that?"

Michael began to understand how his father could have operated so many years without detection. He hid classified material in the burn room itself as well as near his bunk. He routinely brought things off the carrier and no one ever even spot-checked his duffel.

Then two days after his father was arrested, armed Naval intelligence officers arrested Michael and began an intense search of his bunk area. They found a box containing about fifteen pounds of classified documents. Michael was placed in the brig in preparation for a flight back to the United States. The news raced around the carrier, and groups of sailors threatened his life. There was an ugly lynch-mob mood throughout the large vessel.

On May 23, just three days after his father's arrest, Michael asked to meet with one of the Naval Investigative Service agents, Gary K. Hitt, who had originally questioned him briefly at the time of his arrest.

After being advised of his rights, Walker began talking and talking and talking. He had been stealing documents to give to his father at his father's request. He was supposed to meet his father in Naples, according to a tape-recording from his father, where the carrier was scheduled for a liberty call. He admitted writing the letters the FBI found in his father's home. He had referred to classified documents as "photos" and "souvenirs" by prearrangement with his father. He provided Hitt with a sworn statement.

On the following Saturday, May 25, he was flown back to the United States. He arrived at Andrews Air Force Base, where he was arrested by the FBI. He was again advised of his rights, and the next day he made a confession. It was typed and he signed it. He was bitter against his mother for turning in his father, and him indirectly, and he was bitter against his father for enticing him into stealing the documents. Agents played on his feeling of having been used. He told them:

I joined the U.S. Navy on December 13, 1982, and am presently an enlisted man in the U.S. Navy. I completed my recruit and seaman apprentice training on April 16, 1983, was assigned to Fighter Squadron VF102 at the Oceana Naval Air Station, Virginia Beach, Virginia. I worked in the office located in Hangar 200. I performed clerical duties, which included typing letters and memos. I was also the registered mail yeoman and logged in the registered mail which came to the squadron. The mail included official U.S. Navy publications and newgrams. Some of the mail was classified secret, some was classified confidential, and some was unclassified. While at VF102 I never had access to or saw any official U.S. Navy documents that were classified higher than secret. I did see and have access to confidential and secret documents on a regular basis.

While assigned at Squadron VF102, we were deployed on the aircraft carrier USS *America*. We returned from a cruise in June 1983 and approximately one month later [July 1983] I told my father, John Anthony Walker, Jr., of 8524 Old Ocean View Road, Norfolk, Virginia, that I had seen my first piece of classified material. He said something like, "Yeah, there's a lot of jobs in the Navy that require clearances." I don't recall us having any other discussion about classified material at that time. A month or so later my dad told me I could make money if I would take classified material from my work and give it to him. He told me he would pay for the material, but we never discussed how much he would pay. I didn't ask him. I was shocked and afraid at what my dad was suggesting. I knew what he was suggesting was illegal. I think my father said he makes money by doing that [selling classified material], but I'm not positive he said that.

The house in Scranton, Pennsylvania where John and Arthur Walker spent most of their childhood. It has become somewhat of a tourist attraction. *(Photo: Jack Kneece)*

. Patrick's High School where
hn and Arthur Walker went to
hool. *(Photo: Jack Kneece)*

Arthur Walker's senior class high school photo, taken in 1952.

John Walker (top right) on board the nuclear submarine *Simon Bolivar*. To Walker's right is Bill Wilkinson, another radioman aboard the *Bolivar*.

WANTED

$50,000
REWARD
FOR
INFORMATION
LEADING
TO CONVICTION

NO. 1
MOST WANTED

ARMED AND
DANGEROUS!
DO NOT
ATTEMPT
CONTACT

"THE CHAMELEON"
AND KNOWN ASSOCIATES

$50,000.00 REWARD FOR INFORMATION
LEADING TO THE CONVICTION OF "THE
CHAMELEON" AND KNOWN ASSOCIATES. "THE
CHAMELEON" IS KNOWN TO BE A MASTER OF
DISGUISE, INCLUDING THE SUCCESSFUL
IMPERSONATION OF FEMALES.

"THE CHAMELEON" SHOULD BE CONSID-
ERED ARMED AND DANGEROUS. UNDER NO
CIRCUMSTANCES SHOULD YOU ATTEMPT
APPREHENSION OF THIS FUGITIVE OR KNOWN
ASSOCIATES. INSTEAD, NOTIFY YOUR NEAREST
FBI OFFICE AT ONCE.

CONTACT YOUR LOCAL FBI

© 1980 Prof. Bloodgood's Photographic Emporium, Inc.

John Walker and P.K. as Bonnie and Clyde. *(Courtesy Pamela K. Carroll)*

(opposite page) Don Clevenger, now living in Odessa, Texas, was a radioman who served with John Walker aboard the *Razorback* and the nuclear submarine *Andrew Jackson. (Photo: Jack Kneece)*

P.K. and John Walker, as Fidel Castro, go to a costume ball.
(Courtesy Pamela K. Carroll)

(from left to right) Christmas 1983: Michael, Rachel, John, Margaret, and P.K.
(Courtesy Pamela K. Carroll)

John Walker's bar in Charleston, now occupied by VFW Post 3433. *(Photo: Jack Kneece)*

John Walker's house in Norfolk. *(AP Laserphoto)*

The building in Norfolk where John had his detective agency, Confidential Reports. *(Photo: Jack Kneece)*

Arthur Walker's home in Norfolk. *(Photo: Jack Kneece)*

The *Torsk* anchored in Baltimore harbor. This was Arthur Walker's submarine. *(Photo: Jack Kneece)*

The drop site, behind the utility pole to the right. *(Photo: Jack Kneece)*

After their arrests:
John Walker *(AP Laserphoto)*

Arthur Walker *(AP Laserphoto)*

Jerry Whitworth *(AP Laserphoto)*

Michael Walker
(AP Laserphoto)

My father never said who he sold classified documents to, but when he suggested I furnish him with classified documents from my work I believed he must be selling them to the Russians or some other Communist country. When my father asked me to give him classified documents from my work place, I remember that when I was still in high school he commented to me one day that someday he would tell me how he makes his money.

This doesn't jibe with Barbara Walker's telling the FBI that she had told all of her children about their father's espionage activity when they were teenagers. Michael later admitted that he was thirteen when his mother told him.

I now concluded that selling classified documents to the Russians must be what he meant. My father's request of me to furnish him classified documents wasn't a total surprise to me but I really can't explain why not. I knew he had done other illegal things like smoking pot freely in front of us at home. I didn't make any arrangements with my dad to furnish him classified documents when he first asked me.

About three months later, possibly November or December 1983, while at work in my office in Hangar 200, Oceana Naval Air Station, I took a document classified secret from one of the approximately five burn bags in the office. The document was clearly marked *Secret* at the top and the bottom of the front page. It was either a NATOPS (North Atlantic Treaty Organization Publication) or newsgram. I'm not sure which. I don't recall the subject matter but I think the document had a drawing of a jet plane on the front page. It was a current publication. It had the normal classification stamping on it. There were three other people in the office at the time, probably my supervisor, the administration officer, and the master chief, but they couldn't see me because the office is partitioned into sections. I took the document from the burn bag in my partitioned area and put it under my jacket and took it to my dad's house and gave it to him in his den. He looked at it and said it was good. He seemed pleased. He said he'd get back to me about it later. I don't remember that we had any conversation about the document or how I felt about taking it. I don't know what my dad did with the document. I never saw classified documents in my father's house, but I didn't expect him to leave them lying around for people to see.

I took my father approximately five more documents, one at a time, from Squadron VF102, until I was transferred to the aircraft carrier USS *Nimitz* on January 31, 1984. I can only recall they were all classified secret and were clearly stamped. All of the documents were either NATOPS or newsgrams. My dad accepted them from me and told me they were good stuff and things were looking good. He didn't pay me then but said something to the effect that I would get some money for the documents later.

On January 31, 1984, I was transferred to the aircraft carrier USS *Nimitz* CVN68 stationed at the Norfolk Naval Station, Norfolk, Virginia. Because of my job assignments, I had no access to classified documents other than summaries of court-martials and personnel discharge information. I took no classified documents from the *Nimitz* until after I was transferred to Operations Administration, OX Division.

In the OX Division I had daily access to classified documents. The highest classification of documents I had access to was secret. I routinely handled messages regarding U.S. Navy exercises, ship coordinates, Navy operations, and Defense Intelligence Agency messages, which contained mainly information about various countries in the world.

I sometimes had to go through the Communications Center but never handled top-secret material nor did I ever take any. I also routed messages which contained information regarding United States tracking of Soviet submarines. I was responsible for routing messages and deciding who would get them. I was also responsible for deciding whether the messages were of any value or whether they should be thrown in the trash.

I do think the messages regarding Navy exercises, ship locations, and tracking of Soviet ships were properly classified; they were classified secret.

On three occasions, while assigned to the *Nimitz*, I took an examination in an attempt to obtain the rate of Yeoman 3rd Class, or YN3. I was given a YN3 study guide, which I used to prepare myself for the test. The guide contained a chapter on security, which dealt with proper classification and handling of documents. I read and studied that chapter.

"In approximately March or April 1984, while I was still assigned to Special Services on the *Nimitz*, my father paid me

1,000 dollars for the documents I had given him from Squadron VF102. He paid me in twenty-dollar bills. The money was not new and crisp.

Soon after I was transferred to the Operations Administration, I began taking classified documents from the burn bags in the office. This was approximately October 1984. I removed the documents at random and put them in a burn bag which I kept in the fan room where we store the other burn bags prior to their destruction. I was in charge of getting rid of the burn bags and was in charge of the burn-run schedule so it was no problem for me to keep my bag of stolen documents there. I took the documents with the intent of giving them to my father in return for money.

On approximately ten occasions between October 1984 and March 8, 1985, when the *Nimitz* was deployed in the Mediterranean, I took my father stacks of classified documents which I had stolen from the Operations Administration Office. I delivered to my father a total of approximately twenty pounds of classified documents, many of which were classified secret. The remainder were classified confidential. They were messages, all currently classified and clearly marked, such as "rainforms," which contained information regarding Soviet submarine movements, U.S. Navy fleet exercises information, operations messages regarding U.S. Navy ship locations and where the ships were going. About 80 percent of the messages were from DIA and contained geographical information concerning countries throughout the world. I took the stacks of documents, which were several inches thick, off the ship in my duffel bag or in my ditty bag and gave them to my father at his house.

When I gave my father the first stack of documents from the *Nimitz*, I told him I had been gathering them for a while and also told him how I had obtained them and how I stored them on board the ship before I took them off. My father was pleased and said it looked like we were on a roll. He told me to go ahead, keep it up, and kept saying "Keep it flowing." He never paid me for the documents I gave him from the *Nimitz*.

I recall when I was first assigned to the *Nimitz* and had no access to classifed information for several months, my father asked me why I hadn't brought him any documents. He asked me if I was going to stop getting documents for him. He told me to try to get into a job on the ship that was more challenging. I wanted to transfer to Operations Administration and he helped me fill out the paperwork requesting the transfer. I wanted to go to Operations Administration because I thought the work would be interesting and I knew they worked less hours than other divisions on the ship. I didn't know so much classified material was handled in Operations Administration.

I recall one time after I gave my father some documents he said they, meaning the Russians, probably already knew about this stuff or will find out in a few days. I think he said that to try to make me feel better or ease my conscience about giving the documents to him.

I recall after my transfer to the *Nimitz,* my father asked me why I didn't have a top-secret clearance or if I could get one. I told him I didn't have a need to see or know about top-secret material. He kept stressing for me to get an *SI* clearance, which I think is higher than a top-secret.

Before we left Norfolk on deployment on March 8, 1985, my father told me to be careful because it would be a lot harder to store the documents I took while the ship was at sea because of the zone inspection every week.

After the ship left Norfolk, I continued to take classified documents from the Operations Administration office. I put them in a box which was approximately twelve inches by twelve inches and decided to keep the box hidden behind an air-conditioning unit near my bunk and would "trice" [prop the mattress at an angle] up my bunk or rack during inspection. That kept the box out of sight. I was able to fill the box with stolen documents in about two or three days.

In late March or early April 1985 I wrote my father a letter and asked him what I should do with the stuff and told him I was having storage problems and asked if he had any ideas where I should put them. My father sent me a tape-recording in which he told me he would be coming to Gaeta on a case he was investigating and it would be convenient to meet while the *Nimitz* was in port in Naples. The *Nimitz* was scheduled to be in Naples June 26, 1985, through July 5, 1985. I assume my father meant that I could give him the documents during that meeting.

I never was able to give the documents to my father because they

were found during a search of my bunk area by Special Agent Hitt
of the Naval Investigative Service on May 21, 1985.

At the times I was taking the classified documents and giving
them to my father, there was no doubt in my mind that he was
selling those documents to a Communist country, which I believed
to be the Soviet Union."

At this point during the interrogation and confession, Walker
was shown the stack of documents taken from the dead-drop site.
He thumbed through them and told the FBI:

I recognize them to be copies of approximately one-third of the
total amount of documents which I had given my father prior to
March 8, 1985. Each of the documents I looked at came from the
Operations Administration on the *Nimitz*.

A typewritten letter was also among the stack of documents
shown to me by agents Hunter and Kolouch. I believed the letter
was typed on my father's computer. I believe the individual in the
letter referred to as *S* is me, and I indicated that on the copy of the
letter shown to me.

I believe the individual referred to in the letter as *D* is a person
known to me as Jerry Whitworth, who is a friend of my father's
and who I believe lives in California. I indicated that on the letter.

I knew when I was taking the classified documents from VF102
and the USS *Nimitz* that the unauthorized disclosure of them to a
foreign government could harm the United States.

12

Arthur Squirms

If I had to pick the last person in our class at St. Patrick's who would betray his country, it would be Art Walker.
— Vincent Peter Tiberi, classmate, best friend,
Scranton, Pennsylvania, September 1985

After John Walker's arrest, the FBI and NIS focused on Arthur Walker. In spite of Barbara Walker's suspicions and the evidence found in John Walker's house, Arthur's Navy record had been so immaculate—exemplary—that they still had doubts. It was rare that the Navy dipped into the enlisted ranks for officer material during peacetime, but they had done so in the case of Arthur. He was held in high esteem. His record was filled with commendations and glowing praise, such as this:

> Ensign Walker has been impressive in every way in the short period that he has been on board. He wears his uniform with pride and is truly a motivated career Naval officer. In this, my last report, I would like to re-emphasize this officer's value to the Navy and recommend strongly that he be favorably considered for the five-term program for which he intends to apply this fall. The

industry and zeal of Lieutenant Junior Grade Walker's excellent performance has been directly responsible for several favorable comments concerning this ship from superiors in the command chain.

Arthur Walker was past president of the Civic League in the suburban subdivision where he lived. He was a former Little League baseball coach and a participant in a "block security" program to guard against neighborhood crime. Virginia Beach Councilwoman Megera E. Oberndorf described Arthur and his family as "all-American."

Could it be that John Walker was deceiving the Soviets in order to earn extra money—that his brother Arthur was not involved at all? Certainly Arthur's record made him seem an unlikely candidate for treason.

AS WE HAVE seen, Arthur had been worried when in early December 1984 Barbara told him she had informed the FBI about John. Alarmed, he had talked to John, and John had assured him that she was bluffing as she had on so many other occasions.

"Now we are talking about a time when I knew what John was doing, and I knew what I had done," Arthur recalled. I just thought that no matter what she did, it would probably not affect me. Who's ever going to know if I don't say anything and if John doesn't say anything, and if he does is there still any proof?

A few months later, John and his ex-wife talked as they sat in his car outside a fast-food restaurant, and she assured him, after being so instructed by the FBI, that she had merely been trying to scare him after having a few drinks. John relayed this to Art and they both breathed a sign of relief.

That's why Arthur Walker was shocked at 6:50 A.M. on May 20, 1985, when Rita answered the insistent ringing of their doorbell to find a phalanx of FBI agents on the doorstep. They asked if they could come in. Rita asked them to stay outside until she could get dressed. They came in anyway.

Arthur recalled the scene in an interview given to the *Washington Post Magazine*:

It had been a perfect weekend. Everything was going great, really great. My son had graduated from school so there was an end to college tuition payments. I'd gotten a dollar an hour pay raise and that is significant when you think about it. My salary went from $10.50 to $11.50 an hour. And that weekend had been pleasant between my wife, Rita, and me. We were getting along, you know, okay.

John had stopped by the house Friday, and I borrowed his 35-millimeter camera because I was going to take pictures at the graduation. He didn't come into the house, of course. He always tried to avoid that because of Rita. She was cruel to him. It was just an attitude that built up over the years.

I was just on my way down from the bedroom, heading for the kitchen to pour a cup of coffee, when I heard Rita at the door. My first thought was that something had happened in the neighborhood. Then they said, "Your brother has been arrested. . . ."

Oh God, Barbara finally did it, I thought. She turned him in.

Everything was happening fast at this point, but I still felt safe. Only John and I knew what I had done, and I figured they were here just because he was my brother. My next thought was Oh shit. The newspapers are gonna have in there JOHN WALKER, SPY CAPTURED, etc. which is exactly what happened later on, and then all the neighbors will know he's my brother.

Sometime during those first few seconds, it also hit me—Rita. What if she finds out about me? What if she learns what I'd done? I tried to keep calm and even poured coffee for everyone. Two agents and I stayed in the den and two stayed in the kitchen with Rita. That didn't have much impact on me at the time, that they split us up, but I have learned a lot since then—a lot about the FBI.

Arthur thought he could bluff his way out of it. He would play the good brother amazed at the activities of the bad brother. He expressed shock and amazement over his brother's arrest. Special agents Beverly Andress, Carroll Deane, and Kevin Kenneally talked to him at length. After two hours, they asked if he would go down to the FBI offices to continue the discussion. He seemed almost cheerfully cooperative. They questioned him for the rest of the day, concluding at 3 P.M. They talked about his career, his antisubmarine specialty, his relationship with Johnny, and they told Art that they had reason to believe that Johnny had accomplices.

Arthur informed them that John had told him that he had done some contract work for a publication similar to *Jane's Fighting Ships*. "While I don't want to nail my brother, I do want to cooperate," he added.

He was very convincing. Asked if he ever thought of selling secrets to the Soviets for money, he replied, "Never have I passed on anything. It's something I wouldn't even consider, even for my brother. That was why I totally ignored the implications of his first request to me for the *Jane's* information." He told John that he could supply a set of unclassified plans, "but that is it. He never asked me if I could get anything else."

Arthur recalled how he felt during the questioning. "I denied everything when we first started talking, just like you are supposed to do. But as we talked, the first thing that I thought was I've got to help them with John because now he has been caught. They had told me enough that I knew he was nailed." Arthur was trying to save himself any way he could.

"I began to do a damage assessment. As I'm talking to the feds, I'm thinking, How could I tell them stuff about John without telling them about myself because all I know is what I did, okay? I started telling them, and soon I was sliding right down into it. I was giving myself away."

Arthur seemed slightly nervous but under control as he repeatedly said he wanted to cooperate fully. When advised of his right to remain silent and his right to an attorney, he said, "I have no concern along those lines."

Arthur thought that by telling the agents just enough and not asking for an attorney, they would most certainly think that he was innocent. And Arthur knew that Johnny would adhere to the family code of silence that had worked for the better part of the twenty years, even with the children.

Asked if he had any idea how John got started in espionage, he said he did not, adding, "I assume it's been going on for a long time."

He volunteered that his wife, Rita, "had disliked John for some time." Then with a feigned naiveté that immediately alerted the agents to the fact that he might be covering up something, he said, "I wonder if my wife knew about this?"

Arthur was bluntly asked if he was the one who got John started in espionge. "No," he said firmly.

He was asked again if he had disclosed anything, either during or after his Navy career, that would damage the security of the United States. "I am clean. Never had the thought," he said.

He tried to sidetrack the agents with chitchat about his and John's differing methods of raising a family, blaming the strain between Rita and John on that. He said he and John were "very close," but the families were separate because John was single "and lives the life of a single guy."

Arthur told the agents that he had been employed as an engineer with the VSE Corporation, a defense contractor handling classified material relating to repair and overhaul of ships, since February of 1980. In addition, he said he was an officer in John's two companies, Electronic Counterspy and Confidential Reports, but not an active partner. He had conducted "maybe four sweeps" to detect electronic surveillance for Electronic Counterspy. He described the expensive equipment, including a ham radio, that John kept at his home, which had an alarm system to prevent burglary.

The agents asked him to trace his career as it related to John's, if at all. He said he had limited contact with his brother after joining the Navy in 1953, until 1967 when they both wound up in Charleston, South Carolina. He spent four months in Charleston while attached to the SS *Grenadier*, a diesel sub that was in Charleston for an overhaul.

"That was when Johnny opened up a bar called the Bamboo something. He had used up his credit, and he asked me to borrow some money on which he would make the monthly payments." Arthur got a loan from the Household Finance Corporation before returning to Key West with the *Genadier*, and John put a pool table, pinball machines and a jukebox in the bar. He had limited contact with John after that until 1969 when John was stationed in Norfolk. The FBI became convinced that Arthur decided to join John on a joint espionage venture when their tour of duty overlapped in Charleston in 1967.

The FBI asked Arthur if he thought it unusual that John owned an airplane, a houseboat, a camper van, a house, and a lot of expensive electronic equipment, and traveled overseas frequently. Arthur replied that he had not thought so because not only was John making money from the detective agency, but he "is the stingiest son of a bitch who ever lived."

As for the trips, he "always assumed that it was hooked up with the detective business."

He was asked to name some friends of John's. This is the way the FBI listed his response:

> PAMELA K. CARROLL currently dates John Walker. She is a uniformed police officer with the Norfolk Police Department, who worked for Confidential Reports prior to joining the department. He advised she served four years in the U.S. Navy attached to the Shore Patrol and believed she is approximately 24 or 25 years old.
>
> BILL WILKINSON of Georgia. Walker advised that John Walker and Wilkinson served together on a submarine, that Wilkinson was a petty officer or chief petty officer in the Navy, and that he was a grand super dragon of the Ku Klux Klan. He advised that Wilkinson disassociated with the KKK because they became too radical.
>
> JERRY (last name not recalled) from San Deigo. Arthur Walker advised that John Walker has mentioned Jerry's name a few times and that he (Arthur) assumed that John and Jerry first met while John was on West Coast duty. He advised that Jerry's name was brought up in the context of "old shipmates out in California or possibly brought up in discussions of travel."

What he didn't say about Whitworth, P.K. Carroll said in statements to the FBI and two federal grand juries, was that Arthur knew Whitworth well and visited with Whitworth and John each time Whitworth came to Norfolk to make a delivery of secret material to Walker.

Arthur also mentioned Phil Prince, Charlie Smith, Ted Uhlrich, and Pat Marsee, who, Arthur said, was a typist who had "a couple of kids" and worked for the Naval Base Staff College. The agents later learned that Marsee and John Walker had gone to Peru together, ostensibly on an archeological expedition. They wondered if a drop had been made there as well. Authorities said there was no evidence that Pat Marsee knew anything about Walker's espionage activities.

When Arthur was asked what phase of his own career would have most interested the Soviets, he said it would have been when he served as an instructor in Anti-Submarine Warfare and when he was a Communications and Operations officer. But he continued to reiterate that the very idea of spying for the Soviets was repellent to him. He depicted himself as a patriot and a dedicated naval officer who came up the ranks the hard way.

It was convincing, but the FBI is not paid to be convinced. They asked him to come in for a polygraph test. He agreed.

Agent Barry Colvert once more informed Arthur that he had the right to remain silent and the right to counsel.

In response to questioning during the test, Arthur said he was not aware until FBI agents talked to him that John was involved in Soviet espionage. He said that with "hindsight" he had become "suspicious" about six months earlier when John asked him "during a bullshit conversation" what he was doing at VSE. He answered, "The same old stuff—overhauls of warships, gator freighters, and a few carriers." He explained that the term *gator freighters* was Navy slang for amphibious assault ships, helicopter assault ships, and some aircraft carriers. John had asked him whether he knew about only the ships his firm was involved with, and whether he would know at least a year in advance when ships were coming in for overhaul.

"Johnny indicated some people might be interested in something like that." Arthur asked him why, and Johnny said it was because it indicated a ship's movements. John told him that "some people might be willing to pay for ship movement information."

Throughout his questioning, the polygraph needle indicated continual deception. But Arthur continued his "gee whiz, guys" routine.

John's response caused "alarm bells to go off" because he knew that no "legitimate person" would ask for this type of information. He rather flippantly responded to his brother by saying, "If you want to know when a ship's going to be overhauled, I'll be glad to tell you."

The only document he had ever provided his brother, approximately four years earlier, was an unclassified booklet of general plans for an LPH-2 class ship. The booklet had been downgraded to unclassified status and did not contain any updated material.

John Walker had informed him that he could sell photographs and information about warships to *Jane's Fighting Ships*. Arthur told John he didn't think he had anything that would be new or interesting enough to interest *Jane's*.

He insisted that he had never provided his brother with any

other documents and that the only thing he had neglected to tell the FBI earlier was that his suspicions were stronger than he had said.

Four more questions were posed formally:

Q—Prior to 1980, did you know for certain that your brother, John Walker, was working for or cooperating with the intelligence service of another country?
A—No .

Q—Other than what you told me, have you ever provided any sensitive or classified material or information to your brother, John?
A—No.

Q—Have you ever provided any information to John Walker, knowing it was being transmitted to the intelligence apparatus of another country?
A—No.

Q—Have you ever furnished any classified material or information either directly or indirectly to the intelligence service of another country?
A—No.

The polygraph showed that Walker lied in response to all four questions. The FBI agents were particularly alarmed by the first question, because they had hoped, for the sake of U.S. security, that any spying done by Arthur Walker had been done only after he had been employed by VSE and not earlier. It was now apparent that both men has been engaged in espionage for a long time.

Panicky, Arthur tried to explain why he had failed the polygraph. He told Colvert that he had informed Johnny that he had seen such information as "ships information books" and occasionally "CASREPS," or casualty reports, reports of malfunctions and breakdowns on Navy warships. Then Arthur suddenly recalled that he did let John read a CASREP on an LHA-2 class of ship, which was designed to carry helicopters into combat situations. He had let him read just one page about a broken water pump. He denied that he had furnished anything else. CASREPS are marked confidential.

But by this time Arthur knew that the FBI knew he had been

lying. He could not beat the polygraph. The interview was terminated, and arrangements were made for him to return for more questioning.

When Arthur Walker went home he was drained and frightened—more frightened than he had been when the *Torsk* sprang a leak, more frightened than he had ever been. He was now fighting a delaying action only. He was also worried that perhaps Rita had unknowingly incriminated him. In an act of catharsis, he told her details of the spying and, while he was at it, about his affair with Barbara Walker. She cried much of the night.

On May 21, he returned to the FBI office and said he wanted "to start from the beginning." He said his suspicions about his brother did not begin six months earlier but sometime in late 1979 or 1980. No doubt Arthur thought this would account for the deception recorded earlier. He had just begun work for the VSE Corporation when John first indicated that he was able to sell ships' photographs and information. He then felt pretty strongly that "Johnny was doing something illegitimate." Until then, he thought the extra money that his brother always seemed to have came from his part-ownership in the bar and from leasing of pinball machines.

Sometime in 1980 or 1981 John began to ask repeatedly if he were working with any classified information. Because of the persistent questioning, Arthur began to think "Johnny was doing something wrong." Asked to explain, he said, "He could be gathering classified information to sell to someone else."

The only classified information that he could recall having in his possession at that time was a technical manual that had been sent over to VSE dealing with "electronic countermeasure equipment." The manual, classified secret, was sent to VSE because they needed to have access to the information necessary to identify the parts they were required to inspect during overhaul. He did not give this manual to his brother to inspect.

Later that year he took an unclassified book of general plans and met his brother in the parking lot where he was waiting in a van. He did this to show him that he did not have access to anything classified and hoped that John would stop pestering him for classified information.

Then, returning to his naive routine, Arthur told the agents he said, "What can you do with stuff like this?" His brother said nothing could be done with unclassified plans, but for certain other information he could obtain money. When Arthur asked him who, John replied "people in Europe."

Arthur said at this point he became 100 percent sure his brother was trying to coerce him into gathering classified information. Asked what he meant by "people in Europe," Arthur replied, "the Russians."

Arthur could tell from the look on their faces that the agents did not buy his naiveté, but he persisted for a while, with each episode becoming slightly more damaging to himself. He still hoped they would see him as an older brother humoring his younger brother but not really helping him.

Arthur told the agents that he once met Johnny at Charlie's Waffle House in Norfolk. They sat outside in a car, and Arthur told his brother that he was depressed over business failures. He said Johnny then told him that he could make money by obtaining classified material.

Arthur had been required to check out classified material at VSE, and the FBI seized records that showed he had checked out many classified documents—documents that bore no relationship to anything he was working on.

Then, after repeated polygraph failures during two extended sessions, Arthur admitted that it was quite possible that he had provided his brother with the electronic countermeasures booklet marked secret that he had discussed earlier. He said he was fuzzy about when and how he had provided this very damaging document to John. He also admitted giving him other information that may or may not have been classified.

Continuing to depict himself as the duped brother, he told the agents he once asked John, "How do you spy?" John told him how he had gathered information and passed it either through dead drops or by actually delivering it overseas. He recalled his brother going to Austria to deliver material to the Russians, which he called euphemistically "the other side" until agents asked him to be more explicit.

During the questioning, Arthur said John commented with regard to some of the documents he brought from VSE, "I don't know if this is any good, I'll have to let you know. Another time he said the Soviets might tell him that 80 other guys provided the same thing, perhaps an indication of how pervasive spying may be in the military, perhaps just John's imagination."

The FBI then asked a series of six more questions while Arthur was strapped to the polygraph machine:

1. Following your service in the U.S. Navy, other than what you told me did you ever provide any classified material or information to your brother, John Walker?

2. Following your service in the U.S. Navy did you provide more information and material to your brother, John Walker, than you have told me about?

3. Other than what you told me, have you ever caused classified material or information to be provided to the intelligence service of another country?

4. During your service in the U.S. Navy, did you ever provide your brother, John Walker, with any sensitive or classified material or information?

5. During your service in the U.S. Navy did you ever cause sensitive or classified material or information to be given to anyone that represents the intelligence service of another country?

6. Do you know the identity of anyone else that has provided information to your brother, John Walker?

Arthur failed all six questions despite interrupting the exam to tell a little bit of what he knew about Jerry Whitworth, hoping that a backfire would put out the main blaze.

He recalled that during the time period when his brother was continually asking him for classified material, John referred to a person on the West Coast by the name of Jerry. John told him, "I got a guy on the West Coast who helps me out." John described Jerry as "an old buddy of mine."

After he was told of the test failures, Arthur was again advised to get an attorney, but he refused.

"I've always told everybody, 'Don't do anything without a lawyer.' I've always told my kids that. And who was the first dummy that walked through the door without a laywer? Why? Why? I was just dumb."

Arthur appeared before a federal grand jury and, despite the polygraph results, said his espionage had not involved his active duty tour. The foreman proceeded to question Arthur:

> Q—During the time that you served in the United States Navy, did you ever provide your brother, John Anthony Walker Junior, with classified documents?
>
> A—I can't remember ever giving him anything during my tour of duty, my tour of active duty in the Navy.
>
> Q—When you say that you can't remember is it possible that that happened?
>
> A—I cannot remember consciously handing somebody something and saying, "Here."

Arthur continued to insist that he knew nothing of his brother John's spying activities until after 1980.

The foreman also asked him if John used dead drops as a term for dropping material for the Soviets to pick up.

"There were terms like that used, dead drops. He mentioned having to fly overseas at various times, himself, to deliver material, and at times I know he mentioned to bring money back with him."

He admitted to the grand jury that he knew that John had gone to Austria to deliver documents in the 1982-1983 time span.

Then there was a question from the foreman that represented the thoughts of everyone in Scranton and most of America:

> Q—Can you tell us, Mr. Walker, why you were willing to engage in espionage activities that were harmful to the United States of America?
>
> A—At that time the [car radio] business failed, and the amount of money owed was significant and these are my feelings at the time, that I think that I know now, my brother felt this would be a time to approach me. In these past years, I have often wondered why I accepted this, and I don't really have an excuse. . . . The money was there. My wife didn't really know that we were facing such financial difficulty. I don't want to blame it on family, but he was my brother, and there it was.
>
> Q—What were the things that he said to you they [the Soviets] most wanted?
>
> A—The things apparently they were most interested in was

code material, CRYPTO as it's called, any kind of top-secret or intelligence-type information, and it just would work its way down through secret and confidential, which is the lowest classification for classified material.

The foreman, aware of the polygraph results, tried again on Arthur's pre-1980 activities:

Q—And I ask you again for the last time, during the time that you were on active duty with the United States Navy, did you provide your brother, John Walker, or anybody else, classified information or any other kind of information in exchange for money or anything else of value?

A—To anyone, the thought never entered my mind. As I say, I don't recall any discussions where I discussed matters, classified matters in public, although certain classified things get talked about when Navy men are together.

The foreman would not let this obfuscation pass.

Q—Excuse me, let me clarify the question. You have sat here and you have acknowledged under oath that you were engaged in espionage activities against the interest of the United States since 1980?

A—Yes sir.

Q—I am not talking about what you might have told somebody when you were at a cocktail party when you were in the United States Navy. My question is, during the time that you were on active duty in the United States Navy, were you engaged in any kind of espionage activity against the interest of the United States?

A—No sir. No sir. I was not engaged in any type of espionage activity.

Arthur was charged with seven counts of espionage and placed in solitary confinement with a light kept on all of the time. He was watched with a remote, closed-circuit television camera.

"The priest here, he's a little older than me—in his sixties—and real nice and I made a confession and he gave me communion and, man, it had been a long time. We had a chitchat and I mentioned that I had been an altar boy when I was age seven or eight for quite a few years and that John was one too, and I liked it. Everything was in Latin and it was fun and he says, 'Do you remember any of it?' and I said 'I don't know,' and he gives me the first line— '*Introibo ad altare Dei* [I will go to the altar of God],' and the response popped right out of me, '*Ad Deum qui laetificat juventutem meum* [to the God who gives joy to my youth].' He grabs my hand and shakes it and that was really neat, really neat. Of course, they've been saying I have a great memory, haven't they?"

The court appointed two attorneys for Arthur, Samuel W. Meekins and J. Brian Donnelly. They tried to work out a deal whereby Arthur would plead guilty to conspiracy, which could carry up to a life sentence, and nolo contendere to the other six counts. The Justice Department responded through Assistant U.S. Attorney General Stephen S. Trott, "You don't put a knife in your country's back and come in and ask for some kind of deal. . . . We were not going to give up the public's right to see into an espionage case."

Arthur Walker had to pay another kind of penance during his trial, which began August 5, 1985. He had to stare at a photo of his brother that had been propped up against the jury box.

"It's that damned picture," he whispered to Meekins. No matter how he squirmed or sat, he had to look directly into his brother's eyes.

He also had to face his former co-workers from VSE, who testified as to the value and quantity of material he had signed out and turned over to his brother. All of them testified that he was an excellent and intelligent worker. His supervisors admitted that they awarded him "outstanding" job reviews time and again. Others from related industries said he was one of the most knowledgeable engineers around in the specialized area of ship repair and overhaul. Some of what was said was so sensitive that this testimony was expunged from court records.

Attorney Meekins didn't have much to work with after Arthur Walker's admissions to the FBI, all of which were ruled admissible as evidence, but he tried valiantly to depict Walker as a nobody who simply tried to please an overbearing brother by giving him harmless data. It did not have the ring of truth to it in the face of the prosecution's overwhelming case.

Assistant U.S. Attorney Tommy E. Miller told the court, "This person, Arthur James Walker, that Mr. Meekins would have you believe was just a miniscule little rabbit running around in the bushes did more than his brother in the Navy. He achieved officer's rank, outstanding ratings. When he worked at VSE, he was promoted to a supervisor of a department. The people in the Navy said he was the best around. . . . That's not a little rabbit running in the bushes. Your honor, Arthur James Walker is a spy."

After a trial that took more than a week, Judge Clarke took just fifteen minutes (the case was heard without a jury) to find Arthur guilty on all seven counts of espionage.

In an interview from jail a few weeks after the trial, Arthur said, "There's no fairness anymore. I used to go to the movies and you would see John Wayne and there was a sense of fair play, okay? I mean, if you make a mistake and you were sorry and you tried to make up for it, everything would be okay in the end, right? Whatever happened to fair play? It just isn't out there anymore is it?"

"You're wrong, Art," said Meekins, his attorney. "There is fair play for robbers and rapists and even murderers. The courts can cut them some slack, but not you. This case got too big, Art—too many headlines, too much television. It got bigger than you, Arthur, bigger than you."

"The documents that I gave my brother were commonly available," Walker insisted, lying again. "That's what I want the public to realize, commonly available. I can't think of myself as a traitor. I can't think of myself as a spy, although I must be one, right? I mean, I've been convicted."

He paused and looked around for someone who believed him.

"I accept the guilt for what I did, okay? It was wrong, okay? But I don't think that it hurt the U.S.—what I did. Did it, Sam? I am not a traitor am I?"

Assistant U.S. Attorneys Tommy E. Miller and Robert J. Seidel, Jr., were not sympathetic.

"Arthur Walker absolutely is a traitor," said Seidel. "His motive was simple greed. No one who rises from seaman, without a college education, and becomes a lieutenant commander is a sap."

Miller and Seidel are convinced because of the repetitive findings of the polygraph that Walker knows more and did more than he has admitted.

Arthur was spending much of his prison time, he said, trying to assess his feelings toward his brother. "Everything in court was John. His picture. His fingerprints. Was I jealous? No. Well, maybe an occasional twinge of envy. But I think I was satisfied to cut the

165

grass and stay home. John always felt that I was itching to get out and booze it up more often and have more fun, but I was happy to go home at night. I never had any desire to be rich, no more than anyone else. My boys would say when they were growing up, 'Boy, I wish we were rich like so and so.' and I'd say, 'Well, if I wanted to be rich I wouldn't have made the Navy my career because that's not the way that you get wealthy.' It wasn't greed.

"I have mixed feelings about him. It would be wrong to say that I am angry. I don't know if I feel angry, like 'I'm going to punch you in the nose' type anger. I just feel—I don't know what I feel, okay? I just might be forcing myself to be ambivalent, okay?

"He wrote me a letter after he was arrested. He told me not to worry. He said that he would tell them that I didn't do anything, and then he asked me to get him some clothes, short-sleeve shirts."

Arthur, before the plea-bargain arrangement with John Walker obviated the need for a trial, was trying to decide whether he should testify against his brother.

"The moral question is Should I testify against him? John. And in the moral sense, I guess I should, and I probably would and if not out of anger, my sense of guilt, okay? Maybe I am angry. It will still be hard to do. I can psych myself up into doing it. It is my duty. Maybe that's how I will look at it. It will be my duty, the biggest motivation will be that I will finally be doing what is right, meeting my obligation, okay?

"But it will be hard. In some respects I could blame him, okay? But it was still my choice, okay? It was still my choice. I could have said no, but I couldn't say no. Let me rephrase that—what I mean is, well, I should have said no to him, but I couldn't, really. I just couldn't. He is my brother."

ON NOVEMBER 12, 1985, Judge Clarke sentenced Arthur Walker to three life terms and forty years, the sentences to run concurrently. He fined him 250,000 dollars.

Rita Walker appeared at the sentence hearing for her husband. She testified that Arthur had become suicidal while he was spying, and said he once tried to find a shotgun with which he could kill himself. She said he had told her about his affair with Barbara Walker a few days after John was arrested. She had agreed to help her husband tell the FBI about the spying, admitting that she had been aware of it herself.

Arthur Squirms

"I know he wanted to tell the truth," she said, her voice shaking. "I didn't realize, but I was helping him convict himself."

"Arthur Walker was an older brother and an officer and had been entrusted by his government with far greater responsibility than either John Walker or Michael Walker," Judge Clarke said. "I can't treat this as a slap-on-the-wrist case. The evidence is all to the contrary."

When he could speak freely, Arthur told reporters, "I felt like Jell-O when I was doing it. The fact that I even considered it bothered me more than the documents themselves. I'm not even sure how to explain it. I was trying to help him at this point. He is the man, I mean, he needed something that said classified on it. He was trying to prove his value to someone else.

"I don't want to sound naive. I knew what I was doing was wrong. But I just couldn't turn him in, and then the next thing that I did was let him talk me into getting him some documents. I don't know how to put this except to put it in religious terms. Once you start sinning, you either stop sinning or you just keep going and going and you carry this guilt around, subconsciously perhaps, but there is always a bit of tenseness. It's one of those things that you push back inside, you know, that makes you worse for it. It eats on you and it would be nice to tell someone, but who can you tell? Who? Just John. It was strictly John and I, and I would remain pretty upbeat with John when I saw him because I didn't want to disappoint him.

"Then he was under arrest. They had him. I thought, I have to help them now. I can tell someone, okay? It's not me turning him in. I don't have to face our mom. She wasn't going to open a newspaper one day and read 'ART TURNED IN JOHN.'"

Arthur took the opportunity of his last public forum in the courtroom to say, "I want to apologize to all the citizens of this country for what I did. I dishonored myself, I devastated my family. Nobody could be any sorrier."

167

13

Whitworth

The letters the FBI received were tantalizing. Just signed "RUS," they asked for complete immunity in return for breaking up a spy ring that had functioned for 20 years.

Jerry Alfred Whitworth, a shy and introspective man, met John Walker in 1970 when he was transferred to the Navy's Service Schools Command in San Diego. Whitworth served as a communications instructor. Walker was assistant director of the Radioman School. The two hit it off immediately.

Whitworth, who is tall and bearded, looks as if he had sprung straight from the Confederate calvary into modern times. He has a keen sense of the absurd and a sense of humor to rival John Walker's. He also has a serious and meditative side. An avowed atheist, he found kinship in Walker's nihilism, which parallels his own. Walker is just three years older than Whitworth.

The two became as close as friends can get. They discussed everything from Nietzsche to growing up in small towns. They both enjoyed sailing and frequently went out together aboard Walker's boat, *The Dirty Old Man*. They were almost computer-matched in interests and enjoyed joking about the coincidence of having the same initials, JAW. Both wore wire-rimmed glasses and had a fetish about neatness and cleanliness. They often discussed the frustrations of being enlisted men when they considered themselves more intelligent than most officers under whom they had served.

They went to movies together, went drinking together, stayed up late talking, sometimes until dawn. One of the movies they saw together was *Five Easy Pieces*, starring Jack Nicholson. They both identified strongly with the balding, cynical, nihilistic hero. It became a bond between them, and they later referred to it frequently. They also had something else in common: they pursued the wives of friends. Adultery was a game they played as often as they could before Whitworth was married.

One night in a San Diego bar, Boom Trencherd's Flare Path Restaurant, Walker steered Whitworth around to the subject of classified material, the kind of message traffic and cryptographic material both handled on a routine basis. His nihilism included patriotism, Whitworth said, and he volunteered that he would have no pangs of conscience about selling classified information for the right price. He said he'd like to make a big hit, like the one in the movie *Easy Rider*.

At first the *Easy Rider* remark sounded alarm bells in Walker. Was Whitworth part of internal naval intelligence? Was he, Walker, a suspect? Did the Navy instruct Whitworth to buddy up to him? Walker became guarded as he tried to determine whether Whitworth was setting a trap and whether he had any links whatsoever to Navy security.

But Walker had noted that after Whitworth's divorce from his first wife Whitworth continued to indicate to the Navy that he was married in order to get the extra money for a housing allowance. It was this bit of larceny plus the *Easy Rider* remark that encouraged Walker to recruit Whitworth.

He was soon convinced that Whitworth simply was deeply disenchanted with the Navy establishment, along with the ethics and morals of America, just as he himself professed to be. They talked about industrial espionage and how that seemed to be condoned or at least winked at by the American establishment. If anything, Whitworth was firmer in his nihilism than Walker, whose primary motivation was greed. Both men mouthed patriotism, and they played the Navy game around others. It made life much easier.

According to investigators, at one point, satisfied that he could trust Whitworth, Walker asked him if he really wanted to make some extra money by providing information to "people in Europe who pay for that sort of thing." He told Whitworth that he could probably arrange it if he did. He sometimes indicated that it might be Israel that would buy the information—sometimes even the Mafia.

Walker says he waited until 1974 to make the proposal. "He told him," said one federal official who questioned Walker about it, "only after he was certain that the worst that could happen would be that Whitworth would turn him down—and not turn him in."

In an almost childish fashion, he had made Whitworth swear a "blood oath" that he would not reveal the nature of their conversation with anyone.

Walker indicated that there was a routine traffic in such things and that it made no difference because both sides were shuffling paper in a virtual snowstorm of documents. It was the same "everybody's doing it so we may as well get ours" approach that he had used with Arthur and Michael and had tried to use with Laura in Louisiana and later in San Leandro, California.

Walker also told Whitworth that "a black market" was so desperate it would buy almost anything, including such low-level material as technical manuals and data that could be found in the UCLA library. As a safety precaution, Walker did not immediately tell Whitworth that he had been an espionage agent for some time, and he left out any mention of the Soviets as buyers of the information.

"Walker hinted to Whitworth," federal prosecutors said, "that organized criminal groups dealt in drugs and other forms of contraband."

But in no time at all according to Walker, Jerry Alfred Whitworth was on the Soviet payroll. And once he got started, it was like heroin: he found it impossible to quit.

John Walker told federal prosecutors that when it finally became clear to Whitworth that the information was not going to organized crime, they made up a cover story, in the event that they were arrested, that they were dealing with a private intelligence organization. Walker said this is what he first told interrogators after his arrest until he realized they had too much evidence linking him with the Soviets.

WHITWORTH JOINED THE Navy Reserve while still in high school, went on active duty a few years after graduation, attended a number of Navy schools in his radio-communications specialty, and climbed up the enlisted ranks to senior chief petty officer.

He was born August 10, 1939, in Muldrow, Oklahoma, a dusty wheat, soybean, and cattle farming commumity, population 2,000, situated near the Arkansas border. As a junior at Muldrow High School, Whitworth had been voted the class clown. Fellow graduate Anita Green Israel remembered him as "a very likable student."

Whitworth worked as a gas station attendant while going to high school. His vocational education teacher, Don Morton, became a close friend and confidant, in some ways his surrogate father. Whitworth visited Don and his wife, Velma, often after school and never failed to pay them a visit when he returned to Muldrow on leave.

Don Morton was shocked to hear of Whitworth's arrest, remembering him as a fine student and a loyal friend. "I don't believe he's guilty and I'll never believe it," he said.

Whitworth's mother had given her consent to his joining the Naval Reserve at seventeen. "He told me if I didn't, he'd go anyway so I signed for him because I knew he liked the Navy. He's a great person. Has always been and still is." Like Don Morton, her faith in Whitworth never wavered. (She died shortly after Whitworth was arrested. He was not allowed to leave prison to attend her funeral.)

"He was a Libertarian. He showed me his card, and he claimed to be an atheist, too," Velma Morton said. Libertarians believe in the ultimate freedom of the individual without any interference from the government. He liked to read Ayn Rand, a Russian-born writer who espoused an "objectivist" philosophy, individualistic and egoistic in inspiration. It forms the core of such successful novels as *The Fountainhead* and *Atlas Shrugged*. Her books are the favorites of sophomore philosophy majors who like to feel smugly one up on the world and shock their parents. This was a level beyond which Whitworth failed to progress.

On one visit home, Whitworth said to Velma Morton, "You

know, you all really don't know me." She didn't realize the implication of this remark until after his arrest.

According to the Mortons, Whitworth was starved for affection as a boy and followed them around "like a little old puppy."

His uncle Willard Owens remarked on Whitworth's cleanliness fettish. Whitworth would take as many baths a day as he could get and could not stand dirt on himself or in the house. "Jerry was a great big old kid and a hard worker," Owens said. "Triple-A rating—that's what people would give him."

It was Owens, who was Whitworth's mother's younger brother and only sixteen years older than Whitworth, to whom Whitworth was closest throughout his life—closer than to his mother and father. He was estranged from his parents for different reasons. His father left the family and got a divorce, and his mother married a man who did not like Whitworth, forcing him to stay with his grandparents. (This was another thing he and Walker had in common. As a boy, Walker, too, was often moved to the homes of relatives when things got rocky between his parents.) When he first learned that he was under surveillance, it was Owens he called.

Whitworth bad-mouthed his mother to Don Morton and only after his stepfather died would he visit her. He depended on Owens and the Mortons for the kind of family support structure he could not find at home.

After his high-school graduation, Whitworth moved west to live with his father, Johnnie Whitworth, who owned several restaurants in and near the farm town of Mendota, California. He stayed with his father for at least two years while attending a junior college.

Whitworth met Roger Olson while he was still in the Naval Reserve before going on active duty. In 1958 Olson brought him back to Dos Palos in San Joaquin County to meet his parents. Olson's parents had a nice house, a swimming pool, and a backyard barbecue. It was the kind of warm and loving family Whitworth wished he could have had: parents who seemed to love each other and their son, and far away from the Oklahoma farm town. He later told the Olsons and other friends that his relationship with his real father was strained and unpleasant.

"He was a little orphan with no place to go," Adele Olson recalled. She smiled as she remembered the hillbilly boy her son brought home. "He just loved coming home with Roger—just ate it up. So we just adopted him."

Whitworth and Roger Olson roomed together while attending Coalinga Community College, now called Westhills College. Whitworth talked about one day becoming an engineer or geologist. There is little doubt that he had the intelligence to realize those goals under more favorable circumstances.

Then Olson decided to go to a bigger and better college, and Whitworth could not afford to follow. He felt stranded and abandoned by his friend.

"He was just kinda lost," Adele Olson said. "When Roger went to Fresno State, Jerry went back to the Navy, even though he didn't really want to. It seemed he just didn't know what to do with himself. He finally decided he might just as well stay in."

He was self-educated, according to Adele Olson. "When, I first knew him, he was just a little country hick. But now his English is perfect. He reads and studies constantly, and there's not a subject he can't talk on. Put Jerry with any college graduate and he'll hold his own."

He left college to go on active duty with the Navy in 1962 and quickly advanced through the ranks. He decided to specialize in communications. He attended the Navy Communications School in San Diego, served two hitches at the secret base on Diego Garcia in the Indian Ocean, held sensitive jobs handling coded communications aboard ship and shore installations and was granted top-secret clearances twice during the time that the FBI said he was selling information via Walker to the Soviets.

Whitworth's first wife, Evelyn Wodhouse, was nineteen when she met the twenty-eight-year-old career Navy man. Her mother remembers that the two enjoyed long, deep conversations about the meaning of life and philosophy and psychology. But ten months after his wedding, Whitworth was recalled to sea duty, and he soon got a Dear John letter from Evelyn. The failure of the marriage plunged the already gloomy Whitworth into a tailspin of despair from which friends were afraid he might not recover.

Gradually Whitworth got himself together. In 1971, he was asked to be an escort for one of the winners in the National Science Contest sponsored by the Navy. He was assigned to a pretty sixteen-year-old girl, Brenda Leah Reis, and they began a correspondence. Brenda wrote him that she was having trouble deciding what to do with her life. Whitworth offered to pay her a visit at college. It was the classic story of the skinny kid who had blossomed into a beautiful woman. Whitworth was captivated. They spent hours talking about the kind of philosophical questions that intrigue college students who are flexing their intellectual muscles. He got her interested in Ayn Rand. He was constantly striving to be accepted as an intellectual equal. Brenda told friends that "he was dynamic and interesting to talk to."

They fell in love within days after Whitworth arrived, and they were married in Las Vegas in 1976. But they did not tell anyone that they had done anything so prosaic for five years. Then they had a big party, and Whitworth paid the airfare for a host of relatives and a few friends, including John Walker, to celebrate belatedly.

Brenda's adoration was evident in a letter written to a friend about Whitworth's campus visit. "It wasn't until after he left that I realized what an incredible human being he was. In terms of character, he's the type of man a lot of women would want."

They eventually bought a house in San Leandro, but sold it for 91,000 dollars and moved into a rented, oversized house trailer in the Rancho Yolo trailer park in Davis. Brenda was studying for a doctorate in nutrition at the University of California in Davis.

Whitworth bought a Toyota Supra, a Mazda for Brenda, and a 1981 Yamaha 750 motorcycle. He often played classical music on his new stereo system. They were friendly but enjoyed staying to themselves. One neighbor, John Fema, said Whitworth was a "very good conversationalist."

Another neighbor commented that Whitworth seemed obsessed with jogging. "I rarely saw him wearing anything but a gray jogging suit. And I never saw any indication of high living. They didn't even own their own home—they rented it."

From John Walker's records, the FBI was able to determine that Whitworth had received at least 338,000 dollars and probably much more, over the span of years. The biggest single payment he received was 100,000 dollars in June 1980 as an enticement to stay in the Navy, probably the only time the Soviets have ever provided a reenlistment bonus for an American sailor. According to Whitworth's indictment, he received at least another two payments totaling 110,000 dollars in 1981 and 1982. Included in this payment was 10,000 dollars that was used to buy a van. In all, the FBI found evidence of payments made to Whitworth by Walker on twelve different dates. Based on partial records found in the Whitworth home, FBI analysts found evidence of fifteen installments, in amounts ranging from 4,000 dollars to 100,000 dollars.

According to federal officials, "Analysis of John Walker's passport, credit card receipts, pilot's logbook, and various records maintained by him relating to travel reflect that he was frequently in San Francisco or the Far East at times when Whitworth's ship was in the same place. That Walker was meeting with Whitworth is corroborated by the fact that on or about December 5, 1982, Whitworth mailed a letter from the USS *Enterprise*, the ship to which he was then assigned, to John Anthony Walker, Jr., which contained detailed information regarding the itinerary of the *Enterprise* from January 1, 1983, through March 31, 1983."

Whitworth quit the Navy for two months in 1974, and then reenlisted. The FBI speculated that this earlier reenlistment may also have resulted in a fat payment by the Soviets as an inducement to stay in his key communications position.

After leaving San Diego, Whitworth was sent to the Naval Communications Station in Diego Garcia in the Indian Ocean. He was a radioman with access to intelligence communications at this highly secret posting.

In 1976, he was sent to the USS *Constellation*, a nuclear-powered aircraft carrier, as chief radioman. Here he had access to communications about U.S. nuclear attack plans and defense against enemy submarines. Next he was sent to the USS *Niagara Falls*, the same vessel that Walker had served on from 1971 to 1974. In 1979, he was sent to the Alameda Naval Air Station in California, where he became senior chief radioman, the officer in charge of communications security. He held this position until 1982.

From 1982 until his retirement in 1983, Whitworth served as senior chief radioman on board the USS *Enterprise*, a nuclear-powered aircraft carrier. Here he had access to all U.S. nuclear attack contingency plans and defense plans against Soviet submarines.

EVENTUALLY WHITWORTH CLEARLY became aware that Walker was dealing with the Soviets and expressed various forms of concern about this. In 1984, the FBI received three letters postmarked

Sacramento that set off a flurry of activity in the San Francisco and Sacramento FBI offices. The letter writer offered to expose a twenty-year-old spy ring in return for complete immunity. The first letter arrived on May 11 and was dated May 7. It was signed "RUS. Somewhere, USA." No fingerprints were found on the typewritten letter, which said:

> I have been involved in espionage for several years, specifically I've passed along Top Secret Cryptographic Keylists for military communications, Tech Manuals for same, Intelligence Messages, and etc.
>
> I didn't know that the info was being passed to the USSR until after I had been involved a few years and since then I've been remorseful and wished to be free. Finally I've decided to stop supplying material—my contact doesn't know of my decision. Originally I was told I couldn't get out without approval, this was accompanied with threats. Since then I believe the threats were a bluff.

The letter suggested using a newspaper ad to establish contact, and the FBI placed the first ad on May 21, 1984. The ad stated:

> RUS: Considering your offer. Call weekdays 9 A.M.-11 A.M. 415-626-2793, ME, S.F.

The next RUS letter was dated May 21 and offered information in exchange for immunity. "I feel to come forward and help break the espionage ring would compensate for my wrongdoing, consequently clearing my conscience," RUS wrote. But, "there are other emotions: the difficulty of ratting on a 'friend' and the potential of getting caught up in a legal mess." The writer added that his contact had been working for the Soviets for more than twenty years and "plans to continue indefinitely." He "thinks he has a good organization and has no real fear of being caught, less some coincidental misfortune."

On June 11, another FBI ad appeared. This one read:

> RUS: Considering your dilemma. Need to speak with you to see what I can do. This can be done anonymously. Just you and I at 10

A.M. June 21st at intersection of the street of my office and Hyde in my city. I'll carry a newspaper in my left hand. We will only discuss your situation to provide you with guidance as to where you stand. No action will be taken against you whatsoever at this meeting. Respond if you cannot make it or want to change locations. I want to help you in your very trying situation, but I need the facts to be able to assist you.

On August 13, the FBI placed another ad, which read:

RUS, Haven't heard from you, still want to meet. Propose meeting in Ensenada, Mexico, a neutral site. If you need travel funds, will furnish same at your choice of location in Silicon Valley or anywhere else.

A third letter from RUS, dated August 13, stated that he was giving up "the idea of aiding in the termination of the espionage ring previously discussed." He added: "To think I could help you and not make my own involvement known to the public, I believe, is naive. I have great difficulty in coming forth, particularly since the chances of my past involvement ever being known is remote as long as I remain silent."

Whitworth, getting no firm commitment of immunity, and seeing through the FBI's apparent effort to trap him into making an appearance, made no further effort to contact the FBI. Presumably he might also have been apprehensive that if the newspaper ads had gotten any more specific, they might have tipped off the Soviet intelligence apparatus that operated out of the consulate in San Francisco. In that case, he could fear for his life.

The FBI began checking military personnel living around Sacramento for possible suspects, but they did not solve the mystery of the RUS letters until they found Whitworth's name and address and letters to him on computer floppy discs in John Walker's home, and letters from him in Walker's dead-drop package. The RUS letters contained characteristics that "correspond perfectly," according to investigators, with Whitworth's letters to Walker, including postmarks, type style, and paper—quite aside from grammar, punctuation, and writing style. Among the stylistic similarities cited by the prosecutors was the use of rhetorical questions, the phrase "and etc.," the spelling of "though" as "tho," and the use of slash marks in place of the word "and," and "unusually frequent" use of parentheses.

Whitworth's defense attorneys tried to have the RUS letters ruled inadmissible, but the judge in admitting them into evidence cited the "numerous common points between the espionage conspiracy" outlined in the letters and "the known facts of the spy ring."

Whitworth's attorneys protested that the letters were a "virtual confession."

SURVEILLANCE OF WHITWORTH had begun shortly after Walker's arrest. In the days before the FBI arrested him, they deliberately made the surveillance open, hoping that Whitworth would attempt to escape and lead them to a Soviet contact. They sat in parked cars at every entrance and exit to Rancho Yolo and even took over a vacant house trailer as an unofficial headquarters.

But, although Whitworth soon became aware of the FBI surveillance, he made no effort to escape. He later said he thought they were watching him because they happened to find his address in Walker's home. He had no idea at this point that there was far more incriminating evidence in Walker's home and in the drop package.

In addition, the FBI said that because he had dealt with the Soviets only through Walker, he had no escape available to an Eastern bloc nation. He had to hang tough and hope the FBI case against him was flimsy. Had he known how strong it was, he might have fled.

When the FBI closed in, Whitworth made no effort to escape nor did he seem surprised. When they arrived, he told them he was in the midst of writing a letter to his friend Johnny Walker. A crew of agents began a thorough search of the mobile home, including the parrot's cage, even though they were certain that, since Whitworth had known that he was under surveillance for so long, there would be little of interest in the small dwelling. They were wrong.

Inside, they found a number of confidential military documents including contingency plans for war in the Middle East, procedures for handling secret messages at the Alameda Naval Air

Station, and a total of twenty documents relating to high-frequency satellite communications for Navy ships.

They also found documents indicating that Whitworth rented a storage facility in Davis, and they quickly obtained a search warrant for it. Federal officials were poised to announce what was found in the storage bin, then thought better of it. What was in the storage facility remains a mystery—it was never mentioned by federal officials again.

When Whitworth was taken before Chief Federal Magistrate Frederick Woelflen, wearing a leather jacket, green plaid shirt, and faded blue jeans, he looked more like an aging hippie flower child, complete with tinted glasses, than an international spy. Friends and relatives pledged property totaling 250,000 dollars in an attempt to raise bail, but bail was denied on the grounds that Whitworth, suspected of having a cash hoard, would flee the country. Judge Woelflen pronounced that Whitworth was a danger "not only to the community but to the nation as a whole."

The FBI said at this time that Whitworth's fingerprints had been found on sensitive documents that were in Walker's possession.

Investigators began a systematic check of banks in Canada where Whitworth and his wife had been known to travel, but maddeningly, they could not find a cache of cash. All they found was that Whitworth had obtained ten cashier's checks from nine different banks between 1980 and 1983 totaling 22,000 dollars, and that he had deposited hard cash in safety deposit boxes and bought traveler's checks in large amounts.

Special agents of the Naval Investigative Service also learned that Brenda on two occasions met Whitworth in a leased Rolls Royce limousine when he returned from sea duty; but other than that it seemed that Whitworth had been living comparatively frugally in recent years. His standard of living did not seem too far out of line with his 35,000 dollar annual income at the time of his retirement or with his retirement income thereafter. Gradually, however, investigators would find that Whitworth had, indeed, spent money beyond his income. Yet there was still a large pool of cash unaccounted for—and unaccounted for until this day. Some said Whitworth simply spent his money in cash during a time of high living.

WHITWORTH HIRED A local Davis attorney, Louis Hiken, who told reporters that the FBI had misinterpreted the friendship between Walker and Whitworth. Communications between the two were "indicative of nothing except they were friends." After his arrest, Whitworth wrote his uncle Willard Owens that the whole thing was a big misunderstanding because of his friendship with Walker, and added, "I remain an optimist and I'm sustained by the support of family and friends, especially Brenda's undaunting support and love. It's for Brenda's benefit that I most want bail."

Brenda remained firmly behind him. "During the twelve and one-half years that I have known Jerry," she said, "he has never said or done anything which would make me suspect that he would cause harm to the interests of this country. I will stand by him and support him in this difficult time."

She did complain that during two FBI searches of their home, the FBI seized all of the material necessary for the completion of her doctoral dissertation in nutrition.

After the indictment was handed down against Whitworth (later to be modified to include new information when Walker agreed to testify against him), his father tried to see him, but the government turned him down. Then Johnnie Whitworth talked briefly to reporters about his son. "The government seems to have a lot of evidence against him. I wouldn't want to be in his shoes."

One of the first things Whitworth did when he was jailed was request a brush and pail of soapy water to clean his cell.

14

P.K.'s Story

I have this recurring nightmare. I'm almost afraid to go to sleep because of it. I get a call one night that there is a robbery in progress. I go to this store. The suspect runs out. He has a gun and he aims at me. I fire all six shots and he goes down. I run up and turn the body over and it's John Walker—he's dead.
—Pamela K. Carroll, November 6, 1985

Pamela "P.K." Carroll, a lovely blonde whose milky complexion and lynx green eyes often cause passersby to stop and take a second look, was younger than two of John Walker's daughters. She had the kind of startling good looks and lithe figure that he liked to show off. He got a kick out of the young men who eyed P.K. in her swimsuit and wondered what she saw in a man pushing fifty.

"The only kind of women attracted to John Walker were the young, naive, and not-too-bright types," one federal investigator said. "Intelligent women could see right through him," Phil Prince echoed. "Bright and sharp women had nothing to do with Walker," former Wackenhut co-worker Mike Bell said.

"P.K. is not that swift," attorney Michael Schatzow says. "That's one reason she never figured it out."

P.K. was born in Oklahoma and grew up in Spokane, Washington. When she was a girl she decided she wanted to become a policewoman. But she joined the Navy right out of school.

"I figured I would join the Navy—that it would be a good way to kill four years. I wasn't what you would call one of your brilliant students in high school." First the Navy tried to make her a medical corpsman. She didn't like it, "so I flunked out on purpose after eight weeks because it was the only way to get out." Then "I got lucky." The Navy assigned her to the shore patrol in Norfolk, and she learned to subdue and arrest unruly and drunken sailors. She loved it and always volunteered for outside duty.

"Working in an office, sitting behind a desk—that never has interested me," P.K. explains. "I was one of the first Navy females out there on the street—I pioneered it. I had a great chief and I could con him into things."

After her Navy stint was up, she heard of the job opening at Wackenhut. Then Phil Prince, who hired her, invited her to Walker's forty-fifth birthday party.

P.K. was just twenty-two when they met on July 28, 1981. She had come to work for the Wackenhut Corporation seven days earlier.

"It wasn't love at first sight or anything like that," she recalled. "I liked him. And we started seeing each other from time to time.

"I found out about his toupee the first night, when I was running my fingers through his hair. I touched the fabric part and he pulled my hand away. All three of the brothers wear one, you know—Art, John, and Jimmy.

"I thought he was a nice guy. He called me a few days later and asked me if I wanted to go for a speedboat ride. So we went out and rode around the bay. We had a real nice time. If anyone had told me I would be dating a man twice my age, I would have said they were crazy. It just worked out like that.

"John and I were a fluke, really. I didn't want anybody close to me, and he didn't want anybody close to him. But it happened. We had a lot of really good times—a lot of happy times together.

"One of the things that attracted me to John is that he is a strong individual and I am too. I don't like people depending on me. He didn't really like people depending on him. He was outspoken, opinionated, but then so was I. We never fought.

"Well, we had only one fight. It was about business—something

184

I wanted to do. He said no. I got pissed off. I went upstairs and slammed the door. He thought I had left and went off looking for me. But normally if we had things to talk about that were bothering us we just sat down and talked about them. John didn't like to fight, and I don't either. It's just not my nature."

"John was not a romantic person. He would do nice things for me, but I had to train him. The first time we went to the Bahamas, he became very romantic and I told him, 'John, stop. This is just not you. You're making me nervous.' I think he just wanted to try and make things as pleasant as possible. The Bahamas, let's face it, is a romantic place. But we soon got to the point where we were not playing games with each other."

A psychiatrist might conclude that, because P.K.'s father died when she was six, she was looking for a father figure. But she insists that Walker was not a father figure, that she related to him on a strictly female-male level.

"The age thing never really bothered me. He was always active. He was always ready to go. I mean, he drove me. There were times when I just didn't want to do anything. Like roller skating—he loved to roller skate. We bought our own roller skates. We'd go to Northside Park. We'd skate up and down sidewalks in front of his house. We'd go to a church on the corner and skate in the parking lot. He really did have a lot of energy—almost like he was hyperactive, but he wasn't.

"We had a good time. We would take weekend trips, sometimes in his airplane. Sometimes on the houseboat. Sometimes we drove. Once we went to Jamaica. Our best weekend ever was to Natural Bridge. It was when we first really got to know each other and love each other.

"I remember once when we flew to Tangier Island in Chesapeake Bay, and we had lunch in the place called Ma Crockett's where they serve this delicious home-cooked food, including locally grown vegetables and corn pudding, things like that. On the way back a bad storm with lightning and dark clouds came up while we were in the air, flying back in the Grumman. I was scared to death. He said there was nothing to it—not to be afraid. He was cool as he could be. But when we got back to Norfolk and the bottom really dropped out and the stormy rains began, he laughed and told me he had been just as afraid but didn't want me to know it."

She often recalls with longing the trips they used to make

together when they were working on detective cases, times when they seemed most attuned to one another.

"Once in 1983 we went on a case involving adultery. We flew down in John's airplane to Jacksonville, Florida, We stopped in Charleston and topped off the Grumman's gas tank. When we got to Jacksonville, we rented a car. Then we found that the guy had gone to Charleston, but the weather was too bad to fly so we drove. All we knew was that they were at a hotel in Charleston. We called all the hotels and we checked into a hotel—a Howard Johnson's. We got on the phone again. Finally we found him registered under his real name. He was an idiot.

"The guy was staying in a Best Western just five miles from the airport in Charleston where we had gassed up the airplane on the way to Jacksonville. We got a big laugh out of that. I bought this cheap, stupid bottle of champagne and a white dishtowel, a tray, and two wine glasses that didn't match. John presented the champagne to them as compliments from the management on Easter. Then we sat across from the motel, looking at their room with binoculars. Then John gave me an Easter card. I thought it was kind of cute, right there on surveillance. Then the couple left, and we got pictures of them coming out together, going in for breakfast, getting in the car together.

"Later we went around Charleston, and went to one of the plantations. We messed around, went to Patriot's Point. I didn't feel like going through carriers and ships. Then he saw a sub—one of the first subs he ever served on. We went on board. He was so excited. He showed me everything. He was going crazy. He said 'This was my radio shack, this was my bunk!' He was all upset that they cut a hole in the torpedo room for tourists to use. It made me smile because he said it brought back so many memories for him. [The only submarine on display in Charleston is the *Clamagore,* and the Navy said John Walker never served aboard it. He apparently made up his story to impress P.K.]

"Detective work, to John, was the thrill of the hunt. It was always the hunt. He loved it.

"But we could also just be happy at home. Maybe John would watch TV or read. And now and then he would say 'it's hug time,' and we would hug each other. John loved to hug. It was part of his personality. Maybe he would be in the den watching some stupid movie and I would be in the kitchen watching some stupid movie. John didn't like sitcoms. He thought they were stupid. We watched a lot of TV, though.

"A lot of times we'd get together in the dining room and have a hug during commercials. I know it sounds strange but that was a big part of our relationship. We didn't have to have a lot of people around to be happy. We were happy just the two of us.

"He hated the sun even though he liked boating. He thought people who laid out in the sun were ridiculous, that it was pointless. He hated sports. He said, 'Oh, basketball, isn't that where there's this big ball and they try to throw it through this hoop?' and 'Skiing, oh yes, isn't that where there are these two plywood boards with pointed ends and you strap them to your feet ... ?' He thought sports and a lot of other things were absurd.

"Sometimes we'd get together with Uncle Art, his brother, and they would start swapping old sea stories. I would be bored because I had heard them so many times before. I just tuned them out. John loved the Navy. He talked about it all the time. I know it sounds odd in view of everything that's happened, but John really did love the Navy.

"He loved electronics—he was a genius at electronics. There was nothing he didn't know about electronics. He liked gadgets. He had a speaker telephone, a VCR, and, yes, a few blue movies. He had *The Devil in Miss Jones, Insatiable,* and *Taboo.* I saw my first blue movie at his house. I was embarrassed.

"Guns and weapons—he had the Airweight two-inch Smith & Wesson .38 he had when he was arrested. He had a 12 gauge Mossberg pump shotgun I gave him as a present, an AR-15 rifle and he had some knives and other things. He was a weapons expert, but he didn't carry a switchblade. He carried a Swiss Army knife he used for everything. He never went anywhere without it."

P.K. began staying over at Walker's house more and more often until eventually she moved in much of her clothing and set up housekeeping.

She also stored many of her mother's belongings in the house. Her mother was not happy about her staying with a man more than twice her age, but she, too, liked Walker.

"You can't find anybody who didn't like Johnny Walker. John could make anything funny. John could laugh at anything—I don't care how serious it was. He would laugh for days about Barbara. John told Barbara that she needn't get a divorce—that she could go ahead and keep all the benefits that she had. Obviously the reason he wanted to stay married to her was so that she could never turn around and turn him in. A wife cannot be forced to testify against her spouse."

P.K. and Barbara Walker had had an angry confrontation one day when Michael brought Barbara over to John's house. John Walker was busily vacuuming the floors. P.K. said Barbara Walker seemed dumbfounded to see Walker being so domestic.

"She shouted at me, 'I was married to him for eighteen years and he didn't know what a vacuum cleaner was!' I turned around and looked at her and I said, 'At that time in your marriage you didn't have a job, did you? Wasn't your job to take care of the house and cars and yard and take care of the children? And John was the breadwinner? Wasn't that the agreement?' Well, that shut her up.

"I did the cooking. I don't know how the man could have survived without me. He just was not a cook. But he did always make breakfast on the weekends—home fries, or pancakes, or Eggs Benedict. John was an early riser and I liked to sleep late."

John Walker was one of the most methodical men P.K. had ever met, even in little things—things like lists, notes to himself and memoranda.

"He kept a calendar with all of his relatives' and friends' birthdays on it. He never forgot, particularly his mother. He loved his mother a lot. She's a typical Italian mother. She lives for her family. Nobody's good enough for her boys. She's a diabetic and can't eat a lot of Italian foods but she is a very good cook. She makes everything from scratch.

"She didn't speak to me the first few years. She thought that I was a little whore. In fact, she used to refer to me by the Italian word for whore. It came down to the point where when she came down to visit I would not go over to John's at all, because she wouldn't talk to me. Part of that was probably my fault, too, because I sensed her resentment and I just wouldn't put up with it. I wasn't going to force myself into some place I wasn't wanted. But over the years she gradually began to accept me.

"I remember once we went to a big Italian wedding in Scranton. It was one of John's cousins. They rented the hall in the Hotel

Jerman. It was like right out of *The Godfather,* a sit-down dinner for three hundred people. This was the first or second time I had met Margaret, John's mother. She gave me a hard time. It was okay for Uncle Art to smoke in the house but she didn't want me to smoke in the house. Little things like that."

How did John Walker, known throughout his Navy career as a rabid and vocal nonsmoker, tolerate P.K.'s smoking?

"John told me that smoking was my only vice. I don't do drugs. I don't drink a lot. He told me that if smoking was the only unhealthy thing I did I was okay. He said he had got to the point in life where he thought that anything in moderation was okay."

As she began to know him better, P.K. noticed that he had a great many adolescent qualities. "I used to tease him a lot that he had never grown up—had never left his childhood. I remember we went to a party attended by all of the policeman and John was dressed up like Fidel Castro. He really looked like Fidel Castro, with his beard and everything.

"But he didn't overdo things. He didn't drink too much. This business of his picking up two-hundred-dollar bar tabs that I read about, that's junk. Unless it was business. And he gave me gifts but nothing all that expensive. Probably the best gift he ever gave me was an 'unengagement' ring when we became unengaged at one point in the relationship. It's a beautiful ring. It has his birthstone, a ruby, in the center and is surrounded by ten diamonds. But later we decided to get married. We had planned to get married in the summer—the summer after he was arrested. We were going to Switzerland and Italy. Rachel, Michael's wife, was going with us. We were going to meet Michael in Naples. I realize now that he was going to pick up classified documents from Michael in Naples. I now know that he planned to make a drop while he was in Italy."

Walker told her that his childhood was very unhappy—that because of the fighting between his parents the kids often were shunted to the homes of relatives on the big Italian side of the family.

"His mother lavished affection on all the children, but I think John might have been her favorite. He called her every week. But his dad, that was different. You know his dad just disappeared. The only way John found him was that his uncle was driving along on the Eastern Shore one day and just happened to hear John Walker senior on the radio—he was a disc jockey. Then John got in touch with him. John made a concentrated effort to get back with his dad. And yet he was not a good father himself. He was a good father to Michael, but not to Cynthia, Margaret, and Laura. He was never home. Most Navy families are not that close. I used to know a lot of sailors who said 'It's time to go to sea again because my marriage is falling apart.'

"He was always proud of Margaret's independence—the way she became a graphic artist and took care of herself. He may have been proudest of her of all the children. He liked her independence.

"I loved John senior. John senior came over and put his arm around me and gave me a big hug the first time we went to Temperanceville to see them. Art would never go down there with us. I don't think he ever called his father. Art did send tapes to his father for Christmas. John senior is into old jazz—old, old jazz. John and I would try to find old jazz tapes. John bought him a stereo one year for Christmas. He wanted to be a family. John wanted to keep those lines of communication open."

Already strained family relations were further weakened by the arrest.

"There's John's mother. John may have pleaded guilty but he's innocent as far as she's concerned.

"He hates Barbara, but I think John loves his daughters, even Laura. He has a lot of animosity toward her for turning him in. He will never tell Laura that he loves her, and he'll never have anything to do with her again, but I think he loves her. Margaret is the one who is torn. Her father's in jail. Her brother's in jail. Her uncle's in jail, and her mother is the one who got everybody arrested. Think about that for a minute. She loves her mother, she loves her father. She wants to keep the family unit. But her mother turned in her father. She was constantly trying to get John's approval. I used to force John to spend time with her. I think Margaret resented me a lot because I am younger, and she knew I forced John to spend time with her.

"Rachel is sticking by Michael. And I don't know what Laura is doing—I believe she and Cynthia are sticking by their mother."

According to P.K., Barbara had tried to get 10,000 dollars from Walker shortly before she turned him in.

"He gave Barbara the house and she didn't pay the taxes and was about to lose it, so he paid the back taxes and took the house back. She got mad at him one time and threw her wedding ring into the back yard. It may still be there somewhere as far as I know. I don't know whether anyone ever bothered to look for it."

Despite their intimate relationship, P.K. had never seen Walker without his toupee. "He went to the beach with it, went swimming with it. He never took it off, except Monday nights when he washed it. He wanted to be alone on Monday nights. I guess now I know that he probably wanted to talk to Whitworth or do other secret business on Mondays. I went over to his house one day unexpectedly on my way to work and almost caught him without the toupee. He grabbed a hat real quick. He was a little bit upset about my being there, just popping by like that. I guess eventually I would have seen him without it."

Walker took many trips alone. "It used to piss me off when he would go without telling me. I didn't want him going off to North Carolina or South Carolina and the next thing I would know he would turn up dead or something. I wanted to know where he was at. It didn't bother me that he had gone—it bothered me that he didn't tell me.

"With John and I it wasn't his house and his boat. It was *our* house and *our* boat. And he's the one who started this. It was always *ours*. It's hard to explain.

"Our big dream was to buy waterfront property up and down the coast so that we could go south in the winter and north in the summer and always have a place on the water of our own in nice weather.

"I think, though, that the reason he bought the Grand Exuma property was so that he could open a secret account. That's probably where the money is if he's got some stashed away. [The FBI agrees with this assessment and a search was begun.]

"Also, he didn't want the detective agency to make money. He liked the fact that it was losing money so it could be used to launder his money.

"He learned to fly in California when he was at the radio school with Jerry. One time when he had to have a urine test for his pilot's license, he borrowed some of mine because he didn't think his would pass. He also had a boat that he and Jerry went out on all the

191

time. It was a 34-foot sailboat called *The Dirty Old Man*. He showed me a life preserver from it he still has in his garage on Old Ocean View Avenue."

She had gotten home in the early hours on May 21. "I was sleeping. My mom was living with me at the time. She heard someone knocking on my door. It was four-thirty in the morning. I was the first person the FBI came to see after John was arrested. Mom yelled at me. I got up and put on my blue satin bathrobe. I thought some of my friends thought it would be cute to wake me up in the middle of the night—someone from Blue Sector [her police unit]. I figured it was somebody playing a practical joke. I looked through my peephole. I didn't recognize them. I asked who they were and they held their little ID cards up to their faces, smiling, and said, 'FBI.'

"I said, 'What is it?' I didn't know what was going on. I thought, this isn't right. I didn't know what to think. I let 'em in and they introduced themselves. This picture [of P.K. and John Walker dressed like Bonnie and Clyde with a machine gun] was hanging behind the door. They looked at it and chuckled. I really didn't think anything about it. They asked me when it was taken. I said in 1981. Then they asked me if I knew John Anthony Walker, Jr., and I said, 'Yeah, I know him,' and they said well, 'He's been arrested for espionage.'

"Then there was dead silence at that point. I didn't know what to think. I didn't know what to do. I sank down in a chair. They asked me if I wanted to make some coffee or some breakfast or whatever. I went into my mom's room, gave her her crocheting and a Pepsi. My mom is handicapped. She has rheumatoid arthritis. She gets around with the aid of a walker. I made sure she was comfortable.

"I made a pot of coffee and gave some to them. They said John had been accused of passing government secrets to a foreign government. I told them what I knew. I didn't think I knew anything. I just rambled on and on.

"It was like they were killing time at my house. After an hour or two they made a call and said, 'We're at the girlfriend's house now.' I was in shock. I asked them, 'Do I need an attorney?' and they said no. I knew enough about police work to know that if they hadn't read me my rights they couldn't use anything I had said against me. They said they were going to call my chief as a matter of courtesy. I knew that would be the end of my job, but I didn't want to admit it to myself. They stayed at my house until ten-thirty that morning. I had court that morning. I called my partner, Al, and told him, 'Al, this is P.K. Don't ask any questions. The FBI is here. John's been arrested. I can't come to court. Can you handle the cases that we've got together?' Then I called the court and lied and told them I had the flu."

She told the FBI what John had told her he was going to do on the weekend that he was arrested, a subject about which they seemed particularly interested.

"He told me he was going to pick up a check, and he said he was leaving Sunday around noon—I assumed for South Carolina. I said I would take him out to dinner when he came back Monday night. I was excited because we were buying a four-wheel-drive Blazer for me.

"I told the FBI everything I knew about Jerry Whitworth and Billy Wilkinson and a man in Europe John had mentioned to me. John had told me that he and Jerry owned a lot of pinball machines out in California, and to me it seemed reasonable. Pinball machines make big bucks. Jerry and Brenda would always send John a box of California pears for Christmas, and a magazine subscription of some kind.

"Only my mother knew that we had planned to get married in the summer on John's birthday. She felt betrayed when all of this happened. If it hadn't been for her, I probably would have been off the deep end. I haven't allowed myself the luxury of crying. I had to have my phone number changed. The press followed me around constantly. One reporter, a woman from Philadelphia, followed me to work. She stood outside the precinct shouting 'Officer Carroll, Officer Carroll.' Then later she said to some of the officers I worked with, 'Tell her that I'm not a bad person, tell her that I have children—tell her I just want a brief interview, blah, blah, blah.' It was really disgusting.

"As I said, we were going to be married on John's birthday, which was also the anniversary of the day we met. We weren't going to make it public. Now I understand why he didn't want to make it known—Barbara would probably have gotten upset and turned him in when she found out.

"My name even made it into the *International Herald Tribune*. Everybody wants to know what I know. And everybody is after me on that."

She thought Walker was smart to maintain compartmentalization in his own spy ring. Not only did he keep things from her, she said, but "I don't think John let Art know about Mike, and I don't think he let Mike know about Art. John is an intelligent man. He didn't like anyone to be one up on him."

She agreed, however, that perhaps he did have delusions about himself, as some of his former friends have said. "John did live in a James Bond world. I think that maybe the reason that John got involved in all of this was the typical middle-child syndrome. Because of being the middle child, and because of not being the best student, and not being good in sports—not being the best of everything—John felt the personal need to succeed. He had to do better than his brothers, better than everyone else did.

"I still wake up in the mornings and reach for the telephone to call him. Right after all of this stuff started, I couldn't believe that I wasn't going to talk to him any more or see him or that he might spend the rest of his life in jail—that he was gone, probably forever. It's still devastating for me to think about all of this. I couldn't believe he wasn't going to come to my house and knock on the door Sunday night. It's about the only thing on my mind. It's the only thing in my life right now. And not because I want it to be, but because people won't let me forget it. I've lost a lot of friends because of all of this—people that I've known for years, that I thought I could depend on through thick and thin won't have anything to do with me.

"The FBI was convinced beyond a shadow of a doubt when all of this stuff started that I knew what was going on. Art told them that I knew what was going on. It was in the paper. I saw that and I was shitting. I called my lawyer. He said 'Don't worry about it, P.K. I'll tell you when to start worrying.'

"When all of the people in Germany were defecting, John had been in Germany and I think there was a connection. It's frightening when you think of all the information that John had access to. John told me he was the one, when they were having the practice exercises, that he was the one who said yea or nay on flipping the switch, you know, to activate it to go to war. He was the one who decoded messages that said 'station one go' or whatever. He held the world—the fate of the world—in the palm of his hand."

John seemed particularly proud of landing the contract with the shipyard in Norfolk to sweep for illegal bugs. But she agrees with the investigators who believe that he did more than look for them—that he may have added them.

"We had that contract with the shipyard—my name is on it. John went to school when he received all of this Dektor equipment to check for phone bugs that taught him literally how to tap telephones and how to wire rooms for sound. You have to know how to do it to find it. It would have been so easy to replace a telephone with a duplicate phone, complete with a seal, but one that was bugged. You're going to be alone. All you need is about a minute and a half. He could have done it so easily and he probably did."

There is a strange adulation in her voice when P.K. describes John Walker's most sinister accomplishments. "I am convinced that this is the largest espionage in the history of the United States. The Rosenberg case was nothing compared to all of this." She believes the spying began earlier than Barbara Walker said it had, although Walker, in a telephone conversation with her from the Montgomery County Detention Center, had denied that it started earlier than 1968. If I had found out, I would have turned him in immediately. After all, my whole life is law enforcement."

She sometimes had an eerie feeling about John Walker. "There are so many aspects of this case that frighten me. I could have put it together, this espionage stuff. There were so many things. All of his business trips were planned in advance and couldn't be changed. They were set in concrete. I could have put it together, but I never had it all at one time. The closest thing was that I thought maybe John was working for the government. He used to say, 'The less you know the better.' I never, ever, in my wildest dreams believed that John would do anything against this country.

"He was a Republican, extremely conservative in his political beliefs—to the point where he wished that Jane Fonda would be assassinated. He hated Carter—thought he was a jerk—and loved Reagan, you know? He belonged to the John Birch Society at one point. He was a member of the Association of Old Crows, which is an organization of retired intelligence officers."

As for the Ku Klux Klan, "He told me that he was never a member of the Klan, but he has a picture I saw of him and Billy Wilkinson dressed up in Klan garb.

"John did not have close friends. The few he had were me and Jerry Whitworth—Jerry is probably John's closest friend—and Billy Wilkinson. You will note that if other arrests are made, the only people that will be arrested will be those people that remained close with John through the years.

"When we went out on the houseboat it was my friends that came—not his. Everybody who ever went out on the boat aside from his kids were my friends. I remember thinking that this was strange once or twice, because John is personable. But I kind of wrote it off. I wrote off a lot of things, unfortunately.

"Now, Jerry is a nice guy. He immediately puts you at ease. I am not normally the kind of person who opens up to people. Jerry is one of those people—well, I took a liking to him immediately. I heard so many good things about him from John.

"John told me one time that Jerry put his money in jewels rather than spending it like most sailors do. He and Brenda had a big wedding party out in California, and they flew John out to California for the party, picked John up in a limousine, you know, the whole nine yards. They flew in her parents—everybody. Now where did they get this kind of money? I assumed at the time the money came from the pinball machine business.

"John read a lot of spy stories. The thing that is hard to believe is when the spy was arrested last year in California, John went through the ceiling. He went bananas. 'How could he do that—betray his country?' he shouted. And all of a sudden they arrest John for espionage. How can this man be down this line and all of a sudden he is way over here?

"I have a lot of hate for John. I have so many conflicting emotions. I don't know what I feel for him. I'm kinda numb where we're concerned. He's got himself in a world of shit and there's nothing I can do. Not long after the arrest I called his mother, and she made me feel good. She asked me to come up and stay with her. This has been devastating for her. I worry about her. Every letter I write John I ask him how she is doing."

P.K. has often thought about Walker driving to Washington, all the while looking over his shoulder, trying to make certain that he was not being followed, using the techniques he used to teach to new employees of Confidential Reports or in lectures to area students interested in law enforcement careers.

"He was very good at losing a tail or following people. One thing we always drummed into our investigators' heads was 'Watch your six o'clock—know who's behind you.'"

Her strange mixture of feelings toward Walker—fear and love commingled with disgust at his crime, the ash heap her life has become in the aftermath of his arrest—give impetus to a recurrent nightmare, which is as vivid as an Alfred Hitchcock movie, only much more frightening.

"I'm almost afraid to go to sleep because of it. I get a call one night that there is a robbery in progress. I go to this store. The suspect runs out. He has a gun and he aims at me. I fire all six shots and he goes down. I run up and turn the body over and it's John Walker—he's dead.

"Sometimes I think he wanted to protect me—that that is why he didn't tell me or take me to Washington with him on his last drop. [She never knowingly went on any drops.] And he keeps calling me from prison. I'm afraid to talk to him, and I'm afraid not to talk to him. He still has this strange hold over me and I've got to stop it.

"One time he seemed on the verge of telling me all about everything [before he was arrested]. He was talking about the man in Europe he had dealings with and I could tell he was about to tell me everything, but at the last minute he changed his mind. He deliberately tried to make me think he might be a double agent or something. He told me in one of his telephone calls that that is what he wanted me to think, and that is what he would have told me if I had ever figured it all out.

"I'm not sure whether the FBI is still watching me, but I saw them one night. I thought I spotted a tail so I cut down a side street and doubled back and parked and I saw them. John told me that they blew it when they picked up the 7-Up can. They missed their chance to grab the Russian when they did that, John said. They are really dumb in some ways.

"When they were watching John, they rented an office downstairs underneath Confidential Reports in the name of a construction company. It was not much of a cover. We never saw any hard hats or lunch boxes or construction worker types going in and out of there. It was just men dressed in business suits. Of course, it worked somehow.

"And they searched the office and took one old 8-millimeter camera that didn't work and had no film in it and overlooked another one that had exposed film in it. That's not very professional is it? I was also told that the FBI arranged to have Barbara and Laura placed on welfare. [Federal officials denied this.]

"And John told me that part of the secret plea bargain arrangement is that Rachel will not be prosecuted. [Schatzow said there were no secret agreements.]

"In one telephone conversation he said he has become religious, that he now goes to church in prison. I think that's just a con. Of course he's going to start going to church—that will help him in prison. But if I know John Walker, he could care less about religion.

"He was upset at one point because Art had had an affair with Barbara. But I think they're on good terms again, although John was mad when he found out that Art paid his own way up to Baltimore to testify against John before the grand jury. Art always called John 'El Dumbo,' and John called him 'Uncle Art.'

"I was upset when they opened up his juvenile court record, the one with the burglary. Juvenile court records are supposed to be sealed forever. There was no excuse for that.

"And one of the letters he sent from prison says that he had planned to get out—to stop the espionage in about ninety days. I know he was not going to stop—once you start you can't stop. They won't let you. The man has hurt his country so much, and yet I still have some feeling for him. But I know I'll have to cut it off and go on with my life. I'm afraid of him—I'm afraid he'll make up some kind of story about me and get me in trouble.

"Right after he was arrested he told me to more or less pretend he was hit by a Mack truck and he was dead, and to go on with my life, and that he loved me more than anything else. For a while I thought maybe he was a double agent and that this was the ultimate witness-protection program, the trials, the court appearances—everything. But I guess now I know that's not true.

"The man I have been reading about—that's not the John Walker I know. That's a man I have no inkling about. I don't know who he is. It's frightening. I don't know whether I will wait for him. I don't think I will. I know at some point I'll have to get on with my life."

15

Letters from Jail

The very sad thing is that I was almost out of it, maybe less than a year. —John Walker, July 7, 1985

It wasn't until six weeks after his arrest that Walker got around to writing to P.K. His letters were strangely devoid of warmth.

In his first letter, he explained his delay in writing by saying that he had to await a letter from P.K. in order to get her address. He lamented the fact that he had been arrested just when he was planning to stop spying. "The very sad thing is that I was almost out of it, maybe less than a year. I had always planned to hold up on our wedding until I was completely out, although I never planned to tell you my exact background."

He had been looking forward to his "semi-retirement," perhaps doing volunteer work with the Cousteau Society and going into politics.

He explained that Barbara had always been a problem, claiming that she had given him a hard time for years, and adding, "In the movies, I would have had her shot. . . ."

He had always known that "Barbara would push that button

201

sooner or later; Mike was a hope in that she would not turn him in."

One of the main reasons he had wanted to keep their planned marriage a secret was "to keep from pissing Barbara off . . ." and causing her to turn him in.

He told P.K. that Art and Barbara had been lovers. "I thought he had better taste." Unfortunately Arthur had made some very damaging statements to Barbara, and Walker correctly predicted that Art probably would not be able to plea bargain.

He told P.K. that he missed her, but he wanted to be certain of her attitude before arranging a visit. "Times like these show who your real friends are," he wrote. Later he vetoed the idea of a visit altogether. In one letter, he called his situation "so humiliating that I couldn't bear to talk to you or see you."

He blamed many of his problems on the press, which he said "guaranteed" him a maximum sentence. "Thanks to the press, you now know more about me than me. There is obviously very little hope of my ever seeing the outside again."

The press had also hurt "a lot of my friends, you included." But he did admit that he himself was responsible for many of the "side" problems that caused P.K. to lose her job at the police department and caused others to suffer. He was surprised that Margaret had not been fired too.

Adjustment wasn't difficult, he said. "You must keep in mind that I have been expecting this for a long time." The jail was "excellent . . . nearly all white . . ." He had a personal TV and access to an excellent library. He could shave and bathe when he wanted to. He was viewing it as "a much-needed vacation."

He joked that being in jail was like being in the Navy again and added, "in fact, sea duty was much worse."

He told P.K. that he was in touch with Mike, who seemed to be "taking things well," although he has a lot of hate for Barbara and his sister." Walker felt guilty about Michael's situation but added that he could not discuss reasons for the guilt in a letter.

Walker regretted that he might not be able to write a book because of the "Son-of-Sam law." However, Margaret was going to write his story. "We have already been approached, but the first offer was too low at $750,000 for book and movie rights. We're looking at $5 million minimum into a trust with Mags in charge."

Walker planned to use the money to help those who had been hurt, "particularly Mike . . . and others." P.K. hoped that "others" might include her. Federal officials say that Walker had not, to their knowledge, been offered anything for his story and laughed at his grandiose claim of holding out for $5 million.

Before his plea-bargain arrangement, Walker was hopeful that Michael would get out in less than twenty years. And if he received only one life sentence, even he could get out. "Who knows, we may get together for a hug some day." In the meantime, the best he could hope for was that they would become "pen pals."

He claimed to have written a long letter that he could not mail, one in which "I poured my little heart out . . ." But he said it could hurt his case if intercepted.

July 28 had not been a good day for him because it was the day they were to be married and was also his forty-eighth birthday. "God, we really came close," he commented.

He was reading *Shogun* he wrote, and undertook to describe the story line to her. He called it "a definate [sic] analogy to our situation. We're worlds apart and you have to go on with your life." It was best to assume he would never get out again. "There is so much I want to say to you, but I can't for the reasons explained. We'll have time later."

His telephone restrictions had been lifted and he had access to the telephone anytime, he wrote. He promised to call her soon and apologized for having to call collect. "I love you and wish we could have celebrated the twenty-eighth together."

On August 19, he told her he couldn't believe the number of reporters present during two days of court appearances for preliminary legal maneuvering. "I really hate the press and it was fun to laugh at them," he said. He worried that perhaps the press was stealing his mail without offering an explanation of how that might happen.

He lamented that the court had denied a motion made by the defense that the bag found by agents Stauffer and Brahe had not been abandoned, thus making a search warrant necessary (which the agents did not have at the time). But he was glad that the court ruled that he and Michael must be tried separately.

He had written to Art and told him that he forgave him for the affair with Barbara and suggested that they begin to communicate with each other. "He has been so crazy that I'm not sure if I would know him now. I really haven't changed. Art looks destroyed."

He heard that Art would be selling his story, he told P.K., and he hoped this would not "hurt my case any more than he already has."

Michael, in his last letter, "wondered if the two bitches had any idea of the impact of their actions. He feels like they didn't; I feel like they DID!"

"Now and then a pleasant thought flashes through my mind like Natural Bridge or something, and I have to immediately 'change the subject' or go nuts." He thought of P.K. when the other prisoners watched *Love Boat* reruns on television, because it reminded him of the times he had bitched at her about watching it. "God, it makes me miss you."

He was, in effect, tried in Norfolk with Arthur, he told P.K. "The government is going for blood. I believe Art will get life plus—possibly two life terms. He'll then testify against me, then go for a sentence reduction, which he'll get. If they're coming down on a so-called 'lessor [sic] player' like that, you know they're just waiting for me."

He was certain that the FBI was monitoring his mail because a picture P.K. mentioned in a letter had not been enclosed. The FBI probably forgot to put it back when they resealed the letter, he wrote. Then added parenthetically, "FBI, if you're reading this, please forward the picture."

He wrote her in September that he had just finished watching the Washington Redskins squeak by Houston in a football game. P.K. had written him that she was going to the game with a friend. The enormity of Walker's ego was evident when he added, "I didn't see you . . . you should have made a big 'JAWS' flag so the cameras would focus on you."

In October, he told her that he had read her statement to the grand jury and thought it "looked very honest and truthful." He hoped that she would not be called as a witness, however, because the press would "turn it into a circus: ex-wife and girlfriend." He was trying to arrange for P.K.'s statement to be accepted into evidence without her having to appear, but he doubted that the government would go along. He added that if the FBI required her presence, the only reason would be to cater to the press. Most important, "I hate for you to see me in such a humiliating situation, but it will be nice to at least see you again." He thought the trial would last three weeks and predicted it "would be torture."

He had also read Arthur and Barbara's statements, along with ones from Laura and Roberta Puma. "They will kill me. It is difficult for me to fathom Barbara's hate. As for Laura, she reminds me of the WW II Germans who trained their children to turn in their parents to the SS. I wonder if she'll be able to live with it in the future—unfortunately, I believe she will with no problem!"

He was keeping busy, planned to sign up for some college courses after the trial, and hoped that he, Arthur, and Mike could end up in the same prison so they could see each other.

"Writing to you has been painful. I still can't believe you're out of my life. It will take a very long time to get you out of my mind—if ever."

P.K. said that in one letter she got from Walker—the last one before Whitworth's trial began—he boasted of having killed someone during one of his trips to meet a Soviet contact in Vienna.

"John told me that he had to kill a man who was following him in Vienna. He said he just wanted to let me know so I would understand his mood changes." Walker wrote that he determined that he was being followed, then ambushed the man who was following him. Walker told P.K. that he left the man for dead but was not absolutely sure that he had killed him. He didn't say what weapon he used. The story had the aroma of Walker-style fabrication—more John Walker fantasy. But P.K. believed the story. "I don't know why, but I believe it. I believe it really happened," she said.

16

The Trial that Wasn't

We tantalized them a little bit.
—Frederick Warren Bennett

The decryption device was supposed to be the centerpiece of a thorough and exhaustive trial in Baltimore. But the trial of John Walker was not to be. Walker had one last card up his sleeve and it worked. He told his court-appointed attorney, Frederick Warren Bennett, that he had information that the CIA would want to know about. In return, he said, he would like some sort of plea-bargain arrangement. Walker hoped to get a break for Michael, claiming that he deeply regretted roping his son into something that could wind up costing him a life sentence. Bennett did not think a deal was likely and began preparing for an exhaustive trial.

In fact, the new role of deeply caring father was calculated deception on Walker's part, designed to give U.S. intelligence officials a hook on which they could hang a deal, which they were predisposed to make anyway. In the world of international intrigue and espionage, the fate of one person is unimportant compared to the overall goals of national security. It is a big game with certain rules. One of those rules is that any deal is possible involving any given individual as long as the bargain helps protect the safety of a great number of people.

U.S. intelligence decided that it would be worth making a deal if Walker would promise to cooperate in a two-year debriefing during which he would provide detailed descriptions of all the information he had passed on as well as the methods by which he maintained contact with the Soviets.

At the end of the debriefing, Walker would be turned over to a CIA psychiatrist so that his psychological profile might be used to help spot other potential spies in the future.

The CIA wanted the debriefing to be backed up with periodic polygraph tests to ensure that Walker was being forthright. If not, the plea bargain would be declared void.

After much discussion of the terms of the sentence, it was finally decided that Walker would be sentenced to life imprisonment with eligibility for parole in ten years, subject to approval by a federal parole board. Michael would get a twenty-five-year sentence, but would be eligible for parole in eight years and four months. Michael would be freed in sixteen years with time off for good behavior, no matter what the parole board decided.

As the plea-bargain arrangement was read in court, Rachel buried her face in her hands and wept. To her, eight years or sixteen years or twenty-five years were all the same—a very long time to wait for someone while she was young and attractive. Margaret Walker, her auburn hair in a French twist, reached over and massaged Rachel's back in sympathy.

John Walker smiled jauntily throughout the proceedings. Bennett said later it was just a nervous tic—that it meant nothing. When asked if Walker had given the CIA a sample of what he had passed to the Soviets, Bennett said, "We tantalized them a little bit."

Michael, on the other hand was so angry that he wouldn't speak to his father during joint court appearances or even when they were held together outside federal court in Baltimore.

THERE WAS AN immediate outcry from present and former military personnel around the nation, led by Navy Secretary John Lehman, despite the fact that Defense Secretary Caspar Weinberger had approved the deal, along with President Reagan, the joint chiefs of staff, and the national security adviser, and other key members of the cabinet. Reagan reportedly had a hard time swallowing the easy punishment, but he was assured by CIA Director William

Casey that the good to come out of the plea-bargain arrangement would allow the damage assessment to be far more precise and allow the United States to take much faster remedial action.

Lehman had argued that such light punishment would be telling U.S. servicemen that the government would let them off easy, that spying was not as grave as they had been led to believe.

The flap continued at the highest levels of government for several days. Spokesmen for the Reagan administration pointed out that Weinberger and Attorney General Edwin Meese II had approved the agreement and that Lehman, behind closed doors, had voiced only mild objections. They implied that he was showboating for the benefit of the Navy ranks by coming out so strongly against the agreement after the fact. Senior Pentagon and Justice Department officials were angry with Lehman and did little to conceal it. But they admitted that there had been a serious split within the Defense Department, with some demanding severe punishment even if it meant a painstaking damage assessment without John Walker's cooperation.

Lehman and Chapman Cox, general counsel to the Department of Defense, had argued for severe penalties, such as life without parole, for all convicted in the Walker case. Lehman accused the Justice Department of treating espionage as just another white-collar crime. He said the deal reached with Walker would be of little benefit to the military. But his contention was disputed by Colonel Anthony J. Gallo Jr. the Army's chief of counterintelligence.

Gallo and the other members of the intelligence committee hoped for a windfall of information from Walker. "I've said all along that unless John Walker or Whitworth talks, we were never going to know all the damage that was done," he said.

CIA officials said reassuringly that no federal parole board would dare the wrath of the American public by freeing Walker for many decades, if ever. As for Michael, he was a callow, simple young man who had been led astray by his father. All he had wanted was his father's approval; money for the documents was secondary.

Part of the plea-bargain arrangement was that Walker would agree to testify against Whitworth, who was still awaiting trial in California. Whitworth had been hanging tough. This left him hanging in the wind.

17

Whitworth's Trial

John Walker would sell out his mother.

—Roger Olson

Whitworth's trial in San Francisco continued for fifteen weeks in the seventeenth floor U.S. District Court room, which was jam-packed with spectators and reporters. It was often like a soap opera. As the government painstakingly introduced its evidence, the defense and prosecution called relatives and former friends and co-workers of Whitworth and Walker. Many members of the Walker family testified, along with former girlfriends and acquaintances of both men. John Walker, rather than Jerry Whitworth, sometimes seemed to be the defendant as the defense took aim at his credibility and character. It was an easy target.

One of the witnesses to his lack of character was Laura Walker. She titilated the courtroom audience with a story about how her father had threatened to kill her husband:

"He asked me how much I cared about my husband and how I would feel if he suddenly no longer existed. I said I didn't care."

She said John Walker tried "many, many times" to talk her into spying for him when she was in the Army. "He told me the offer was always open—that it would never be closed," she said. "I didn't come out and say no, but I tried to explain that I wouldn't—that I couldn't do it." She said her father encouraged her to have an abortion in order to remain in the Army and become a spy. Then, after she left the Army, she said he offered to adopt her son, "hire a nanny, and I could go into the Army and spy for him."

Arthur told the court what he had told the FBI—that he was recruited by John Walker while at the VSE Corporation. But he didn't say that his polygraph answers indicated deception when he was asked if he had been spying earlier. Barbara's testimony about when Arthur began spying—which would come later in the trial—would be at odds with his timetable.

Throughout the trial, Whitworth spent his time methodically arranging pencils at the defense table, taking notes, and whispering to his attorneys. He always looked neat and clean, with pants well pressed. But his two suits—one blue-gray and one light brown—were ill fitting, with the sleeves too short for his gangling, Li'l Abner frame. They were suits that Brenda hastily purchased after his arrest. Brenda was usually in the courtroom. Whitworth had a manila accordian file he brought with him each day. He would remove papers from the file and shuffle them, first on the long side and then the short side. He grew progressively more gaunt, and jailers told reporters that he was very choosy about his food and often sent meals back scarcely touched.

THE STAR WITNESS against Jerry Whitworth was John Walker. He said, as Whitworth and Brenda listened, that he had passed secret material to the Soviets—much of it from Whitworth—in such diverse places as Casablanca and a Zayre's department store in Northern Virginia near Washington. He had carried a *Time* magazine under his arm so his Soviet contact could pick him out in the department store. He also told the court he had flown to various ports around the world to pick up classified material from Whitworth, whom he described as his "best friend." Whitworth stared ahead with no display of emotion as Walker spoke, averting his gaze from his accuser.

He said one method the Soviets used in Vienna involved a quick swap of camera cases on the street—his filled with stolen secret documents and theirs filled with 50-dollar bills.

Walker kept the courtroom enthralled as he described a tearful parting in Vienna when his longtime Soviet contact was re-assigned. The two men had become close friends. They usually met, he said, on the street—often in the dead of winter. He was forced to purchase a pair of electric socks to withstand the cold Austrian winters as he talked to his contact.

"That's so you wouldn't get cold feet on your face-to-face meetings?" joked assistant U.S. Attorney William S. Farmer, causing the courtroom audience to burst into laughter. Walker seemed irritated by this.

Walker admitted he could never remember the letters the Soviets had given him to use for identifying members of the spy ring. That is why, he said, he kept them on an index card—the card that was discovered by the FBI in his home. Even so, he said he once wrote the Soviets about Whitworth but mistakenly used Arthur's code letter.

When Farmer asked him about a "spy calendar" with various dates and entries on it, Walker snapped testily:

"This is not a spy calendar—it's a planning calendar. It just happens to have spy entries on it!" He spoke of spying as if it were as innocuous as delivering milk. He even seemed boastful as he described getting a stack of secret material from Whitworth that was over a foot high.

Walker said at one point that the Soviets told him that the KWR-37 broadcast system for which Whitworth had been providing the daily changing key lists had "ceased to decrypt." He told Whitworth that the two of them "should be able to figure out what was going wrong," and, although Whitworth reacted with surprise, they began a study of the diagrams and tech manuals, and they solved the problem together.

Walker also testified that Whitworth had told him that he created a cover story just for his wife. Whitworth had told Brenda that he was working for the United States in "a secret kind of way." Noting that he had not fooled his own wife, Walker told the court, "You can't keep anything from your wife. Every married man knows that."

The Soviets at one point fell behind in payments, deciding to check out the value of the material before paying up front, and he and Whitworth later split a $200,000 lump sum payment, Walker told the court.

Once, after Whitworth had decided to leave the Navy, Walker

213

said he warned him that making such career changes without first informing the buyers of the secret information would wind up getting both of them killed. He said his Soviet contacts were upset by Whitworth's decision to retire from the Navy in 1983 without completing his planned tour of duty on the aircraft carrier *Enterprise.*

"In the field of espionage," Walker somewhat pompously said he told Whitworth, "one does not play games with one's contacts." He told Whitworth that the "buyers" were constantly monitoring their behavior for any irregularities that would signal that the two had been found out by the authorities.

"It would foul up the money flow and it would put us in danger of being assassinated," he warned Whitworth.

One of Whitworth's defense attorneys, James Larson, had Walker read parts of his own Navy evaluations for the jury, evaluations that described him as a man of "impeccable appearance and demeanor" involved in "vigorous self-improvement." It also described him as "intensely loyal" with a "fine sense of personal honor and integrity."

Larson then showed the jury four canes found in Walker's home: one concealing a two-foot long dagger, another a pistol, a third a blackjack, and the fourth, glass vials. This did not seem to be the accoutrements of a man of "honor and integrity."

Walker denied the suggestion that he got them from the Soviets, telling the jury that they were ordered through the U.S. mails from various men's magazines.

In a carefully constructed case, the prosecutors showed that between 1979 and 1984, Whitworth and his wife spent at least 138,465 dollars more than he and his wife earned. The prosecution also showed that in many years, Whitworth spent none of his Navy income. The government said he put his Navy earnings in savings accounts and spent his espionage money on such things as a Fiat sports car, a 20,000-dollar personal computer system, a 2,000-dollar home burglar alarm and—during one shopping binge —853 dollars worth of lingerie for Brenda.

Although Whitworth used cash to avoid leaving a record that might be found by the Internal Revenue Service or the FBI, he kept receipts for cash purchases, which were found in his home by FBI agents after his arrest. Agents said they found records of 42 bank accounts and 44 credit card accounts, plus assorted safe deposit boxes where he stored cash he got from Walker. Agents also found among his possessions a copy of a letter he had written to an airline praising the efforts of airline employees, who had found his money clip containing over 800 dollars in cash.

Agents said Whitworth also bought two boxes for the San Francisco Opera for the summer of 1983 and gave a 200-dollar contribution to the opera.

In 1983, Brenda sent Whitworth a telegram asking permission to purchase two Salvador Dali prints for 4,000 dollars. And he sent her a telegram in 1983 instructing her to purchase 10,000-dollars worth of gold Krugerrands, and some silver, cautioning her to use "discretion please."

When friends inquired about his spending habits, said the FBI, Whitworth tried to create the impression that he was a successful investor in the stock market. Actually, he failed a stockbroker's examination and lost almost 30,000 dollars in investments in the stock market. Even with the Krugerrands and silver, Whitworth lost 1,000 dollars on his investment. If anything, he seemed to have a knack for making bad investments.

Barbara Walker told the court of Walker's longtime friendship with Whitworth, and she said she knew that Walker was trying to recruit Whitworth. She even told Whitworth that she knew.

Whitworth asked her if she would turn Walker in to authorities after their divorce, and she assured him that she was "not after revenge." She told Whitworth that Walker had once told her that Whitworth was bisexual.

At this point, Barbara Walker said something that indicated possible perjury by Arthur and John Walker. Both brothers said Arthur's espionage began in 1980, but Barbara said Arthur had told her he was involved in spying in 1968 while stationed at a submarine base at Groton, Connecticut. This would have been while he served aboard the submarine *Grenadier,* a mission that was so secret that even today the Navy will not publicly discuss it. It was also during this time that the two Walkers overlapped duty assignments in Charleston, South Carolina.

The defense had planned to call P.K. Carroll and Laurie Robinson to the witness stand in an effort to undermine Walker's credibility as chief witness against Whitworth. They later changed

215

their minds about P.K., but she testified instead for the prosecution. They also called Roberta K. Puma, who once managed one of Walker's apartment buildings, and Whitworth's college buddy, Roger Olson.

Laurie Robinson said Walker once perjured himself in a trial involving a Navy case against a friend. The friend was accused of using a tape recorder for an unauthorized wiretap. She said the tape recorder was Walker's, but Walker denied under oath ever having owned it or even having seen it. Walker had also asked her to lie in court, and she had refused.

She said Walker became so angry at the friend during the trial that he tried to get her to use her feminine wiles to lure him from Florida to Virginia Beach "in order to bump him off."

Robinson also said that, during a plane trip with Walker, he once asked her to toss a manila envelope out of the aircraft into a wooded area of North Carolina. She and Puma said Walker had involved them in operations that, after his arrest, they realized could have been exchanges with the Soviets.

ALTHOUGH P.K. WAS to have been a defense witness and was flown to San Francisco for this purpose, defense attorneys decided her testimony would be too damaging to Whitworth. She was about to walk out of the courtroom after learning this when the prosecution asked her to testify.

Whitworth grinned strangely at her throughout her brief testimony, P.K. said. She told the court that John had told her he would tell the truth about his and Whitworth's espionage. P.K. said the defense decided not to call her when she told them that she would not try to help out Jerry Whitworth by undermining Walker's testimony.

Michael Walker testified about how he took the secret material from the *Nimitz.* "I did it for money and to please my father. My father was pleased I actually had the guts to do it." There was the same note of aberrant pride in his voice that his father had as he described receiving secret documents from Whitworth.

Puma testified that Walker seemed more like Peter Sellers playing a comic role than a spy—a klutz who bumbled his way through what appeared to be a dead drop. At the time, she said, she didn't know what Walker was doing but figured it out after his arrest.

Defense attorneys decided not to call Whitworth to the stand because he could not adequately explain the origins of his non-Navy income. One of the charges against him was tax evasion.

Whitworth's college friend, Roger Olson, now a construction superintendent at a New Guinea copper mine, said he was Whitworth's "best friend." He said he considered Whitworth "like a brother." He had met John Walker through Whitworth in San Diego, and he took an instant dislike to Walker. "John Walker would sell out his own mother," he said.

Olson said Whitworth had told him that the source of his money was "the underground economy," or more specifically, the purchase of scrap gold at low prices, which Whitworth said he resold for a profit.

Near the end of the trial, the defense asked Judge John P. Vukasin, Jr., to instruct the jury that they could find that Whitworth unknowingly passed information that he did not know would hurt the United States, and did not know it would wind up in the hands of a foreign government. Judge Vukasin agreed, and so ruled.

Prosecutors were furious at this ruling, which they thought was far too lenient and favorable to the defense based on the evidence. The prosecution asked a federal appeals court, in an emergency petition, to overturn Vukasin's ruling. The appeals panel agreed to hear the petition. Assistant U.S. Attorney Farmer said Vukasin's ruling created a "significantly greater chance of acquittal," but the appeals court upheld Vukasin and the trial resumed July 7.

The U.S. District Court jury of five men and seven women returned from the July 4 break to determine Whitworth's fate. The jury was out for ten days and deliberated fifty-two hours before reaching a decision. The prosecution began to worry about the possibility that Vukasin's ruling and instructions might have confused the jury, which could result in a hung jury and a mistrial. But the jury found Whitworth guilty on all but one of the thirteen counts. They reached no decision on one count involving some of the data found in Whitworth's home. They could not decide whether it had been in his possession as a legitimate part of the job.

Although sentencing was delayed, the prosecution asked for the maximum penalty on all counts: seven life terms plus seventeen years for tax evasion.

Whitworth sat stoically as the verdict was read, showing no emotion. Brenda was not in the courtroom.

18

Damage Assessment

We always consider the worst case. We have to assume that any sensitive information that could have been passed was actually given to the Soviets.

—Rear Admiral James D. Watkins,
chief of Naval Operations, June 11, 1985

For years a faction in the Navy had believed there was a mole somewhere with access to top-secret and cryptographic information as well as other technical data. It seemed to them that the Russians had made remarkable strides in technology without paying their dues in research time and effort. Others argued that we Americans, in our arrogance of technological superiority and power, had habitually underestimated the Soviets—they simply obtained all the technical data publicly available via their information-gathering branch in the United Nations then used their own research to fill in the blanks.

The mole proponents insisted that the Soviets had skipped steps *A, B,* and *C* to jump straight to *D.* Our intelligence showed a sophistication in Soviet submarine advances that could not be accounted for without penetration of American technology or, worse, American communications and American defense contractors. The arrest of the Walker spy ring ended the debate on the side of the Navy mole advocates.

After the arrests of the three Walkers and Whitworth, the Navy began a top-secret damage estimate based on worst-case and best-case scenarios. Initially this was done on the assumption that Walker would not cooperate.

Rear Admiral John L. Butts, director of Naval Intelligence, was appointed to head a thirty-five-member board charged with coordinating the activities of investigators and producing a damage assessment. They worked virtually around the clock, sifting through reports of their own and FBI investigators. There was a speed and urgency about the investigation that rivaled wartime planning. Navy investigators began to retrace the careers of the men to determine just what they could have provided the Soviets.

Former Deputy CIA Director Bobby Inman said shortly after the arrests, "All we know, really, is where they served. If you look at their duty stations, there are some judgments that you can make about worst-case kind of losses. First would be service on SSBN, a U.S. ballistic missile submarine—that would have been at or near the top of Soviet interests. How the SSBN operated, where, when did it come to the surface to communicate, did it transmit communications, if so, exactly what time, when, where, on what frequencies.

"The second major area of possible loss," Inman continued, "would be from the service with attack submarines—the ability to see the communications from the attack submarines. Revealing details on how we went about detecting Soviet units, the effectiveness of it, how we operated, what kinds of tactics we used, what kinds of tactics we might use if we were to move into a time of crisis or hostilities. There could have been insights into our other means of locating foreign submarines, including some impact on both surface and air capability. And there, because systems stay in place a lot longer, the damage could be enduring.

"The third area that is still pretty murky," Inman said, "is the degree of exposure to surface, amphibious, and naval air warfare areas, where there is potential that message traffic could have been provided on the details of exercises, exercising our war plans, candid assessments of weaknesses of equipment or of tactics and doctrine."

The fourth area would be "the security of communications . . . I inherently worry when I see that one of these individuals was a crypto repairman, and at the prospect that they were in position to provide materials for years. Now that is clearly a worst-case look."

The potential damage was worse than even Inman imagined. He had spoken before finding out that Walker had not only stolen the rotor encryption technology but had kept the Soviets abreast of communications changes on a continuing basis, using the small testing device manufactured in the Soviet Union.

Investigators were particularly worried about how much the Soviets had learned about U.S. communications. There was little, they found out, that Walker and Whitworth—between them—did not know or to which they did not have access.

One of the most crucial functions of U.S. submarine operations is to guarantee communications to the submarine and surface fleet in the event of a nuclear war. Without such guaranteed communications, there is no capacity for ordering a massive retaliation or second strike. And without this deterrent capacity, the nation is particularly vulnerable.

The Defense Communications System has ground-based transmitters transmitting at high, low, very low, and extremely low frequency bands. The transmitters were designed to be nuclear-bomb proof and to operate with the rotor encrypters. The technology allows compressed messages to be sent so that a long message can be transmitted in only a fraction of a second.

Relays of such messages are also possible via satellite, along with emergency rocket transmissions. Investigators had to assume that John Walker and Whitworth were familiar with even the most sophisticated nuances of Navy communications methodology and technology. While officials were publicly stating that it didn't look too bad, privately there was much wringing of hands and gnashing of teeth. Walker had provided the Soviets with enough information to enable the duplication of American cryptographic equipment, allowing the interception of our fleet messages and top-secret war-plans messages for well over a decade.

If the Soviets thoroughly understood our complex system of communications, they could also knock it out of operation as part of a first strike. This would leave the fleet and much of the rest of our defense network "deaf and blind."

Arthur was an expert in all forms of the most sophisticated sonar equipment. John also knew a great deal about sonar. Also, sonar technical manuals and state-of-the-art documents were certainly part of his hoard of gathered materials. Both were familiar with the sonar net, SOSUS, and how it helped keep track of Soviet submarines and surface vessels. Whitworth, the last to leave the Navy, had kept up with any state-of-the-art advances in cryptography, as well as the periodic changes in key lists.

John was an expert on the Lafayette class of nuclear-powered submarines and all of its strengths and weaknesses. He had also been assigned to the *Bolivar* while it was under construction and had a first-hand look at its structure and 15,000 horsepower nuclear-driven engine, its guidance systems, the layout of its equipment, its vulnerabilities, its maximum speed, and its silent-running technology, measurements, and idiosyncracies. The knowledge he had and probably transmitted to the Soviets on this class of sumbarine was in itself devastating, but there was much more.

Arthur and John were familiar with every kind of missile used, their careers having spanned the time from the old liquid oxygen-kerosene missiles through the post-Loon, Triton, Rigel, Regulus, Polaris, Poseidon, Trident, and Tomahawk. Arthur was so knowledgeable that he was used by the Navy as a lecturer and teacher of sonar. He could probably write enough material from memory to provide the Soviets with a head start in duplicating American sonar, which had been far superior to that of the Soviets, particularly the new "towed array sonar."

As it became apparent that John Walker was the most damaging spy in U.S. history, grown men wanted to cry. Navy Secretary John Lehman toyed with the idea of recalling the Walker brothers and Whitworth to active duty so that they could be court-martialed to the fullest extent of the law. What they had done, it was feared, in addition to opening up our cryptographic technology, was no less than nullify the postwar advantage the United States had gained in missile guidance technology.

To understand the damage fully, it is necessary to know how the United States pursued missile technology after World War II. Americans studied German research avidly. It was thought that perhaps a sophisticated V-1 rocket bomb could be mated to submarines. The project began under the code name Loon. Early guidance technology was simple by today's standards, as missiles used a hyperbolic technique in which pulsed or continuous radio wave emissions from two fixed points—picket ships or picket submarines—interacted to form a fixed pattern of hyperbolic lines. The missile would guide itself to target with input from these lines. It was crude by today's standards, but effective. Another method was astrotracking, in which a gyro-stabilized tracker on board the missile locked onto a star or other heavenly body and navigated by a computerized version of the traditional seaman's sextant.

By the time the Walkers arrived on the scene, a more sophisticated inertial navigation or guidance system, INS, was well along in research and development. For this system to work, the missile's guidance system must "know" the missiles precise location at the instant of firing. Given this factor, it continuously computes speed along with time and attitude throughout its flight path with startling accuracy. It also factors in the speed of the submarine at launch.

Admiral W. F. Raborn and a team from Lockheed put together the Polaris missile with a highly accurate inertial guidance system that was more precise than anything the Soviets had at the time. It included miniature inertial guidance systems, miniature nuclear and thermonuclear warheads, cold gas launch techniques that would do no damage to a submerged submarine, noise reduction techniques, and many other classified features. When the missile was tested near Cocoa Beach, Florida, there were a number of interested observers: Soviet technicians on trawlers, and John Walker, who was on board the launch platform of the SSBN *Simon Bolivar*, then our state-of-the-art nuclear submarine.

The Navy did not rest on this accomplishment, however, but immediately began upgrading the sophistication and reliability of the Polaris, producing the Polaris A-1, A-2, and A-3 before it was replaced by the Poseidon, which became operational in March 1971. The Poseidon is already giving way to the Trident, which may be the Navy's operational missile for the rest of this century. The Soviets kept pace with their own SS-N-8 missiles, some of which had superior range. How much help John Walker was to the Soviets in perfecting their own guidance systems, if any, may never be known. But it is known that he was an intelligent and resourceful participant in the early testing of the Polaris-class missiles. For planning purposes, the Navy had to assume the worst.

The Navy also feared that Whitworth might have penetrated the computer system used by naval ships and subs, ARPANET, or Advanced Research Projects Agency's Communications Network. He was chosen for his specialty, crypto repair, because of his exceptional intelligence. A student at the University of California at Los Angeles was arrested November 2, 1983, for breaking into ARPANET, along with more than two hundred other computer systems, including the Naval Research Laboratory's own system. Surely Whitworth was equally as capable. Naval authority Thomas Allen noted that "the lack of adequate computer protection was conceded in the Department of Defense computer security manual in effect when Whitworth was serving aboard the *Enterprise.*" The manual read:

> Operating in a true multilevel security mode remains a desired operational goal. . . . However . . . this goal cannot generally be obtained with confidence due to the limitations in the currently available software state-of-the-art.

Another fear was that Whitworth may have been paid to insert— program in—defects in the computer system that would only be found in a state of war, defects that could give false signals and messages, nullifying our war effort. The Chief of Naval Operations, Rear Admiral James D. Watkins, in a June 11, 1985, press conference assessing the probable damage, hinted at concern over computer penetration. "Some technical design communications information has probably been lost," he said. That he would publicly state this much spoke volumes about Navy concern over computer penetration.

Watkins said the technology gap between the United States and Soviets was significant in 1975, but had rapidly closed. For the first time he made public the Navy's worst fears based on its study of the damage, saying, "There is some indication in the past ten years—because of the amazing capabilities of the Soviet Union to demonstrate improvements in a variety of their systems—that this could have been influenced by the information gleaned out of the Walker tragedy here."

Soon after the arrests, Watkins ordered the number of uniformed and civilian Navy personnel with access to classified information cut form 900,000 to 810,000, and he announced that the Navy's goal would be to remove such clearances from 50 percent of its personnel. The Navy would no longer allow field commanders to issue such clearances, and the use of polygraphs, then required for only a few Navy officers with the very highest clearances, would be broadened to include thousands more.

After Watkin's announcement, Secretary of Defense Weinberger expanded the 10-percent cut in security clearances to include all service branches' military personnel and civilian workers for defense contractors. That number included an astounding 4.3 million people, but one statistic was even more astounding: 600,000 of those people had access to top-secret materials, sometimes cryptographic. This was placing a lot of confidence in human nature and the laws of probability. How many other Walkers were there lurking about in the nooks and crannies of the Defense Department, the armed services, and private defense contractors? What no one seemed to realize in the rush to slam the door was that the new regulations would scarcely affect submarine radiomen.

These men should undergo thorough background checks. Those with felonies in their backgrounds, such as John Walker's burglary, should be weeded out because a felony has to be interpreted as a weakness of character that could be a precursor of later security damage. Strict enforcement of this or routine polygraph examinations or even drug testing would have weeded out John Walker, who was an habitual pot smoker.

The Navy's first concern after cryptographic espionage was the highly secret SOSUS, or Sound Surveillance System, the undersea sonar network that allows accurate tracking of Soviet subs, and "Ivy Bells," a SOSUS system actually in place in Soviet harbors.

Submarine experts say Walker probably provided the Soviets with enough communication data to allow them to monitor U.S. submarine movements via radioed position checks. This would allow them—at the very least—to correct weaknesses in their own submarine movements. One intelligence source said some Navy officers had long suspected, from watching changes in Soviet submarine movements, that the Russians had learned something, somehow.

The worst-case scenario would be if Walker—as feared—provided the Soviets with maps of where the hydrophones are situated. It would take no great genius to determine that the United States has hydrophones at the entrance to the Mediterranean in the Strait of Gibraltar; near the Suez Canal, Cape Horn, Havana, and the Straits of Magellan; off the northern coast of Turkey to monitor movement in the Black Sea; near Copenhagen to monitor traffic in and out of the Baltic; and other key places any schoolboy could name. But where the rest of the listening devices are placed is highly prized intelligence.

Rear Admiral Gene R. LaRocque, retired, an expert in antisubmarine warfare, said the Navy might need to replace and upgrade the entire SOSUS system. Presumably he had reason to believe this from preliminary checks into what Walker had access to during his career.

Relocation of the SOSUS detectors would not only be enormously expensive, but would now be far easier for the Soviets to watch via new satellite technology. Satellites also make it more difficult to change the system. The new look-down radar can see through cloud cover and reconstruct, through computers, amazingly accurate images that in many respects rival clear-weather photographs.

Walker also knew about U.S. listening labs in the mountains of North Carolina and Virginia, highly secret places where sounds and radio messages—down to the walkie-talkie level—are analyzed twenty-four hours a day.

The CIA began a 10 million dollar study to determine whether the submarine fleet is as invulnerable as the Navy alleges it to be. This is a separate and distinctly different undertaking from the Walker damage study. But the stakes are high, based on the outcome of both. If the submarine fleet operation has been mortally wounded, the MX missile program will seem far more necessary, and even the MX's severest critics on Capitol Hill will have to reassess their arguments.

The CIA study, to be finished by mid-1986, is focusing on advanced techiniques—using satellites, infarared photography, radar and other sensing devices—that the Soviets may have devel-

226

oped. Lending urgency to the study, besides the Walker damage or perhaps because of it, according to Navy sources, is the recent Soviet success in tracking U.S. submarines, with both hunter-killer submarines and aircraft. Navy officers were surprised when Soviet Bear-D reconaissance planes based in Cuba flew patrols over submerged U.S. submarines, almost as if flaunting a new-found technology.

The White House continues to insist that no new Soviet technology has been detected, but this, of course, would be the wisest thing, from a strategic point of view, for the White House officials to say no matter what the actual case.

American defense scientists fear that the Soviets may be using a new technique called SAR (Synthetic Aperture Radar) in their Salyut 7 space station. The technique bounces radar signals off the surface of the ocean, then processes computer-generated images that show up as a track made by a submarine. No matter how deep within the 3,000-foot range, a submarine will generate waves on the surface of a different pattern—a pattern not distinguishable by the human eye but apparent after computer enhancement. Such faint surface turbulence, however, is obscured if the ocean surface is too roiled.

Some defense scientists have told Congress, in partially censored testimony, that the SAR technique is still ineffective. But combined with SOSUS, infarared photography, and other still secret methodology, it is believed that the process has a future.

WITHIN WEEKS OF Walker's arrest and the succession of arrests that followed, intelligence experts had a rough handle on what the Walker ring had provided the Soviets. It made all previous espionage seem paltry by comparison. They were reasonably certain it included much of the following:

- Cryptographic rotor information that enabled the Soviets to intercept U.S. naval wireless messages for more than fifteen years, including reports on location of U.S. nuclear submarines and a vast amount of information during the Vietnam War
- Key lists, as often as Walker or others could get them to the Soviets, for use in the cryptographic machines known as KUR-37
- The stations where U.S. nuclear subs cruised on mission, the

227

special duties of each mission, and the number of subs on various stations

• Information on harbor mining battle plans, and ship movements during the Vietnam War, some of it provided while acting as a courier

• Technical manuals or wiring diagrams for the SOSUS system hydrophones or sonar net, but most important, an undersea map of where the hydrophones are placed

• Technical manuals and wiring diagrams for the submarine's several radio systems showing how they dovetail into cryptographic machines

• Towed array sonar, a top-secret method of listening that was provided to the Soviets by an industrial spy in California and probably cross-checked against information provided by Walker

• A layout of the submarine's equipment, machinery, and quarters, down to evaporators used for converting sea water to fresh water and other relatively basic technology

• A report on everything Walker gleaned while participating in the testing of the Polaris A-1 fired from the *Bolivar* in its testing stage, including any malfunctions or technical data on board the sub that he could copy

• A list of those Navy men Walker thought might be "turned" to Soviet espionage, based on his work with polygraph operators while stationed in San Diego

• Details commonly obtainable on the submarine's navigation systems

• The pattern of U.S. submarine deployment, length of cruise, overlap of other submarines, and any window of vulnerability based on deployment

• Methodology of low-frequency radio transmission and reception based on Walker's shore duty at Norfolk, where much of the radio contact with the submarine fleet is maintained

• Performance data on function testing of limited-warfare missiles such as the Tomahawk, Harpoon, and acoustic and wire-guided torpedoes

• Top speed of various classes of submarines and surface vessels

• Latest in Antisubmarine Warfare (ASW) techniques

• Maximum depth capacity of various classes of submarines

• Target data, information on Soviet sites targeted by U.S. submarine missiles

- Advances in silent-running technology, in which the Soviets had lagged noisily
- U.S. methodology in tracking and observing Soviet submarines via a combination of satellite observation, infrared photography, Synthetic Aperture Radar (using changes in surface patterns of waves), SOSUS, and routine aircraft patrol
- Information on American assistance given Allied nations in detecting intrusion of Soviet submarines in fjords and other closed-in bodies of water
- A rundown on all messages other than "eyes-only" received by the captain on a given cruise—before the Soviets were able to construct their own decoders
- War plans involving the submarine and surface fleets in the Atlantic, Pacific, Mediterranean, and Indian seas and oceans
- Undersea mapping technology and progress
- How the submarine and crew prepared to react after undersea encounters such as the Gibraltar incident
- A list of submarine equipment malfunctions
- How computers are used in determining acoustic signatures of Soviet vessels
- How computers are used in war plans and how such computer programs could be penetrated and sabotaged
- Equipment failure data of various ships from the VSE corporation

This list does not include the intelligence data that a gifted espionage agent can pick up randomly by overhearing chitchat among officers who have SI clearance.

19

Aftermath

You have tirelessly worked for the best interest of your country and you may be sure that your efforts were in keeping with the highest traditions of the FBI.
—FBI Director William Webster, August 13, 1985

Soon the public's attention was diverted by a rash of espionage arrests. They ranged from a runner who was charged with trying to sell some of the material he was assigned to deliver, to a Naval employee charged with trying to sell secret information to Israel. But none of the new cases had the scope and long-lasting damage of the Walker case.

Arthur was sent to a federal prison in Lewisburg, Pennsylvania. Michael remained in Petersburg, Virginia, at a federal prison. John was moved to a federal prison in Norfolk during the debriefing period. Whitworth remained in a federal prison in San Francisco. John hoped to be sent eventually to Lewisburg so he could be near Arthur or to Petersburg to be with Michael.

Agent Hunter was detailed to the team in charge of debriefing John Walker, a tedious process expected to last more than a year.

P.K. was unable to find another law enforcement job because

she was honest about her romantic involvement with John Walker. She finally took a modest-paying job with a convenience store.

Margaret Walker began work on a book of her own. Her father cooperated by mail.

Barbara Walker remained at her job in Massachusetts, but Laura reported that her mother's struggle with alcohol "has gotten worse. This has all just been too much for her."

Rachel remained in Norfolk and began spending more time with her parents.

Laura also began work on a book, and she said her mother might do one too. "We all decided to do our own thing."

The whole ordeal had been easier for Laura to bear because of her religious convictions. "When I was fifteen I gave my life to the Lord. I would say that has given me the strength of Jesus and God in my life. I prayed a lot—I still do. Even when I don't pray, He's there—He's very faithful."

Even before she learned of her father's espionage, "I suspected it when I was seven or eight."

Even now, she says of her father, "I love him. I really do." But she feels no guilt for turning him in—"none. I only hope that now he can start doing something a little better for himself and the people around him instead of living to please himself." She thought Don Clevenger's loyalty remarkable and said, "I hope I can have friends that loyal."

She has not talked to her father since his arrest: "He doesn't speak to me. He has no desire to." She has not been to visit either her father or brother. "I'm not on his visitor's list."

If the two Walkers had not been "my father and brother," Laura probably would have liked to see them severely punished, possibly even executed. But because they are who they are, "it is hard for me to say I would like for them to have the firing squad."

Does she think that her father feels remorse?

"This has turned his life upside down. He's a human being. I hope he feels remorse, but I really am not certain."

The big Walker and Scaramuzzo families have turned against her. "They aren't happy with me at all."

Asked to be more specific about certain family relationships, Laura talked about the book she was writing. "I am writing it because there are enough people who have questions that I think there will be enough people to buy it to find the answers. I feel that God's opened a door for me to show people how He comes through for people who believe in Him, and He's come through for me."

When someone suggested that she might share some guilt for not informing on her father and trying to profit from the family heartbreaks and divisions, she said, "To imply that I am profiting off of his treason—first of all, let's say what if I were? Even if I were, am I to be held accountable for my father's treason? No, you can't judge my Christianity or my faith in Jesus on the fact that I didn't turn my father in for three years."

A pretty brunette, Laura has a job working in the Department of Biblical Studies at the Christian Broadcasting Network University in Norfolk.

Don Clevenger began to think more and more about Barbara Walker. They were both divorced. He toyed with the idea of asking her to visit him in Odessa.

"I'd really like to see Barbara again," he said. "I hope we can get together soon. We talk on the phone now and then."

Phil Prince started a new job as director of security for the Tandy Corporation. His wife kids him about being a good judge of character.

Mike Bell hoped the publicity might help the detective agency he had started in Richmond, Virginia.

Nora Moody now lives with a son in St. Stephens, South Carolina.

Bill Wilkinson built that trailer park he'd always wanted, along with some apartment buildings. He also bought a house with a pond in Denham Springs, Louisiana. Now and then he looks at the faded photographs from his days as a submarine radioman or gets out the ukulele he made from a crypto box. "I still find it hard to believe," he says.

One day agent Hunter found a letter in the FBI's interoffice mailboxes. He opened it and found a check, but the letter meant a lot more to him. It stated:

August 13, 1985
PERSONAL
Mr. Robert W. Hunter
Federal Bureau of Investigation
Norfolk, Virginia

Dear Mr. Hunter:
Your exceptional performance in the WINDFLYER Investigation has been brought to my attention, and I am proud to commend you. The enclosed check represents the incentive award your actions have so richly merited.

As the case agent in this matter of vital importance to the FBI and our nation as well, you skillfully managed the overall investigation conducted by the Norfolk Division. You minutely planned the exhaustive surveillances that were put into operation, arrested two major subjects implicated in this espionage ring, and conducted key interviews with the subjects. Your knowledge in regard to this case enabled you to provide expert testimony before two federal grand juries and other judicial hearings. You have successfully served in this position under the intense scrutiny of public attention and the necessity for the careful coordination of a tremendous accumulation of investigative material. You have tirelessly worked for the best interest of your country and you may be sure that your efforts were in keeping with the highest traditions of the FBI.

Sincerely Yours,

William H. Webster
Director

Bibliography

Bentley, John. *The Thresher Disaster*. New York: Doubleday and
    Company,
Burgess, Robert F. *Ships Beneath the Sea*. New York: McGraw-Hill,
Janes Fighting Ships, 1966-1984 editions. New York: McGraw-Hill.
Latimer, Edward, *Submarine*. New York: Holt, 1952.
Lipscomb, Fran W. *Historic Submarines*. New York: Praeger,
Miller David. *An Illustrated Guide to Modern Submarines*. New
    York: Arco,
Polmar, Norman. *Death of the Thresher*. Philadelphia: Chilton,
Preston, Anthony. *Sea Power*. New York: Exeter Books,

In addition, I found invaluable information in *The Cape Cod
Times* of Cape Cod, Massachusetts, the *Norfolk Virginian-Pilot,*
the *Washington Post,* the *Los Angeles Times,* the *Scranton Times,*
The New York Times, and the *Sacramento Bee.* Thanks, too, to
Edwin Karpowicz, the custodian of the submarine *Torsk,* now
docked in Baltimore Harbor, for his patient explanations and tour
of the submarine.

Index